Fro Michael ~~Davitt~~

to

James Connolly

'Internationalism from Below' and the challenge to the UK state and British Empire from 1879-95

Allan Armstrong

Allan Armstrong, November, 2010

Published by
INTFROBEL PUBLICATIONS

An Eleconmac Paperback

intfrobel@hotmail.co.uk

ISBN: 978-0-9567412-0-2

Front cover - Michael Davitt and traditional Irish cottages in Connacht

Back cover - James Connolly and the Cowgate in Edinburgh

Printed by Clydeside Press,
37, High Street, Glasgow G1 1LX

Dedicated to Brian Higgins

A Glasgow bear, Celtic mad, Irish-Scottish migrant worker, bolshie brickie, blacklisted militant, republican, internationalist and communist, whose political activity has followed in the great tradition of 'internationalism from below' established by Michael Davitt, James Connolly and John Maclean.

With thanks to Nick Clarke

Nick is an extremely patient English Scot, republican communist comrade and a good friend, who has spent a great deal of time on the layout of this book.

With thanks to Alister Black, Mickey Keenan and Sean McGuinness

Alister laid out the front and back cover of this book. Mickey and Sean respectively have produced the cameo portraits of James Connolly and Michael Davitt. They are in the style of the image of James Connolly originally designed by the Irish artist, Robert Ballagh, in 1971.

With thanks to my partner, Myra Galletly, and our daughters, Caitrin and Eilis

We have visited a great many of the locations in Ireland, Scotland, Wales and England mentioned in this book. Together, Myra and I have made firm friends and thoroughly enjoyed all the craic and the music. Caitrin and Eilis may have been bemused at the choice of some of the places we have visited, but both have developed a great passion for seeing new places - only now, of their own choice!

Contents

Contents

1. Introduction

Why should Socialists spend time examining a period of history from over a hundred years ago? Perhaps the best reason is that between 1879 and 1895 there are striking parallels to the situation we find ourselves in today. This was also a period of increasing inter-imperialist competition as the previously dominant world power began to lose its leading position. In the late nineteenth century it was the UK that found itself in this new situation; today it is the USA, with the UK continuing to fall well down the global pecking order.

Furthermore, when we compare the UK over the two periods, we can see the continuing significance of national democratic challenges to the unionist state. 'The Irish Revolution'[1] (1), which began in 1879, triggered a series of economic, social and political movements, which led to a questioning of the very existence of the UK. As a result profound divisions emerged amongst the British ruling class over how best to maintain its rule over these islands and their wider empire. Major economic and social struggles became linked to demands for national self-determination in Ireland, Scotland and Wales. Clearly, there are important echoes of this situation today.

The rise of 'New Imperialism' fortifies the British Union and Empire

From 1875, with the beginnings of the 'New Imperialism'[2] (2), Disraeli's Conservative government had begun to pursue increasingly aggressive colonial

---

[1] 'The Irish Revolution' is the term given by the Irish historian, Theodore Moody, to describe the major period of social and political upheaval between 1879-82, initiated by the Irish National Land League and the 'Land War'.

[2] 'New Imperialism' developed in Europe, the USA (and later Japan) in the 1870's. This followed the defeats of the Paris Commune in 1871, and the overthrow of Radical Reconstruction (the concerted state-backed attempt to bring about black emancipation after the Civil War) in the USA, by 1877.

policies. These reflected the growing concerns of a British ruling class, now facing global competition from a larger number of European states. These states had followed the British road to economic development through industrialisation with its need for overseas raw materials and markets.

Prior to this, in the middle of the nineteenth century, British capitalism had enjoyed such a dominant economic position that its leading spokesmen declared their support for a non-colonial, 'free trade' world order[3] (3). By the last quarter of the century, however, the leaders of the UK state increasingly abandoned this model, joining others in the scramble for colonies.

From 1879, a new challenge developed to this recharged British imperialism. It drew its politics largely from the **social republican** tradition found in Ireland, and from the **Radical** tradition found in England, Scotland and Wales. This opposition was formed in response to the failure of traditional Liberals, led by William Gladstone, to uphold their earlier support for civil rights and opposition to colonial expansion.

The most significant figure in this opposition was Michael Davitt. He had been an infant Irish immigrant and child textile worker, losing his arm in an industrial accident. He joined the Irish Republican Brotherhood (the Fenians) as a teenager in 1865 and was imprisoned in 1870.

After his release in 1877, Davitt initiated the 'New Departure', with the support of American social republicans in the Fenian movement. This led to the setting up of the Irish National Land League (INLL) in 1879, to challenge the Anglo-Irish Ascendancy landlords and to win 'land for the people'. It was one of the biggest 'lower orders' movements in the nineteenth century UK. As well as enjoying a truly mass basis, the INLL was a revolutionary movement involved in legal and extra-legal struggle, as well as political campaigning. It had major economic, social, cultural and political effects, not only in Ireland, but also upon the wider UK.

Davitt attempted to unite land and labour struggles across the four nations constituting the United Kingdom – Ireland, Scotland, England and Wales - and beyond into the British Empire and the USA. He developed an **internationalism from below** approach to win wider support for the INLL. Furthermore, he deepened this alliance by contributing to the development of land and labour organisations in Scotland, England and Wales.

The Land Leagues, whether in Ireland, the Highlands and Islands of Scotland,

---

[3] The historian, Bernard Semmel has termed this period, when the UK did not face significant industrial competition on the world market, as 'Free Trade Imperialism'.

or Wales, all organised in areas where there was still considerable support for religion and a strong identification with particular denominations. Davitt and his allies were able to unite Catholic and Protestant tenant farmers and, sometimes, landless labourers and cottars. The Irish Land League even made some inroads amongst tenant farmers in the Orange Order, despite the extreme hostility of the Order's leadership.

The Catholic Davitt was well received by the largely Free Church crofters and cottars in the Highlands and Islands. Calvinist Methodist slate quarriers welcomed him in North Wales. The first Catholic MP to be elected from a Scottish constituency to Westminster was the Land League candidate for the overwhelmingly Protestant Argyll in 1885.

Michael Davitt - former IRB member and leading figure in the Irish Land League

Davitt was prepared to take on the Catholic hierarchy whenever it opposed the Irish Land League. The Radical wing of the Highland Land League, in its fight against landlordism, also took on the Free Church leadership. Social republican and Radical leaders in the Land Leagues were trying to develop a secular approach, which set aside religious differences, the better to unite people behind their economic, social and political struggles.

However, the President of the INLL, Charles Parnell, an atypical Irish Protestant landlord, decided to follow a different course. The full potential of the INLL had to be curtailed in a 'counter-revolution within the revolution'. Parnell looked to a growing Irish bourgeoisie and the better-off tenant farmers to support Irish capitalist interests. He came to depend more and more upon the Catholic hierarchy to contain the 'lower orders' component of the INLL.

Parnell represented an 'internationalism from above' alliance, seeking supporters amongst the liberal wing of the British ruling class, particularly Gladstone's Liberal Party. In 1882, Parnell and his allies closed down the INLL in order to form a purely constitutional nationalist party, the National League. It had the aim of winning Irish Home Rule, promoting peasant proprietorship and Irish industry.

The First Irish Home Rule Bill, adopted by Gladstone's Liberal government, was defeated in 1886. A new government led by the Conservative Lord Salisbury took office. Parnell's attempts at political wheeler-dealing with top British politicians had come unstuck.

Davitt and his allies now had to further develop an 'internationalism from below' strategy to confront a thoroughly jingoist, racist and sectarian Unionist alliance. The Unionists would countenance no concession over Irish Home Rule, and revelled enthusiastically over every latest imperial exploit. This was the conservative unionist approach to maintaining British ruling class domination at home and abroad. It vehemently opposed the liberal unionist approach[4] and its support for Home Rule (Devolution) for the constituent nations of the UK.

As 'New Imperialism' increased its stranglehold over British politics, the Liberal Party, including many on its Radical wing, were drawn into its slipstream, just as today New Labour, including many once on the Left, has become the servant of a new corporate imperial order. In the late nineteenth century, however, a section of advanced Radicals reacted against these political retreats and made the first tentative steps towards socialism. Robert Cunninghame-Graham and Keir Hardie were just two such examples in Scotland. Nevertheless, many former Radicals, who went on to become Socialists, still retained much of their earlier politics.

One contrast, though, compared with today, was that the Conservative Party, hitherto seen as a major impediment to any democratic advance, began to develop a Tory Democrat wing. Its adherents made appeals to the newly enfranchised workers. They were offered limited reforms in return for giving their support to British ruling class attempts to expand the Empire. The Conservative leader, Benjamin Disraeli, was one of the first to see the possibilities of harnessing the link between reform and Empire; but it was Randolph Churchill, who attempted to push this further, by appealing directly to the working class, as a Tory Democrat. He strongly linked expansion of the British Empire with the defence of the existing British Unionist state. He looked to the local dignitary-led and plebian-supported, Orange Order in Ulster for inspiration in forming his pro-imperial, cross class, Unionist alliance.

Many workers were drawn into reactionary Conservative and further right populist organisations. They hoped to gain economically from the Empire, or to draw some psychological comfort by celebrating their 'racial' or religious 'superiority', in the confusing, rapidly changing world they lived in. The growing

---

[4] Here, liberal unionism refers to one of the two overall approaches taken by the British ruling class to defend the Union. It is not to be confused with the Liberal Unionists of the day, who were adherents of a conservative unionist approach.

number of wars directed against the peoples of the colonies took only a small number of British lives. The real cost was to come later, when the inevitable consequence of growing inter-imperialist competition led to the mass slaughter of the First World War. By then, though, the leaders of the Conservative Unionists could look with smug satisfaction as their Liberal, Irish Home-Rule, and some Labour and Socialist 'opponents', all threw themselves into the promotion of the carnage.

However, back in the 1880's, a few Tory Democrats, such as Henry Hyndman and Henry Champion, broke with the Conservative Party and became leading figures in the new Socialist movement. Like many former Radical Liberals,

Henry Hyndman - founder of British Marxism

who joined them, first in the Democratic Federation (DF), and then the Social Democratic Federation (SDF), these individuals retained aspects of their old politics, especially their lingering support for English/Anglo-Saxon/British supremacy and racism. Some of the clashes, which took place in the early Socialist movement, reflected this prior division between Radical Liberals and Tory Democrats.

The launching of the Irish Land War, in 1879, and the formation of the INLL, had been the main inspiration behind the formation of the DF in 1881. Its members began by opposing Gladstone's Liberal government's newfound support for state coercion. By 1884, the majority of DF members had come to the conclusion that Radicalism was inadequate, and they changed the organisation's name to the SDF, reflecting their conversion to Socialism.

The SDF showed many of the characteristics which have plagued later attempts at Socialist organisation – whether to concentrate on militant actions coupled with Socialist propaganda, or to seek political office by advocating limited reforms; or whether to seek constitutional or economic changes. Failure to develop a coherent programme, along with the lack of an integrated strategy, contributed to many of the setbacks and consequent splits amongst Socialists at the time, just as they continue to do today.

One early breakaway from the SDF was the small, but quite influential, Socialist League (SL), formed in 1885. It soon became divided between those who wanted to make propaganda for Socialism, and those, mainly in its affiliated Scottish Land and Labour League (SLLL), who wanted to orientate upon trade union, crofter and cottar struggles.

These early Socialists joined the wider struggle against those forces, both Conservative and Liberal, which were either aggressively advancing the Empire and defending the existing Union, or meekly bowing before the new onslaught. Due to the massive impact of the Irish Land League struggle on British politics, economic and social struggles became closely linked to the political battle for Irish Home Rule. Furthermore, as new Land Leagues were formed in Scotland and Wales, the demand for Home Rule was taken up in these nations too. The majority of the independent Crofter candidates of 1885, and those in the new Scottish Labour Party formed in 1888, supported both Irish and Scottish Home Rule.

Many key individuals, from the land and labour struggles of the 1880's, contributed to the massive wave of 'New (Trade) Unionism' which burst out in 1889. They faced a similar situation to that faced by Socialists and trade unionists today. Only then, Socialists were up against the politics of Lib-Labism[5]. Trade union leaders were still tied to an earlier Radical Liberal vision of a 'British Free Trade Empire' and a 'fair day's wage for a fair day's work'.

Gasworkers - one of the first of the New Unions

Today we are up against the politics of New Labour, with trade union leaders locked into the politics of 'social partnership'. Some of these misleaders still hanker back to the disappearing vision of the post-war, 'British Welfare State Empire', when workers in the UK were looked after 'from the cradle to the grave'.

---

[5] Lib-Labism first described attempts made by trade union leaders to win parliamentary influence, by getting adopted as official Liberal Party candidates. Lib-Labism was to develop in two more ways. Sometimes individual, independently promoted, Labour candidates would end up giving their support to the Liberal Party. Later, the leadership of the Independent Labour Party also became involved in various electoral deals with the Liberal Party.

Furthermore, prior to 1889, the vast majority of unskilled and casual workers lay outside the New Model unions[6], which had developed since the 1850's. Today, union membership has shrunk back to a minority of workers, mostly concentrated in the public sector. This has left vast numbers in the private sector unorganised, particularly women, migrant, part-time and casual workers.

The majority of the British Left today is tied to a Broad Left strategy of recapturing the 'old' unions by replacing their existing leaders (many of whom are earlier Broad Left leaders) with new Left leaders. In contrast, any contemporary 'New Unionism' would aim to thoroughly democratise existing unions and bring them under rank and file workers' control; or, where necessary, build completely new unions to bring together those workers who are now completely unorganised.

Nor is the Left nationalist notion of breakaway national unions much use against the global corporations that workers confront today. Yes, national (and sectoral) union sections need much more autonomy, but unions should encompass as many workers as possible. The key issue is not the existence of a union HQ flying a national flag (e.g. the tricolour or saltire), but the need for union sovereignty to reside with workers at the workplace level, not in national union HQs. The nationally-based Scottish teachers' union, the Educational Institute of Scotland, is one of the most fervent upholders of the embrace of government and employers, not so much in social partnership, more a morganatic marriage[7].

Today, some may take comfort from the fact that the majority of the British ruling class has opted for the liberal devolutionary unionist, and not the conservative direct rule unionist option, in order to maintain its rule over the UK. New Labour promotes (and the Conservatives have reluctantly accepted) 'Devolution-all-round' (i.e. for Northern Ireland, Scotland and Wales). This goes along with the all-party joint UK/Irish government promotion of the 'Peace Process', by which British influence is also maintained, albeit indirectly, over 'Twenty-Six Counties' Ireland.

Increasingly the Nationalist parties are being drawn into the running of the British state's devolved administrations. This includes the one time revolutionary nationalist Sinn Fein, now in partnership with the UK's most reactionary

---

[6] The New Model unions first developed in the 1850s, after the collapse of Chartism. With the appearance of 'New Unionism' in 1889, the New Model approach was characterised as 'Old Unionism'. This 'Old Unionism' looked to arbitration as the best way to solve disputes with the employers, and to the Liberal Party to advance working class interests.

[7] A morganatic marriage was an arrangement by which a king married a queen who was entitled to none of his property and whose children had no inheritance rights. In other words she only had the right to be screwed.

11

governing party, the Democratic Unionist Party (DUP). These British and Irish ruling class political initiatives have been backed by the social partnerships of compliant trade union leaders and aggressive governments and employers.

Yet, the aims of today's liberal unionists and constitutional nationalists are the same as those of the conservative unionists of the nineteenth, twentieth and twenty-first centuries. They want to create the best political environment for their principal class backers. Today this means allowing corporate capitalists to lower wages, undermine working conditions and undermine pensions, and supporting deregulation and privatisation. It means fawning before the requirements of finance capital.

The British ruling class may indeed have learned some political lessons from the failures of their earlier support for intransigent conservative unionism. When Conservative and Liberal Unionists tried to face down the rising demand for Irish Home Rule, in the 1880's, '90s and the first two decades of the twentieth century, this eventually proved to be a disastrous strategy for them. By 1922, direct rule over twenty-six counties of Ireland had been ended, and the UK state had begun to break-up.

The British government then turned for help to the very Irish Nationalists they had been attempting to crush. Shared class interests proved stronger than national differences. The British promoted the 1922-23 Irish Civil War to ensure that their favoured conservative, Empire-accepting Nationalists triumphed over their Republican opponents in 'the Twenty Six Counties'. The Republican institutions set up in the War of Independence were systematically dismantled, paving the way for many of the British-inspired institutions in the new Irish Free State. Thus the British ruling class added a new weapon to its wide armoury of mechanisms for exercising their political and social control – the neo-colonialist manipulation of Nationalist parties.

Within a decade of the establishment of the Irish Free State the position of the conservative Catholic Church was enshrined in the constitution, in an analogous way to the conservative Crown Powers in the UK. Meanwhile the British state's Unionist allies in 'the Six Counties' resorted to the Belfast pogroms from 1920-22, with their use of sectarian police and paramilitary forces, followed by the electoral gerrymandering of the new Northern Ireland constituencies to establish and consolidate a 'Protestant Parliament for a Protestant People'[8].

---

[8] It was one of the ironies of history that Northern Ireland ended up, in 1922, with the sole devolved parliament in the UK, in the form of Stormont, despite the Ulster Unionists' earlier vehement opposition to Home Rule. Stormont, far from being liberal in inspiration, more resembled the old reactionary, pre-1801, Irish Parliament, in its attempt to exclude Catholics (or Irish Nationalists) from any share of power.

After these particular traumas, this British imposed settlement seemed so permanent that the dramatic failings of pre-1922 conservative unionism were largely forgotten for almost half a century. However, in the late 1960's, new national democratic movements began to challenge British rule in Northern Ireland, Scotland and Wales. These movements also coincided with major working class struggles in the late 1960's and early 1970's.

The British ruling class experimented with both liberal devolutionary[9] and liberal centralist[10] measures to deal with the new national democratic challenges. To deal with the simultaneous working class challenge, the Labour government produced the liberal Bullock Report in 1975, which advocated forms of worker participation in industry. However, following Labour's capitulation to International Monetary Fund dictates in 1976, they increasingly resorted to more draconian measures to suppress working class discontent, including the use of troops to break the strikes of the Glasgow binworkers in 1977 and the firefighters in 1977-8.

To cope with the national democratic challenges they faced, both the Conservatives (in the late 1960's) and the Labour Party (in the later 1970's) made half-hearted liberal unionist devolutionary moves[11]. However, once the British ruling class had reasserted its control over events between 1977-79, it returned to the old failed conservative unionist strategy of Direct Rule, defence

---

[9] The proposals for Scottish and Welsh devolution enjoyed wider support, both from liberal unionists (more so in Scotland) and constitutional nationalists in these two countries. However, political support for a liberalised and reformed Stormont was much more narrowly based, and found primarily amongst Irish constitutional nationalists. Those Ulster Unionists reluctantly drawn into the British government's weak liberal devolutionary schemes were soon seen off by Loyalist reaction. The latter were quite prepared to act unconstitutionally and illegally to maintain the British unionist, monarchist and Protestant order.

[10] The Conservatives' closure of Stormont in 1972, and their resort to Direct Rule, was initially a very weak, liberal, centralising, political measure. However, British military and security forces were given responsibility for implementing Direct Rule on the ground, thereby negating any hesitant liberal intentions. After the collapse of the liberal devolutionary Sunningdale Agreement, in 1974, Labour accepted Direct Rule. They also relied primarily on military and security forces and the attempted criminalisation of the Republican opposition, which eventually led to the Hunger Strikes, in 1980 and 1981, once the Conservatives returned to office.

[11] In 1973, the Conservatives initially, if in a somewhat lukewarm manner, accepted the findings of the Royal Commission headed by Lord Kilbrandon. These recommended Devolution for Scotland and Wales. The Conservatives also supported the Sunningdale Agreement, which promoted a reformed devolved Stormont. The incoming 1974 Labour Government initially supported the Sunningdale Agreement too, but backed down in the face of Loyalist reaction. A divided Labour government also introduced the Scotland and Wales Act in 1976. Its devolutionary proposals were defeated in referenda in 1979.

of the constitutional status quo, backed by threats and coercion.

Meanwhile, under Thatcher's post-1979 Conservative government, anti-trade union laws soon tamed most union leaderships. The TUC and the Labour Party leaders left the National Union of Miners (NUM) isolated, when it defied these new laws. Between 1984-5, the NUM faced a wide range of the coercive powers available to the UK state, some developed in 'the Six Counties'. The Labour Party and TUC leadership's adoption of 'New Realism' was but the beginnings of the road back to the Lib-Lab 'Old Unionism' of the nineteenth century, and its complete and unquestioning acceptance of capitalist rule. Neo-liberal New Labour became the end product.

Thatcher's British Unionist, "Out, out, out" [12] intransigence towards any democratic change in Ireland first began under Labour, in the late 70's. The attempt by then Labour Northern Irish Secretary, Roy Mason, to criminalise any effective opposition had its parallels in the introduction of coercion to Ireland in 1881 by the Gladstone Liberal government's Irish Secretary, William 'Buckshot' Forster. This occurred long before Lord Salisbury's Conservative Irish Secretary, 'Bloody Balfour', was given free rein in 1887.

The failure of the UK state to meet the constitutional and economic reform demands, initially raised by the Civil Rights Movement in the 'Six Counties', in the late 1960's, produced another period of political and constitutional

'Buckshot Forster' and 'Bloody Balfour' - Liberal and Conservative architects of repression in Ireland

instability, lasting over a quarter of a century. An overt and determined Republican challenge emerged within the UK's frontiers. Thatcher's later

---

[12] "Out, out, out", was Thatcher's response, in 1984, to then Irish Premier, Garret Fitzgerald's 'New Ireland Forum' proposals. These would have given the Irish government a very limited role in representing, but also curbing, the aspirations of Northern Nationalists.

attempt to deny even limited political self-determination, for either Scotland or Wales, made the 'National Question' an even wider and more volatile political issue. Her attempt to use Scotland as a testing ground for the poll tax just highlighted the unionist state's democratic deficit.

A diffuse Scottish social republicanism emerged in Scotland, However, the largest Socialist organisations (Militant and the Socialist Workers Party) remained committed to a 'British road to socialism' and still supported, albeit critically, the British Labour Party. Socialist republicanism, with its advocacy of 'internationalism from below', was only able to establish a toehold on the Socialist spectrum.

Nevertheless, the massive opposition to the poll tax, across the whole of Britain, and the inability of the British state to break the Irish Republican challenge by brute force alone, led to Thatcher's downfall, and the ending of the British ruling class commitment to intransigent unionism. In their majority, they now unceremoniously dumped Thatcher in 1990 and, under John Major's government, adopted the Downing Street Agreement in 1993 to bring the Irish Republicans on board.

Conservatives were now committed to a liberal unionist strategy to defend the Union. When this proved too limited to contain the wider national challenges, the ruling class turned instead to New Labour's policy of 'Devolution-all-round' for Northern Ireland, Scotland and Wales. This is, in effect, a return to the old nineteenth century Liberal 'Home Rule-all-round' strategy.

However, as in the case of the nineteenth century divide between Conservatives and Liberals, there is little difference behind the strategic aims of today's Conservatives and New Labour. Both are committed to maintaining a British imperial presence in the wider world. Both accept that the British ruling class can now only achieve this as a junior partner to US imperialism. This political path leads to continuous wars, attacks on civil rights, austerity welfare provision, and the scape-goating of migrant workers. There is indeed now a tension between New Labour's and the Tories' shared liberal unionism at home and their conservative militaristic imperialism abroad. But, under today's prevailing political conditions, it is the liberal unionism that is more likely to give.

Each retreat from the initially more liberal unionist, Good Friday Agreement (1998) - first the St Andrews Agreement (2006) and now the Hillsborough Agreement (2010) - has further entrenched conservative unionism. The emergence of the True Unionist Voice, to the right of the DUP, and the latest electoral alliance between Cameron's Conservatives and the Ulster Unionist Party (an alliance broken in 1974 and 1985) demonstrates the continued growth of reaction in 'the Six Counties'.

New Labour has also fallen back on the nastier traits, usually associated with conservative unionism and imperialism. Indeed, as international competition becomes more pronounced, in the wake of the current 'Credit Crunch' and the deepening worldwide recession, New Labour, in defending the interests of finance and other corporate capital, and attacking workers' livelihoods, has prepared the ground for even more jingoistic, racist and sectarian forces.

Former New Labour Immigration Minister, Philip Woolas, has shown that it is not only Conservatives, who will stoop to the gutter, when it comes to racist attacks to divert attention from the real causes of the economic crisis. Meanwhile, the rise of the BNP, and the continued presence of malevolent Loyalist forces in 'the Six Counties', shows that even more sinister forces are lurking not far below the surface in the UK. Events in Berlusconi's Italy demonstrate that it is but a short step from government promoted racist policies to assaults upon and murders of migrants and members of ethnic minorities.

As we try to build a new Socialist movement, an appreciation of the Left's politics, between 1879 and 1895, provides us with useful insights. The Radicals were then the dominant force on the Left, from whom the infant Socialist and Labour movements inherited much of their politics. The Radicals wanted to return to the mid-century 'glory days' of free trade and international peace.

Today's Left includes those 'Marxist Radicals' - the entrants and outriders of the British Labour Party - who hope to re-establish the welfare state and to prolong the long period since 1945 without a world war. This is often tied to their Broad Left strategy for reclaiming the trade unions for 'real Labour'. They mimic the attempts by 'real Radicals' in the 1880's to reclaim the Liberal Party from the 'sham Radicals'.

However, just as the rise of 'New Imperialism', at the end of the nineteenth century, spelled out the end of the old international 'free trade' capitalist order, so the development of corporate capitalist imperialism today means that the post-1945 social democratic world has changed irrevocably. New answers and approaches are required.

'Marxist Radicals' in the SWP and Socialist Party (former Militant)[13] often defend

---

[13] Whilst the tradition of the Tory Democrats soon lost any remaining political purchase upon Socialists in Britain, it enjoyed a longer afterlife in the Labour Unionism found in 'the Six Counties'. Furthermore, even the virulently anti-Tory, Socialist Party (ex-Militant) has been known to flirt with plebian Loyalism, particularly that of the Progressive Unionist Party (linked to the paramilitary Ulster Volunteer Force).

the formation and continued existence of the UK as a 'progressive' achievement. They claim this historical gain, bringing working class unity, needs to be defended against the attacks of the Nationalists in Scotland and Wales. They completely fail to see the wider democratic issues at stake, or to understand the real nature of the UK's unionist and imperialist state, with its anti-democratic Crown Powers. 'Marxist Radicals' take some consolation in the 'Peace Process' in 'the Six Counties'. They believe this has reopened the possibility for raising 'bread and butter' issues, i.e. traditional Labourist politics.

When 'Marxist Radicals' are forced to address major democratic and constitutional issues, they tend to follow their nineteenth century Radical predecessors. They either see the 'National Question' as a diversion from the 'real struggle', or begin by giving their support to liberal unionist options to defend the UK. When the 'National Question' refuses to go away, some 'Marxist Radicals' end up tailing the more liberal sections of the British ruling class, when they call for more powers for the existing devolved assemblies. A few go so far as to advocate a new federal arrangement between the constituent parts of the UK. This last ditch liberal option has a long pedigree, whenever the British union state is under real threat from national democratic movements.

When even these tactics become untenable, 'Marxist Radicals' may then transfer their support to the schemes offered by the Nationalists. They hide behind the formulation of support for the 'right of national self-determination'. The political effect of this is to leave it to the various Nationalist parties to take the lead in formulating the politics of the national democratic movements. The only consistent aspect of all these 'Marxist Radical' approaches is their tailending of the constitutional 'solutions' offered by others.

Thus, by examining past history, we can see that the politics of those advocating various 'British roads to socialism' are but continuations of an older British Radical tradition, the 'British road to progress', which dominated the Left in Britain, in the late nineteenth century. Radicals tended to leave the political initiative over constitutional reform to the Liberal Party and their Irish Home Rule allies. Following these traditions, today's 'Marxist Radicals' usually take their political lead over the UK constitution from the liberal wing of the British ruling class, or sometimes from the Nationalist parties – Sinn Fein or the SNP.

Yet during the last quarter of the nineteenth century, an alternative tradition developed, which recognised some of the weaknesses of the Radicals of the day. In 1888, the Scottish Socialist Federation (SSF) was formed. It brought together SDF and SL/SLLL members, as well as other Socialists, to try and go beyond the politics of Radicalism and the subservience of Lib-Labism to the

Liberal Party.

In some respects the SSF was a forerunner of the Scottish Socialist Alliance (SSA), formed in 1996, in the aftermath of the Anti-Poll Tax Struggle, and the continued failure of the Labour Party to meet workers' needs. The SSA recognised the need for Socialists to take new look at the 'National Question'. Left nationalist and Left unionist tendencies united and clashed in the SSA and its successor organisation, the Scottish Socialist Party (SSP).

The Left nationalist tradition[14] came with the Scottish Republican Socialist Movement, and was taken up by sections of the former Militant/CWI, International Socialist Movement.

The Left unionist tradition[15] has been passed on through the British Labour, Communist parties and various Trotskyist organisations. In particular, the SWP, Alliance for Workers' Liberty and the CPGB-*Weekly Worker* brought this tradition into the SSP. Those remaining in the CWI, forming the International Socialists, adopted a Left nationalist approach on paper towards Scotland, but remained essentially Left unionists in practice.

The originally small socialist republican tendency, which emerged from the Anti-Poll Tax Struggle in Scotland, and from solidarity work with the ongoing social republican struggle in Ireland, went on to form part of the Republican Communist Network (RCN). The RCN became a growing influence in the SSA, then the SSP (4).

However, the historical fates of Davitt's social republicanism, the Scottish Labour Party's social Radicalism and the SSF's hybrid socialism offer a warning to Socialists in Scotland, Ireland, Wales and England today. Davitt's social republicanism collapsed into populist nationalism in Ireland, in the 1890's. After 1894, the SLP and the SSF, collapsed into the old Radical and social Radical traditions of the 'British road to progress' inherited by the Independent Labour Party, or its 'Marxist Radical' variant - 'the British road to socialism' - found in the SDF.

Today, after a major internal crisis, both the SSP and the breakaway Solidarity

---

[14] Those Left nationalists, in both the SSP and the breakaway Solidarity, tend to tail the constitutional proposals of the SNP, or its populist fringe and organisations like Independence First.

[15] The two main Left unionist groups in Scotland, the Trotskyist Socialist Workers Party and the International Socialists/Socialist Party Scotland (Committee for a Workers International) are to be found in Solidarity, although the much smaller Trotskyist left unionist and social imperialist Alliance for Workers Liberty has remained in the SSP.

face strong pulls in the form of Left nationalism and Left unionism, accompanied by tendencies to populism. Socialist republicanism remains a significant force only in the SSP[16].

Meanwhile, 'over the water', the near total eclipse of the social republicanism, once associated with the Irish Republican Movement, has contributed to a political vacuum amongst the working class, particularly in 'the Six Counties'. A pure physical force Republicanism, which originally developed amongst a section of the nineteenth century Fenians, has tried to fill this political vacuum.

It was the curtailment of the INLL's social republican offensive in 1881, and the defeat of the First Home Rule Bill in 1886, which allowed the pure physical force (as opposed to the social) Fenians, the Invincibles, and then the Dynamiters, to make their presence felt; just as today, the continued economic deprivation and social isolation experienced by sections of the Nationalist working class in 'the Six Counties', in the aftermath of the Good Friday, St. Andrews and Hillsborough Agreements, has led to the re-emergence of the physical force Republicanism of the Real and Continuity IRAs.

Dissident Republicans believe that nothing has changed since the 1960's and early '70's, when 'the Six Counties' were ruled over by Ulster Unionists and their Orange statelet. Today, however, continued British rule does not depend on unconditional support for a local Unionist-led Stormont regime, but on its ability to broker and manipulate constitutionally recognised Unionism and Nationalism in the reformed Stormont. Therefore, the military actions of the dissident Republicans, divorced from wider social aims and from any significant political support in the Nationalist community, tend to lead to further political fragmentation and demoralisation.

Over a century ago, by 1895, the limitations of Davitt's social republican and Radical politics had also become quite apparent. He had been unable to develop a new **socialist republican** politics, which could have united the economic, social and political movements in the face of 'New Imperialism' and conservative unionist triumphalism. The British ruling class was able to regain the political initiative and derailed the Home Rule challenge. At the same time, the Socialists

---

[16] Socialist republicanism now enjoys considerable support in the SSP. This was shown by the SSP's initiation of the Declaration of Calton Hill, and the very successful demonstration against the royal opening of the new Scottish Parliament building on October 9th 2004. After the split, the SSP's socialist republicanism was further highlighted when it organised the Republican Socialist Convention on 'internationalism from below' principles, in Edinburgh on November 29th, 2008, with representatives from Scotland, England, Ireland and Wales, and the political course adopted in relation to Scottish self-determination at the 2010 conference in Dunblane.

of the day were unable to take the vigorous post-1889 'New (Trade) Unionism' challenge forward. This militant workers' opposition went into retreat, as the New Unions took on some of the characteristics of 'Old Unionism'.

However, it was within the SSF milieu that the needed socialist republican alternative began to emerge, in the figure of James Connolly. Like Davitt, Connolly, born in 1868, was a member of an Irish migrant family. His family had settled in Edinburgh's 'Little Ireland' in the Cowgate. Initially he worked as a child labourer in the *Edinburgh Evening News* printshop, but enlisted in the British Army, between 1882-9, and was sent to Ireland.

James Connolly - member of Scottish Socialist Federation in Edinburgh, founder of Irish Socialist Republican Party in Dublin

Upon returning to Scotland, Connolly joined the SL/SLLL in Dundee in 1889. He also became a member of the SSF. He moved back to Edinburgh, taking on the job of manure carter with the City Corporation, just at the time the New (Trade) Unions were being introduced to the city, particularly amongst Leith dockers and Edinburgh carters.

Through Connolly's friendship with SSF Secretary, the Irish-Scot, John Leslie, he probably became more fully acquainted with the tradition of alliance in Scotland between United Irishmen and Scottish Radicals in the 1798 period, between Young Irelanders and Scottish Chartists in the 1840's, and between Fenians, Irish Land Leaguers and Scottish Land Nationalisers, social republicans and Socialists in the '70's and '80's.

Connolly became active in Scottish Socialist circles, just as the Irish Home Rule movement was splitting, and Davitt's own Irish Nationalist politics were found wanting. Nevertheless, Connolly drew considerable inspiration from Davitt's contribution to the struggle for control of the land. Connolly further developed Davitt's earlier secular approach to win over religiously influenced workers.

Connolly became a member of the Scottish Labour Party (which was supported by the SSF). He joined the ILP after the Scottish party dissolved itself in 1894.

The next year Connolly, at more or less the same time as Edward Aveling, Eleanor Marx and William Morris, joined the SDF. With the demise of the SL/SLL, and its collapse into Anarchism, the SSF had decided to merge into the SDF. However, Connolly did not follow the SDF's 'British road to socialism' but made a quantum leap in his approach when he moved to Dublin and founded the Irish Socialist Republican Party in 1896.

Here Connolly developed the socialist republican politics that took Davitt's social republican and radical 'internationalism from below' alliance on to a higher level, during the heyday of 'High Imperialism' from 1895. Connolly's early involvement in the 'New (Trade) Unionism' in Edinburgh also ensured that his socialist republicanism remained grounded in the working class. Connolly's consistent anti-unionism and anti-imperialism offered a clear strategy, which opposed both the 'British road to socialism' and the Irish constitutional nationalism supported by most of the British and Irish Left of his day. Instead, Connolly promoted a 'break-up of the UK and British Empire road to socialism'.

In today's world, Imperialism still calls the shots. The continued existence of the UK state provides the British ruling class with a powerful bastion of support. This unionist and monarchist state gives the ruling class a whole host of draconian Crown Powers to maintain its rule. Even the formally independent Irish Republic has to bow to British ruling class needs. This was highlighted by Irish politicians' recent acceptance of the liabilities of UK-owned banks in Ireland. Nor did the Irish government get thanks for their pioneering bank rescue plan to save domestic capitalism, much of which Gordon Brown and Alistair Darling so quickly copied and took credit for.

However, the current financial crisis has also highlighted the close links between leading Scottish Nationalists and the British banks. In panic, they have quietly rushed into the arms of the UK government to develop a common approach to address shared capitalist concerns. New Labour and the SNP both push for public sector cuts at workers' expense. Meanwhile, in public, the SNP and New Labour continue their political squabbles over the constitution, jockeying for position to gain relative advantages for their particular capitalist backers.

British politicians, whether they are Labour, Conservative or Liberal Democrat, continue to argue with SNP politicians over the extent of power to be awarded to the devolved Scottish Parliament at Holyrood. However, they all agree that the monarchy and the ruling class's Crown Powers have to remain in place; that the Bank of England will control the economy through the continued use of sterling; and that suitable arrangements have to be made to accommodate NATO and to protect US imperial interests. All these parties are wedded to neo-liberalism and are in hock to corporate capital.

The Nationalist parties represented in the various devolved assemblies, in Holyrood, Cardiff Bay or Stormont, make no attempt to mount a joint challenge to continued British rule, or to the all pervading corporate capitalist power over these islands. Whilst Plaid Cymru leaders may be envious of the powers already devolved to the Scottish Parliament, it is pretty clear that, if parity were to be achieved by the Welsh Assembly, this would merely signal their intention to compete more effectively for inward corporate investment. When Donald Trump threatened to abandon his exclusive golfing complex project in Aberdeenshire, in the face of local opposition, in stepped the then DUP Northern Ireland Minister, Ian Paisley Junior, to offer an alternative site on the Antrim Coast. However, the SNP-led Scottish Executive moved quickly to give Trump the green light.

Just as Davitt and Connolly realised, in their day, that they faced the combined forces of British imperialism (whether it be Conservative or Liberal) and Irish nationalism (whether it be Parnell or his successors), so Socialists face the similar combined opposition of Labour, Conservative and Lib-Dem unionists and the Nationalists today. By studying our class's history, we gain the advantages of hindsight. This is why we need to look once more to rebuild an 'internationalism from below' alliance, but now of republican socialists in Scotland, England, Ireland and Wales. The Republican Socialist Convention, held in Edinburgh on November 29th, 2008, represented the SSP's first attempt to develop such an alliance (5).

References

(1) **see** T. W. Moody, *Davitt and Irish Revolution, 1846-82*, (Oxford University Press, 1990, Oxford)

(2) **see** http://en.wikipedia.org/wiki/New_Imperialism

(3) **see** Bernard Semmel, *The Rise of Free Trade Imperialism - Classical Political Economy and the Empire of Free Trade and Imperialism, 1750-1850* (Cambridge University Press, 1970, London)

(4) **see** http://republicancommunist.org/blog/

http://en.wikipedia.org/wiki/Declaration_of_Calton_Hill

http://www.scottishsocialistparty.co.uk/republicansocialist/

(5) **see** Republican Socialist Convention Conference Report, 29th November 2008, Edinburgh (International Committee, Scottish Socialist Party, 2009, Dundee)

2. The growing conflict between Liberal and Conservative unionism in the period of new imperialism

British labour history, when dealing with the later nineteenth century, tends to focus upon the sudden explosion of 'New Unionism' in 1889 (1), and the creation of the Independent Labour Party in 1893 (2). Sometimes it investigates the earlier work done by Social Democrats and other Socialists in certain key areas, such as the East End of London. These certainly contributed to this dramatic flare-up of class struggle. Irish socialist historians have tried to recover the previously, largely hidden, indigenous roots of an Irish Labour and Socialist tradition (3). Some labour historians examining Scottish (4) and Welsh (5) history have also adopted this approach.

Much of this work is excellent, but sometimes its findings get caught up in the political debate between those upholding an all-Britain (occasionally all-UK) working class history, and those trying to locate the various national working class struggles within their particular Irish, Scottish or Welsh contexts. These alternatives could perhaps be termed Left unionist and Left nationalist approaches. They represent responses to the wider and continuing debates over the development and future of the UK and Irish states in a changing world.

In early and mid Victorian Britain, when the UK was the unquestioned dominant economic power in the world, it was the Whigs and Liberals who had best expressed the pressure for reforms. These removed traditional barriers to effective industrial capitalist development and 'free' waged labour. By late Victorian Britain, with 'New Imperialism' becoming the dominant economic and political force in the world, the Conservatives' jingoism and racism better reflected these pressures.

In the mid-1880's, a major section of the Liberal Party, the Liberal Unionists, joined the Conservative Party in a reactionary defence of the Union and the jingoistic celebration of the Empire. By the mid-1890's, the leadership of the truncated Liberal Party had also fully capitulated to the politics of 'New Imperialism'.

However, it is necessary to go back to 1879, and the launch of the 'Irish Revolution' (6), to appreciate the nature and extent of the new wave of struggles that spread across the UK. These contributed to the break-up of the prior British ruling class consensus over the existing unionist form of the UK state. This wave of opposition led to the sequence of events that contributed, not only to the 'New (Trade) Unionism' of 1889, and to the birth of the Socialist and Labour movements, but to a wider political struggle against this new intransigent British Unionism and jingoistic British Imperialism.

The 'Irish Revolution' helped to bring new groups into independent action throughout the UK. First in action were the Irish tenant farmers and their allies. As their struggles developed, tenant farmers and the landless from Scotland and Wales, as well agricultural and industrial workers from England, Scotland, Wales and Ireland, were all drawn into the economic, social and political maelstrom. Furthermore, these struggles enjoyed considerable support from US (including Irish-American Fenian) and Australian social republican, radical and labour figures.

Migrant labour played a key role. The constant changes in the class composition of the 'lower orders', leading to the fall or rise of certain categories of labour, initially made working class organisation more difficult, as employers deliberately promoted ethnic or sectarian divisions amongst their workforces[1]. However, migrant labour also brought its ready-made traditions of struggle, imported by workers from other nations and regions. These traditions were drawn upon and modified in the course of struggle. They contributed to the political awareness and fighting capability of a new ethnically mixed working class.

---

[1] In the UK, this divide was strongest in north-east Ulster, Clydeside and Merseyside. Here the Orange Order helped the employers by promoting sectarianism. Of course, there were much deeper divisions in the colonies, where trade unions also promoted racist, white, skilled labour policies and social segregation.

[2] Social republicanism was represented by that wing of Irish Republicanism that linked the struggle for an Irish Republic with economic and social issues, particularly the demand for land.

[3] Radicalism changed its social basis over the nineteenth century. It began as an ideology of a section of the rising industrial bourgeoisie confronting the old aristocratic landowners. There was also a plebian anti-capitalist Radicalism, which often came into conflict with bourgeois Radicalism, highlighted by the epic struggle between the Chartists and the Anti-Corn Law League. Once the bourgeoisie made its peace with the landlords, after 1845, Radicalism became more the preserve of the smaller bourgeoisie, now backed by trade union leaders wedded to the 'Old Unionism', which originally took root with the New Model unions in the 1850's. These Radicals looked to a reformed capitalism and opposed Socialism.

[4] Socialism had originally appeared in the UK as an idea amongst the followers of Robert Owen. A Socialist current later emerged amongst the Chartists led by Bronterre O'Brien. It reappeared as a force within the British section of the First International. However, Socialism fell into retreat and was only to re-emerge again in a politically organised form after 1884, in the Social Democratic Federation, followed a year later by the breakaway Socialist League.

The impact of social republican[2], Radical[3] and Socialist[4] propaganda, along with labour agitation, ensured that important struggles, undertaken by one section of the 'lower orders', provided lessons and inspiration for other sections. Furthermore, key economic and social conflicts were tied in with the political struggles that developed first around the issue of Irish Home Rule but were later extended to Home Rule for Scotland and Wales too. These helped to overturn the existing British and Irish party set-up, and to undermine the existing constitutional order in the UK.

Left unionist historians tend to assume that the continued development of the UK state and what they describe as the 'British nation', created a wider, more united British working class, marked by the creation of all-British (occasionally all-UK) trade unions and the eventual emergence of the Independent Labour Party, the Labour Representation Committee and the British Labour Party.

However, the UK state framework did not provide an organisational template, which could be replicated by oppositional forces, except at considerable political cost. The all-Britain and all-UK political, trade union and other bodies, which attempted to adopt this approach, were strongly tainted by British unionism and imperialism. The continued rise of 'New Imperialism' shifted the mainstream political centre of gravity sharply to the Right. Ultra-unionism and 'gung-ho' imperialism produced liberal unionist and 'ethical' imperial responses, not only amongst Liberals and Radicals, but also within both Social Democratic/Socialist and independent Labour organisations, when they appeared from the mid-1880's.

An 'internationalism from below' approach better appreciates the impact of the constitutional monarchist, unionist and imperialist UK state (and later, a divided Ireland) upon class struggles. It recognises the political and social significance of the national democratic movements, which have contested the UK's union-state constitution. It is also more able to account for the connections between the class struggles which emerged and influenced each other in England, Ireland, Scotland and Wales.

From the early 1880's, an 'internationalism from below' alliance, of Irish social republicans and Scottish, Welsh and English Radicals, was created in the course of the growing class struggles. This did much to contest the wider political accommodation to 'New Imperialism'. Those adopting an 'internationalism from below' approach were informed by a sharper awareness of the problems brought about by 'New Imperialism' and the rise of conservative unionism. Struggles launched on this basis were better able to avoid the restraints enforced upon those 'wearing' an all-Britain, or an all-UK, organisational straitjacket. They were also able to produce wider alliances, which in turn brought about cross-national struggles.

Some of those struggles, which began within a distinct national (Irish, Scottish, Welsh or English) arena, based on their own particular organisations, were still able to extend beyond their initial areas, without falling under the moderate or conservative sway of existing all-Britain or all-UK bodies. Sometimes, these struggles then lifted the political tempo in their original national locales, bringing other class forces into play, which had previously been weaker there. The infant Socialist and Labour movements, in the UK and beyond, were all profoundly affected by the spreading waves of class conflict originally centred upon Ireland.

The demand for Home Rule, initiated in Ireland, but extended to Scotland, Wales, and occasionally to England too, meant different things to different classes and people. Social republicans, Radicals, Socialists and Liberals all held to their own visions. However, it was to be the liberal unionist[5], or middle class version of Home Rule, that eventually gained political ascendancy amongst those contesting, first the landlord-led Conservative, then the new business-led, Conservative and Liberal Unionist alliance.

The liberal unionist demand for a devolved Irish parliament only really developed after the failure of the First Irish Home Rule Bill[6] in 1886. In the new official Liberal version, Home Rule was designed to create protected jobs for the middle class in their particular constituent nation – Ireland, Scotland or Wales. Just as important, though, the continuation of the UK state and of the British Empire also left the way open for careers at an all-UK or imperial level.

Some liberal unionists were concerned to downplay the wider national democratic aspect of the demand for Home Rule. They came up with the idea of 'Home Rule all-round'. The idea behind this was to severely reign in the more advanced Home Rule demands coming from Irish Nationalists, and to

---

[5] Here it is necessary to once more emphasise the distinction between the liberal unionism of the official Liberal Party, and the somewhat misleading name given to the breakaway Liberal Unionist Party. The Liberal Unionists gave their support to the conservative unionist strategy of opposing Home Rule. Eventually this labeling anomaly was resolved when the Liberal Unionists followed the logic of their politics and merged into the expanded Conservative and Unionist Party.

[6] The First Irish Home Rule Bill was not based upon devolving certain Westminster powers to a subordinate Irish parliament, but upon Ireland achieving similar (what would later be called Dominion) status to certain British white colonies like Canada. This would also have met the traditional Irish nationalist demand to break the 1801 parliamentary union, by re-establishing an Irish Parliament, albeit still under the British monarchy and within the British Empire.

limit them to the much more restricted demands which, at that time, might satisfy Liberals in Scotland and Wales[7]. In contrast, when the 'internationalism from below' alliance of the 'lower orders' developed, it drew in the more advanced Home Rulers from Ireland, Scotland and Wales. Social republicans and many Radicals tended to accept the leading role of Ireland. They did not ask for Ireland to wait until others had caught up.

However, in the gung-ho, jingoist climate created by 'New Imperialism', even the very moderate official Liberal demand for Home Rule was violently opposed by the Conservative and Liberal Unionists, particularly in north-east Ulster, the Clyde Valley and on Merseyside. Conservative unionists tried to make the very notion of Home Rule as unacceptable as American neo-conservatives try to make the word 'liberal'.

Nevertheless, the political division, between the Conservative and Liberal Parties' chosen strategies, disguised the fact that they were both united in wanting to preserve the United Kingdom and British Empire. Conservative unionism saw the demand for Home Rule as a dangerous stalking horse, designed to break up the Union and British Empire. Liberal unionists, however, saw Home Rule as a means to try and win wider support from the peoples of Ireland, Scotland, Wales, and hopefully in England too, for the British Union and Empire.

Now, there may well be political circumstances, in which social republicans in the nineteenth century, and socialist republicans today, would fight alongside others for some more limited extension of democratic powers. However, such a situation arises because of the relative weakness of the politically organised class forces, which would be needed to bring about a more fundamental democratic advance - the break-up of the unionist and imperialist UK state, and the whole host of anti-democratic Crown Powers used to buttress the rule of the British ruling class.

Engels was to make acute observations on the different political conditions that may prevail, at a given time, when he tried to outline political demands for Socialists addressing the linked land and national democratic struggles in

---

[7] In the 1990s, New Labour was forced to recognise the national democratic nature of the Irish, Scottish and Welsh challenge faced by the British ruling class. Their strategy to try to control this was to promote 'asymmetrical devolution'. This concedes the minimum devolutionary measures in each constituent nation or region, which the government thinks it can get away with. This model was first developed in Spain in the 1970s and '80s, in the face primarily of Basque and Catalan opposition.

Ireland. He chronicled the changing political conditions brought about by the 'Irish Revolution'. Furthermore, Eleanor Marx and Edward Aveling, the other two key remaining members of the 'Marx Party' living in the UK, were very active, in both England and Ireland, in making the link between the rising forces of New (Trade) Unionism, and the need for a new socialist republican political approach to carry the 'internationalism from below' alliance forward.

References

(1)   **see** Yvonne Kapp, *The Air of Freedom: The Birth of the New Unionism*, (Lawrence & Wishart, 1989, London) **and** Terry McCartney, *The Great Dock Strike, 1889 – The Story of the Labour Movement's First Great Victory* (Weidenfield & Nicholson, 1988, London) **and** Eric Hobsbawm, *The 'New Unionism' in Perspective* in *Worlds of Labour – Further studies in the history of labour* (Weidenfield & Nicolson, 1984, London)

(2)   **see** http://en.wikipedia.org/wiki/Independent_Labour_Party

(3)   **see** W.P. Ryan, *The Irish Labour Movement, From the Twenties to Our Own Day* (The Talbot Press, 1919, Dublin) **and** Peter Berresford Ellis, *The History of the Irish Working Class* (Pluto Press, 1985, London) **and** Fintan Lane, *The Origins of Modern Irish Socialism, 1881-1896* (Cork University Press, 1997, Cork)

(4)   **see** W. Hamish Fraser, *Conflict and Class, Scottish Workers, 1700-1830* (John Donald, 1988, Edinburgh) **and** William Kenefick, *Red Scotland! The Rise and Fall of the Radical Left, c. 1872 to 1932* (Edinburgh University Press, 2007, Edinburgh)

(5)   **see** David Smith, edit., *A People and A Proletariat – Essays in the History of Wales, 1780-1980* (Pluto Press, 1980, London) **and** Gwyn A. Williams, *When Was Wales?* (Penguin Books, 1985, London)

(6)   **see** T. W. Moody, *Davitt and Irish Revolution, 1846-82* (Oxford University Press, 1990, Oxford)

3. 1879 - Michael Davitt and the launching of the 'Irish Revolution'

Michael Davitt (1) was the key political figure associated with the first phase of the 'internationalism from below' alliance. He, perhaps more than any other figure, amongst leading Labour leaders in the UK, demonstrated the greatest political awareness and the most advanced strategic thinking at the time. Davitt, as much as Keir Hardie[1] (2), considered the whole of England, Ireland, Scotland and Wales to be his theatre of struggle, whilst showing a strong interest in political developments within the British Empire and the USA too. The social republicanism and Radicalism, which informed Davitt's politics, provided him with a way of thinking that placed him ahead of most of his contemporaries in the 1880's, until the limitations of his politics became more apparent after 1889.

Michael Davitt was born in Straide, County Mayo, in 1846, within a small tenant farming family. They had been forced to emigrate to Haslingden in Lancashire as a result of the Great Famine (3). Here his experiences as a young millworker contributed to one side of his politics - Radicalism. Davitt's remaining strong links with Ireland contributed to the other side of his politics - social republicanism.

Davitt joined the Irish Republican Brotherhood (IRB) in 1865. He was jailed under harsh conditions in

Davitt worked as a young millworker in Haslingden

Portland Prison from 1870-7. He was only released on a ticket-of-leave basis[2].

---

[1] Keir Hardie unsuccessfully stood for the Scottish Mid-Lanarkshire constituency in 1888. He won the English West Ham seat in 1892, and five years after his defeat there, won the Welsh Merthyr Tydfil seat in 1900.

[2] Ticket-of-leave meant that he could be re-arrested at any time the authorities thought it expedient. He was re-imprisoned on 3rd February 1881 at the height of the Irish Land War.

Soon after Davitt's release from prison he developed what Marx had called a 'socialistic', although more accurately, a social republican tendency which he had inherited from Fenianism (4).

Davitt worked with key Irish-Americans, including Clan-na-Gael³ (5) leader, John Devoy (6), William Carroll, and Patrick Ford (7), editor of the influential *Irish World*, to promote the latest manifestation of social republicanism – the 'New Departure' (8). Other Fenians, such as Jeremiah O'Donovan Rossa (9), opposed this. They still upheld an older, largely physical force strategy for achieving their ideal Irish Republic.

Patrick Ford - editor of "Irish World"

The 'New Departure' was designed to involve tenant farmers and their allies in militant action to break the power of the landlords. In Davitt's mind, the 'New Departure' revived the strategy, which had originally been advocated by the Irish Confederate leader, James Fintan Lalor (10), in 1847, in order to win an Irish Republic. In 1879, however, this action was to be supplemented by a political campaign, led by a strengthened and more radical Home Rule League (HRL)/Independent Irish Party (IIP)⁴ (11) presence in Westminster. Clan-na-Gael would ship arms across to Ireland clandestinely. These would be made available to those who resisted the inevitable UK state and landlord clampdown. IIP MPs would then put forward a Bill in Westminster to end the Union, which, when refused, would lead to their walkout, and their summonsing of a National Convention in Ireland (12). As it turned out, there were to be considerable problems in coordinating these three strands of the 'New Departure'.

The role of leading the political strand of the 'New Departure' largely fell to

---

³ Clan-na-Gael was the Fenian organisation in the USA that replaced the Fenian Brotherhood there, after the failure of the 1867 Irish Rising and the Fenian invasion of Canada.

⁴ The Home Rule League had been set up Isaac Butt in 1870. After the 1874 election it had 60 MPs in Westminster, but they were not a very cohesive group. Their membership included landlords and ex-IRB members.

Charles Parnell[5] (13). Despite being a Protestant landowner, Parnell was an advanced nationalist. He was aided in his attempt to radicalise the HRL by Radical middle class supporters, such as Joseph Biggar (14) from Belfast, John Ferguson (15) from Glasgow, and John Barry from Newcastle-upon-Tyne (16). They were all businessmen, ex-members of the IRB, and current members of the Home Rule League or Home Rule Confederation of Great Britain (HRCGB)[6]. Beginning in Scotland and England, Parnell's supporters helped him to marginalise the old landlord element in the HRL, previously led by Isaac Butt (17), and to rally support behind the 'New Departure'.

Parnell became the new leader of the HRL/IIP, after many earlier landlord MPs had been deselected or challenged as parliamentary candidates for the 1880 General Election. This occurred in the middle of the recently launched Irish Land War. It paved the way for an increased and radicalised IIP presence at Westminster. Parnell's religious and class background, atypical for Irish Nationalists, meant that he could project himself as being above narrow clerical and class influences, and an indispensable coordinator of the different forces involved in the new movement. Parnell emerged as a populist, rather than a democratic, leader.

As Engels appreciated at the time, "Violent insurrection had no prospect of success for many years... Hence a legal movement remained the only possibility, and such a movement was undertaken under the banner of the Home Rulers" (18). For Davitt and others, Home Rule was but a stage on the road to the Irish Republic. It was Parnell, who later in 1885, best expressed this view of Home Rule[7] - "No man has the right to fix the boundary of a march of a nation" (19). This, though, went further than the understanding of Home Rule held by many of the Irish middle class, who still saw this policy as quite compatible with remaining part of the UK and British Empire.

---

[5] Charles Parnell had been elected as a Home Rule League (HRL) MP for County Meath in 1875. He opposed the conciliatory tactics advocated by the then HRL and IPP leader, Isaac Butt. Parnell built up an advanced nationalist wing amongst the IIP MPs by utilising the tactic of obstructing the government's bills in Westminster. He was careful in his choice, choosing issues like the government's proposed annexation of Transvaal, and its Mutiny, Prison and Army Reform Bills to put forward amendments, which would draw British Radical support.

[6] The Home Rule Confederation of Great Britain was the official organisation of the Irish Home Rule League in Britain. It enjoyed certain legal advantages here denied to its parent body in Ireland.

[7] It is a moot point though, by this time, whether Parnell believed this himself, rather than using such rhetoric to win over others to his now one overriding idea – an Irish National Party alliance with Gladstone to achieve whatever limited form of Home Rule he could get.

In contrast to Parnell's particular class appeal to the better-off tenant farmers and Irish bourgeoisie, Davitt sought to win a new and active mass base of support amongst the poorer tenant farmers, the landless, the agricultural, and later the industrial workers. The road to a future Irish Republic lay through an immediate campaign of 'Land for the People'. This was to be the main, and the most successful, strand of the 'New Departure'.

The first meeting to launch the 'New Departure', and which started the train of events leading to the 'Irish Revolution', was held in Irishtown in County Mayo, on the 20th April 1879. The west of Ireland was experiencing the Gorta Beag[8], or Small Famine, at the time (20). A leaflet was issued, under the heading, *The West Awake*[9]. The organisers' strong anti-imperialist sentiments were demonstrated in its text. "From the China towers of Pekin to the round towers of Ireland, from the cabins of Connemara to the kraals of Kaffirland, from the wattled homes of the isles of Polynesia to the wigwams of North America the cry is 'Down with the invaders! Down with tyrants! Every man to have his own land – every man to have his own home" (21).

A national organisation was officially launched at Westport, also in County Mayo, on the 16th August (22). The Irish National Land League (INLL) (23) was set up in Dublin on the 21st October (24). Many from the earlier Tenants Defence Associations[10] had been persuaded to join, and leading member, Andrew Kettle, was brought into the new leadership (25). Philip Johnson, of the Irish labourers' union in Kanturk, County Cork, also joined the leadership, despite the tensions that existed between tenant farmers and agricultural labourers (26). Catholic priests and a few Protestant ministers were also involved (27).

Davitt thought that Parnell's detached social position and political skills made

---

[8] The name 'Gorta Beag' was to distinguish it from the much more severe 'Gorta Mor', or Great Famine from 1845-9. If Mayo witnessed the launching of the most progressive secular movement yet witnessed in Ireland, it also saw the rise of its obfuscatory religious counterpart, with the first 'sighting' of the 'blessed Virgin Mary' at Knock, during the same period.

[9] *The West Awake* also signalled the entry of the West to the Irish national struggle. This area had previously had been marginal compared to Dublin, or the North (Ulster), and South (Munster). The West continued to be the focus of land struggles long after the issue had died down elsewhere in Ireland.

[10] These had been associated with the earlier land reform policy of the 'Three Fs' - Fair Rent, Fixity of Tenure and Freedom to Sell - accepted by Butt's HRL and Irish Liberal Party MPs alike. However, tenants had made little headway in achieving these aims, except in the North, where the 'Ulster Custom' prevailed and provided tenants there with greater security. This, and the concerted opposition from the landlords and Orange Order leadership, helped to limit the appeal of the INLL's new policy of peasant proprietorship in most of Ulster.

him an ideal person to become President and, in effect, act as the INLL's main public face (28). Parnell, however, maintained his distance from the Fenians. They were meant to represent the third 'armed strand' called upon when the time was right. After a great deal of effort on Davitt and his allies' behalf, the Fenian leadership had been persuaded to allow IRB and Clan-na-Gael members to take part in the 'New Departure' as individuals, although they did not officially support the INLL (29). As the Land League's struggle developed further, both Parnell and the official Fenian leadership, from their own different standpoints, were to undermine the social republican approach initially promoted by Davitt and his supporters.

The INLL put forward the immediate demand of lowering rents, and the long-term aim of replacing landlord ownership with peasant proprietorship. Davitt, and his principal lieutenants, Patrick Egan (30) and Thomas Brennan (31), were the League's key organisers. It was Brennan who first pointed out the hollowness of national liberation without social emancipation. "As long as the tillers of the soil are forced to support a useless and indolent aristocracy your federal parliament" would be a bauble and your Irish republic but a fraud[11]" (32).

Davitt gave his support to the setting up of the Ladies Land League. This had been initiated by Parnell's sister, Fanny, in New York, and was then spread to Ireland by his other sister, Anna (33). Davitt did this in the teeth of opposition, even from some of his closest allies, including Brennan, as well as from a scornful Parnell. The Ladies Land League was first involved mainly in relief work. However, it was later to develop a much more central role in the struggle.

The ongoing Long Depression[12] (34), and the famine conditions in the West, meant that many tenants had been unable to pay their rents and, as a result, were being evicted by the landlords and their agents, with the aid of the courts and the Royal Irish Constabulary (35). Davitt developed the tactic soon to be

---

[11] Brennan's reference to a federal parliament was a dig at the demand put forward by Isaac Butt's moderate HRL, whilst his mention of the Irish Republic was a dig targeted at those Fenians, who opposed social republicanism in the name of 'pure' Irish nationalism won through armed struggle only. It also anticipated James Connolly's more famous statement, (**see** Chapter 20, reference 41).

[12] The Long Depression is the name given to the economic situation prevailing between 1873 and 1896. Thus particularly affected the price of agricultural products, as a result of cheap food exported from the USA and colonies flooding the European markets, and undermining traditional agricultural production here. Ireland was particularly badly affected.

known as boycotting[13]. It was directed against anyone attempting to buy evicted tenants' land. Here, Davitt made use of his knowledge of the tactics used in industrial struggles in Lancashire against blacklegs, and directed them against land-grabbers and their agents (36).

Soon boycott action was extended to anyone who offered any help to the

Captain Boycott - target of Land League action

landlords whatsoever. This proved to be very effective, but where landlords were more obdurate, some tenants went beyond the methods advocated by the League, and adopted violent tactics directed against the landlords' property, their agents and occasionally the landlords themselves. These tactics were attributed to 'Captain Moonlight'. They followed a long tradition going back to the Whiteboys (37), Defenders (38), and Ribbonmen (39), clandestine organisations of Catholic tenants in the countryside.

When it came to Catholic clerical interference and Orange sectarianism, Davitt confronted these head on. As a secular Catholic, Davitt was acutely aware of the reactionary stance of the Vatican, which went out of its way to help the UK government, and to pressurise the Irish clergy to denounce the League (40). In the 1880 General Election[14], he successfully fought in support of League-backed parliamentary candidates in Counties Mayo and Wexford against the hierarchy's preferred candidates (41). Furthermore, Davitt was able to win the support of many clerics, particularly at the parish level, where priests often had close family links with the tenant farmers. Davitt also held meetings in Orange Ulster strongholds, even winning over some of its members, who were tenant farmers (42).

---

[13] Named after Captain Boycott, whose estate in County Mayo was to witness the most celebrated instance of the use of this tactic.

[14] Strictly speaking, the INLL was constitutionally prevented from funding election candidates. This hurdle was imposed by the Fenian members amongst its leadership, less than impressed by the performance of Isaac Butt's old IPP, which had initially enjoyed some Fenian support. However, the INLL was still able to provide funds 'under the counter' for its preferred candidates in the 1880 General Election, and their successes were perceived by friends and foes alike as a victory for the League.

Davitt had a number of allies in Ulster, including the Reverend Harold Rylett[15] (43), who campaigned relentlessly in the face of landlord-backed reaction. The Orange Order[16] leadership, however, demonstrated its usual reactionary role by acting on behalf of the landlords. The Order provided fifty labourers to work the lands of Captain Boycott, in 1880 (44), and then set up an Orange Emergency Committee to counter the League in 1881 (45).

---

[15] The Reverend Harold Rylett was a Presbyterian Unitarian minister from Moneyrea in County Down. He had been an associate of Joseph Arch in setting up the National Agricultural Labourers' Union in England in 1870. Rylett campaigned vigorously in Ulster for the INLL. He later attended the founding conference of the Independent Labour Party in 1893.

[16] The Orange Order had begun its life as a counter-revolutionary organisation for Church of Ireland (CoI) members only, in 1795, at a time when many Irish Presbyterians were members of the republican United Irishmen. However, after 1801, most Presbyterians joined their CoI brethren in support of the Union. A new Rightist and theologically conservative leadership emerged in their ranks in the nineteenth century, leading to an ultra-sectarian Presbyterian street preacher tradition in the 1850's from which the Reverend Ian Paisley also emerged a century later.

References

(1)   see http://en.wikipedia.org/wiki/Michael_Davitt

(2)   see http://en.wikipedia.org/wiki/Keir_Hardie

(3)   see http://en.wikipedia.org/wiki/Great_Famine_(Ireland)

(4)   see Karl Marx, Letter to Frederick Engels, 30.11.1867, in *Ireland and the Irish Question,* p. 157 (Lawrence & Wishart, 1978, London)

(5)   see http://en.wikipedia.org/wiki/Clan_na_Gael

(6)   see http://en.wikipedia.org/wiki/John_Devoy

(7)   see http://places.galwaylibrary.ie/history/chapter140.html

(8)   see *1878* on http://en.wikipedia.org/wiki/New_Departure_(Ireland)

(9)   see http://en.wikipedia.org/wiki/O'Donovan_Rossa

(10)   see http://en.wikipedia.org/wiki/James_Fintan_Lalor

(11)   see http://en.wikipedia.org/wiki/Home_Rule_League

(12)   see T. W. Moody, *Davitt and Irish Revolution, 1846-82 (DatIR),* p. 207, (Oxford University Press, 1990, Oxford)

(13)   see http://en.wikipedia.org/wiki/Charles_Stewart_Parnell

(14)   see http://en.wikipedia.org/wiki/Joseph_Biggar

(15)   see Elaine McFarland, *John Ferguson, 1836-1906, Irish Issues in Scottish Politics* (Tuckwell Press, 2001, East Linton) **and** T. W. Moody, *DatIR,* op. cit., pp. 125, 188-9, 335.

(16)   **see** T. W. Moody, *DatIR*, op. cit., p. 134.

(17)   **see** http://en.wikipedia.org/wiki/Isaac_Butt

(18)   Frederick Engels, *The English Elections*, in Karl Marx and Frederick Engels, *Articles on Britain*, p. 370 (Progress Publishers, 1975, Moscow)

(19)   **see** http://en.wikiquote.org/wiki/Nations

(20)   **see** http://en.wikipedia.org/wiki/Irish_Famine_(1879)

(21)   T. W. Moody, *DatIR*, op. cit., p. 289.

(22)   ibid., p. 317.

(23)   **see** http://en.wikipedia.org/wiki/Irish_Land_League

(24)   **see** T. W. Moody, *DatIR*, op. cit., p. 334.

(25)   ibid., p. 325.

(26)   ibid., pp. 340-1.

(27)   ibid., p. 335.

(28)   ibid., p. 335.

(29)   ibid., p. 288.

(30)   **see** http://en.wikipedia.org/wiki/Patrick_Egan_(land_reformer_and_diplomat)

(31)   **see** http://en.wikipedia.org/wiki/Thomas_Brennan_(Irish_Land_League)

(33)   T. W. Moody, *DatIR*, op. cit., p. 343.

(34)   ibid., p. 291.

(35)   ibid., p. 457.

(36)   **see** http://en.wikipedia.org/wiki/Long_Depression

(37)   **see** http://en.wikipedia.org/wiki/Royal_Irish_Constabulary

(38)   **see** T. W. Moody, *DatIR*, op. cit., p. 419.

(39)   **see** http://en.wikipedia.org/wiki/Whiteboys

(40)   **see** http://en.wikipedia.org/wiki/Defenders_(Ireland)

(41)   **see** http://en.wikipedia.org/wiki/Ribbonmen

(42)   **see** Michael Davitt, *The Fall of Feudalism - or the Story of the Land League Revolution* (*TFoF*) pp. 397-408 (Harpers & Brothers Publishers, 1904, London)

(43)   ibid., pp. 372-3.

(44)   ibid., pp. 447-8.

(45)   **see** T. W. Moody, *DatIR*, op. cit., p. 490.

(46)   **see** Michael Davitt, *TFoF*, op. cit., p. 424.

(47)   ibid., p. 434.

4. Davitt adopts an 'Internationalism from Below' strategy to spread the revolution

After his key role in organising the INLL, Davitt's most important contribution was his promotion of an 'internationalism from below' strategy. This was also to provide him with a new basis to reinvigorate the struggle, when Parnell eventually compromised and backtracked. Davitt reinvented this 'internationalism from below' approach, following the precedents set by the United Irishmen, United Scotsmen, London Corresponding Society and the American Society of United Irishmen in the 1790's and early 1800's, and by the Chartist Left and the Irish Confederates in the 1840's.

With Davitt's support, and the help of his overseas allies, an INLL solidarity organisation, the National Land League of Great Britain (NLLGB), was formed in March 1881, often making use of existing branches of the Irish Home Rule Confederation (1). Other support organisations were set up in the USA (2), Canada and Australia. These bodies provided both moral support and financial help, supplementing that which also arrived clandestinely from Fenian sources.

A certain Jim Connell[1] became involved in the Poplar branch of the NLLGB in London's East End. He was to join its National Executive (3). In Scotland, close allies of Davitt's, such as John Ferguson, Edward McHugh (4) and Richard McGhee (5) were to provide a bridge to the next stage of the land struggle. They became organisers of cross-national land, labour and political campaigns.

Davitt, on the invite of Patrick Ford and others, made a public tour of the USA on behalf of the INLL. Whilst there, he also privately consulted leading Clan-na-Gael figures as to the progress being made by the 'New Departure'. The tour was a great success. Furthermore, Davitt also met another figure, Henry George (6), who was to influence him greatly, in his attempts to revitalise and extend the movement, after Parnell's clampdown in 1882.

Henry George had recently published the massively popular *Progress and Poverty*. This book advocated a 'Single Tax'[2] to fall upon ground rent. Local

---

[1] Jim Connell was a former Fenian, and would later join the SDF and the Independent Labour Party (see Chapter 14, reference 30).

[2] In Henry George's thinking a 'Single Tax' on ground rents could replace all other taxes and raise sufficient revenue for the community's needs.

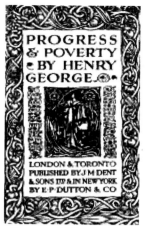

'Progress & Poverty'
by Henry George

communities could then use this revenue to finance economic and social reforms. George was sent by Patrick Ford to work in the UK as a correspondent for the *Irish World*. In this capacity he followed the activities of the INLL closely. He wrote a pamphlet, *The Irish land question: what it involves and how it can be settled.* George's wife, Annie (nee Fox), also got involved with the Ladies Land League, providing valuable help, at a time it was threatened with government proscription (7).

George was a politically ambiguous figure. In a sense, he was a late representative of the American 'White Republican'[3] tradition, at the point when other radicals were beginning to move towards the new Socialism. George supported new labour organisations and had expressed sympathy for the Workingmens Party (WP), when he lived in San Francisco. The WP was strongly opposed to the big tycoons. However, the WP was also virulent in its agitation against Chinese migrant workers.

Land was now providing its owners with previously undreamt of incomes from mining royalties and railway speculation. Therefore, control of this wealth was no longer just a concern for those competing to control agricultural land. George saw land as the source of all unearned income. He opposed Socialism, and did not recognise the existence of surplus value extracted by capitalists' from their workers. He claimed that capitalists, as well as workers, created new value.

Marx accepted the need for taxing landlords' unearned rental income, as part of a wider armoury of transitional measures. However, he dismissed George's

---

[3] The 'White Republican' tradition was mainly upheld by American small farmers and artisans. It had been particularly associated with President Jefferson and later, President Jackson. It envisaged a democratic and egalitarian republican order, opposed to the imperial republicanism of the bankers, lawyers, land speculators, plantation owners and larger manufacturers. However, the African American population was largely excluded from this 'White Republican' vision, whilst Native Americans were viewed as 'savages' who needed to be cleared off their land. In this sense 'White Republicans' too were imperial, but they did not recognise the incorporation of Native American lands as imperialism. They considered their removal as necessary for the productive use of 'empty' or 'underutilised' US territory.

underlying economic theory[4]. Nevertheless, Marx appreciated the impact George was having in undermining the dominant Liberal laissez-faire political economy of the Manchester School[5] (8). The effects of the Long Depression, coupled to the very visible emergence of a new capitalist 'aristocracy', began to dent previous Liberal complacency about the 'natural', 'fair', and self-regulatory nature of their economic system.

George himself remained wedded to a capitalist order, albeit one without landlords. Yet, he still opened the door to Socialist thinking in the USA and the UK, through his questioning of the Liberals' political economy. Although his own political solution was the 'Single Tax' upon ground rents, nevertheless, his campaigns gave the issue of land nationalisation a major boost. This also connected with the earlier political work of the Land and Labour League, which had been formed by members of the First International in the 1870's (9).

Davitt quickly appreciated the superiority of this policy of land nationalisation, compared to the existing INLL policy of peasant proprietorship. The revenues accruing to the state could be used to tackle the problems faced by the landless, and the rural and urban labourers. Davitt wanted to fight their cause more effectively. In adopting this course, he was reflecting the reality of many Irish lives, including his own, when countless poverty stricken or evicted tenant farmers joined the industrial working class throughout the UK, British Empire and the USA.

Divisions between tenant farmers and agricultural labourers had already emerged in County Cork, leading to strike action there in 1881 (10). Davitt was aware that Parnell's policy of asking tenant farmers to show consideration towards the landless and agricultural labourers was hardly an adequate approach. Davitt had earlier been able to persuade Parnell to drop Isaac Butt's

---

[4] Earlier, the classical political economist, David Ricardo, had demonstrated the unearned nature of ground rent at a time when the rising industrial capitalist class was still involved in major struggles with the old landlord class. By 1845, their 'free trade'/laissez-faire system had largely triumphed in the UK. After that, fear of any working class challenge to property was the capitalists' main concern. The political consequences of a general defence of property in capital, land and labour had already been seen as far back as the first Whig/Liberal administration in 1833. Although chattel slavery was abolished in the British colonies, the government also ensured that the slave-owners were given financial compensation for the loss of their property. The slaves, of course, received no compensation for their enslavement.

[5] Some Chartists, such as John Francis Bray, had already further developed Ricardo's 'Labour Theory of Value', showing workers' own surplus labour to be the source of capitalist profits, thus prefiguring later Socialist thought. However the demise of Chartism also marginalised early Socialist thinking, until its reappearance in the British section of the First International.

old IIP 'fair landlord' policy of the 'Three Fs' (11), so perhaps he hoped to push him further still.

Land nationalisation was a policy that could be taken to England, Scotland and Wales, and hence open up new fronts in the struggle. The moderate Land Law Reform Association had received money from the INLL's funds. John Ferguson, Davitt's supporter, pointed to the

Alfred Russel Wallace - prominent scientist, Darwin's co-thinker in theory of evolution, socialist and member of the Land Nationalisation Society

importance of links with labour organisations, such as the Miners Association. Soon, the Durham Miners Association gave a £100 donation to the League's relief fund (12). The issue of mining royalties linked industrial and land struggles. Furthermore, George's tour provided a direct inspiration for the foundation of the more radical Land Nationalisation Society (13), launched by Dr. G. B. Clark[6], John Morrison Davidson[7], Helen Taylor[8] (14), Alfred Russel Wallace[9] (15), and others in 1881.

Meanwhile, things were stirring in Scotland. Glasgow had its own branch of the INLL, led by Ferguson. George spoke at one of its meetings. *Progress*

---

[6] Dr. G. B. Clark was a Radical and former member of the First International. He later became a Crofter MP for Caithness.

[7] John Morrison Davidson was an advanced Radical and staunch republican. Initially he was a supporter of Radical Liberal MP, Henry Cowen, then later of Michael Davitt. From the 1880's, he worked closely with Socialists and was inspired by the writings of Karl Marx, Frederick Engels, Henry Hyndman, William Morris, Leo Tolstoy and Peter Kropotkin.

[8] Helen Taylor was John Stuart Mill's stepdaughter, and a leading campaigner for Women's Rights. She had helped Mill draft his unsuccessful amendment to the 1867 Reform Act to give women the vote on the same basis as men. She was an important Radical activist involved in a wide range of issues, including the Irish Land League struggle. She later joined the Democratic Federation and became an Executive member, when it changed to the Social Democratic Federation.

[9] Alfred Russel Wallace was a biologist who discovered natural selection independently of Darwin. He was involved in a number of Radical causes, and came to strongly oppose both Social Darwinism and eugenics, whilst supporting democratic reform, including women's suffrage.

and Poverty was published in Glasgow in March 1881 (16). Skye crofter-fishermen had made contact with Land League members at Kinsale, in County Cork, and had begun discussions about action to be taken against the ongoing Clearances, and land shortages in the Highlands and Islands (17). John Murdoch's (18) pro-crofter, pro-Irish land reform, and pro-Gaelic newspaper, *The Highlander* (19) already received a subsidy from William Carroll of Clan-na-Gael (20). Murdoch was also invited to directly attend the INLL's Central Committee (21), rather than that of the NLLGB.

By early 1881, the INLL "had about a thousand branches in Ireland comprising fully 200,000 members, another 200,000 in the United States and Canada, and branches springing up in all the principal cities in Australasia which would bring the total membership of the extended league to about half a

John Murdoch - editor of 'The Highlander', member of Irish Land League Executive, initiator of Highland Land League and founder member of Scottish Labour Party

million" (22). Boycott and other actions had rendered the landlords' traditional control of the Irish countryside untenable. Gladstone's government was trying to come up with some emergency measures pending a new land reform bill (23). Furthermore, the British government was involved in a war against the Boers in South Africa, which was not going well (24).

Engels, who had previously thought that the adoption of the Home Rule political banner was the correct tactic, sensed that the revolutionary upheaval in Ireland now needed more advanced political aims. "While in the *social* field the *Land League* pursues more revolutionary aims (which are achievable *in* Ireland) — the total removal of the intruder landlords — it acts rather tamely in *political* respects and demands only Home Rule, that is, an Irish local Parliament side by side with the British Parliament and subordinated to it" (25).

Davitt had originally hoped that the Land League's mass organisation could form an alternative 'second power' in Ireland to that constituted by the British government and the Anglo-Irish Ascendancy. This would provide the launching pad to give new life to the Fenians' struggle for an Irish Republic. That situation had already arrived. The INLL "was, in truth, nothing more nor less than a provisional Irish Government, stronger because based on popular suffrage[10], than the Government of the Castle" (26). Some of Davitt's supporters, particularly Egan, were already raising the demand for "general strike against rent on the precedent of industrial strikes in England" (27). Such a course of action would have led to a decisive battle between the 'second power' against the 'first power' – the UK state.

Davitt, however, procrastinated. He saw his job as being first to try and persuade Parnell of the necessity for such a course of action. Although Parnell had moved politically since 1879, he was not going to sanction an immediate social and political revolution. A different strategy was already forming in his mind – a slow transition to peasant proprietorship and to Irish Home Rule. He was planning his own 'counter-revolution within the revolution' – the 'revolution' being "The Fall of Feudalism"[11], or the breaking of landlord power; the 'counter-revolution' being the cementing of bourgeois political, economic and social power in Ireland, with the backing of the larger tenant farmers. Parnell knew of Davitt and his allies' thinking. He kept his own thoughts to himself, the better to put them off the scent, and to prepare his own counter-offensive.

Realising that the British government was planning to introduce coercion, Davitt, Brennan, Egan, Harris[12] and Kettle approached Parnell in late January 1881, to persuade him of the need to adopt a 'No Rents' strategy (28). In effect this would have represented another 'new departure' to reinvigorate the original 1878 'New Departure'. "A no-rent movement coinciding with the British disaster at Majuba Hill {in the First Boer War on February 27th} would probably have won for Ireland a land act fulfilling the proposals of the {Land League's} conference of 29 April, and a home rule bill anticipating that of 1886 with much more likelihood of becoming law" (29).

Such was the opportunity Davitt and his allies missed. Parnell refused to commit

---

[10] The Independent Irish Party held 60 seats in Ireland after the 1880 General Election, compared to the pro-Dublin Castle, Conservative and Liberals combined total of 44. However, even this favourable political balance massively under-represented the lower orders, many of whom, as poor male tenant farmers or agricultural workers, were not to get the vote until 1884.

[11] The *Fall of Feudalism* was the title Davitt chose to give to his account of the Irish Revolution and the role of the Land League.

[12] Martin Harris was another ex-IRB man and ally of Davitt's with experience in the tenants' rights struggle in Connacht. He was opposed to graziers as well as to landlords, since sheep and cattle farms also displaced small tenant farmers from the land. This economic and political divide was to grow wider in the future.

British defeat by the Boers at Majuba Hill undermined government's position in Ireland

himself to the 'No Rents' strategy. Davitt was arrested on February 3rd, his ticket-of-leave terminated by Lord Harcourt, Gladstone's Home Secretary (30). He was sent to Portland Prison. However, Davitt was now held under considerably better conditions than the first time he had been imprisioned. Nevertheless, he was still isolated from events in Ireland, his letters severely restricted, subjected to censorship and his few visitors confined to non-political friends (31).

References

(1)   see T. W. Moody, *Davitt and Irish Revolution, 1846-82* (*DatIR*), p. 481 (Oxford University Press, 1990, Oxford)

(2)   ibid., p. 383.

(3)   Andrew Boyd, *Jim Connell – Author of the Red Flag*, p. 22 (Donaldson Archives/ Socialist History Society, 2001, Oxford)

(4)   see Andrew C. Newby, *The Life and Times of Edward McHugh (1853-1913)* (Edwen Mellen Press, 2004, Ceredigion) and http://en.wikipedia.org/wiki/Edward_McHugh

(5)   see Elaine McFarland, *John Ferguson, 1836-1906, Irish Issues in Scottish Politics* pp. 163-4 (Tuckwell Press, 2001, East Linton)

(6)   see http://en.wikipedia.org/wiki/Henry_George

(7)   see Henry George, Jr, *The Life of Henry George* (*TLoHG*) p. 366 (Double Day, Doran & Company Inc, 1930, Garden City)

(8)   see http://www.cooperativeindividualism.org/marx_henrygeorge.html

(9)   see Henry Collins and Chimen Abramsky, *Karl Marx and the British Labour Movement*, pp. 164-5 (Macmillan 1965, London)

(10)   **see** T. W. Moody, *DatIR*, op. cit., pp. 423-4.

(11)   **see** F. Sheehy-Skeffington, *Michael Davitt, Revolutionary Agitator and Labour Leader, (MDRAaLL)* p. 71 (MacGibbon & Kee, 1967, London)

(12)   **see** T. W. Moody, *DatIR*, op. cit., p. 368.

(13)   **see** Roy Douglas, *Land, People & Politics, A History of the Land Question in the United Kingdom, 1878-1952, (LPaP)* pp. 45-46 (Allison & Busby, 1976, London)

(14)   **see** *Helen Taylor* in *Oxford Dictionary of National Biography*, Vol. 53., p. 898 (Oxford University Press, 2004, Oxford)

(15)   **see** http://en.wikipedia.org/wiki/Alfred_Russell_Wallace

(16)   **see** T. W. Moody, *DatIR*, op. cit., p. 505.

(17)   **see** Roy Douglas, *LPaP*, op. cit., p. 63.

(18)   **see** James Hunter, *For The People's Cause – From the Writings of John Murdoch (FTPC)* (HMSO Books, 1986, Edinburgh)

(19)   **see** T. W. Moody, *DatIR*, op. cit., p. 359.

(20)   **see** James Hunter, *FTPC* , op. cit., p. 33.

(21)   **see** T. W. Moody, *DatIR*, op. cit., p. 343.

(22)   ibid., p. 458.

(23)   ibid., pp. 455-6.

(24)   **see** T. W. Moody, *DatIR*, op. cit., p. 459 **and** http://en.wikipedia.org/wiki/First_Boer_War

(25)   Frederick Engels, *Engels to Eduard Bernstein*, 26.6.1881, in Marx and Engels, *Ireland and the Irish Question,* pp. 451-2 (Lawrence & Wishart, 1978, London)

(26)   R. Barry O'Brien, *The Life of Charles Stewart Parnell*, p. 188 (Thomas Nelson & Sons, 1910, London)

(27)   T. W. Moody, *DatIR*, op. cit., p. 419.

(28)   ibid., pp. 457-8.

(29)   ibid., p. 459.

(30)   ibid., p. 464.

(31)   ibid., pp. 473-4.

5. The struggle against coercion and for land triggers off a new movement in England and Scotland

The Liberal government, which the INLL was now confronting, had taken office, in 1880, on the basis of Gladstone's Midlothian Campaign (1), with its attacks on Tory jingoism. There had also been high expectations that it would seriously address the problems of Ireland, so mismanaged by the Tories and their landlord backers. However, the one thing that Liberals were not going to countenance was a social revolution, and that was what they were facing in Ireland. The Secretary of State for Ireland, William Forster (2), urged on by the Ulster Liberals[1], was preparing an eventual land reform measure based on the 3Fs (3). The time for such a solution had now passed, but it was going to be a number of years before landlords and British governments saw the economic and political benefits to themselves of peasant proprietorship.

Furthermore, in the dire economic climate of 1880, the number of evictions of Irish tenant farmers for inability to pay rents continued to rise. In response to this, the number of 'outrages' increased too (4). In a repeat of the official attitude demonstrated during the Great Famine of 1845-9, Forster declared, "We have no discretion as regards humanity or the moral justice of the eviction, but have simply to consider whether we will allow the law to be defied or not" (5), i.e. the landlords' law backed by the landlords' courts. Therefore, Forster's more immediate concern was to introduce a general coercion measure, following the imprisonment of Davitt, the League's main organiser.

This retreat from liberal principles outraged many of the Liberal government's Radical supporters. In 1880, the advanced Radicals set up the Anti-Coercion League to try and prevent Forster's planned bill becoming law. They campaigned with their new weekly paper, the *Radical,* for 'real radicalism' against 'sham radicalism' (6). This campaign failed and the Protection of Persons and Property Act was passed on March 2nd 1881 (7). Furthermore,

---

[1] The main concern of the Liberals in Ulster was to separate the Protestant tenant farmers from the INLL, after the inroads Davitt had made amongst their ranks. However, the Conservative landlords preferred to use sectarianism and intimidation, with the backing of the Orange Order leadership, to deal with this threat to their continued control posed by the INLL.

once passed, any remaining opposition from the government's own Radical-Liberal members collapsed. John Bright[2] (8) had capitulated in the vote, and soon Joseph Chamberlain[3] (9) was supporting the Act's use (10).

Advanced Radicals were growing more alarmed. Moves were made to set up a Democratic Federation (DF) to unite the 'real Radicals'. A leading light behind this was Joseph Cowen[4] (11), the maverick Radical MP (10). However, there was growing unease amongst Radicals over the setting up of an organisation that was opposed to Gladstone, 'The People's William'. Some, including Cowen, got cold feet (12). Others in attendance, such as Henry Hyndman[5] (13), soon to be joined by Henry Champion[6] (14), came from the Tory Democrat tradition, with its paternalistic appeal to workers and support for England/Britain's leading role in the world.

An impressive range of Radicals, a handful of former Tory Democrats, and some Socialists, attended the DF's founding conference, held on 8th June 1881, in London (15). The politics of Radicalism dominated proceedings. The conference debated the adoption of an advanced Radical programme and a campaign of action. Helen Taylor (16), a leading Radical campaigner, won

---

[2] John Bright was a mill owner and early bourgeois Radical, associated with Manchester. Along with Richard Cobden, Bright had led the middle class campaign to end the Corn Laws to its successful conclusion in 1845. He remained committed to free trade and opposed colonialism.

[3] Joseph Chamberlain was a Birmingham manufacturer. Unlike the earlier generation of Radicals, he was more concerned with social issues, but also supported a forward colonial policy. Despite this latter political retreat from former Radical principles, he regained wider support, when he campaigned on his unofficial Radical Programme in the 1885 General Election. Ireland, however, was to prove his Achille's heel. He joined the Conservatives in their opposition to Irish Home Rule in 1886.

[4] Joseph Cowen was Radical Liberal MP for Newcastle-upon Tyne. He enjoyed close relations with the local Irish community, including one-time IRB figures. Nevertheless, in relation to the UK's connection to the wider world, Cowen was still a British imperialist, who wanted the Empire reformed as a confederation. He even anticipated the trajectory of later Radical Liberal imperialists such as Joseph Chamberlain, when Cowen gave support to the Disraeli government's attacks on the Boers.

[5] Henry Hyndman was a financial businessman and was considered by some Radicals to be a Tory. He was in the process of switching his support to Social Democracy, although he still retained many of his earlier pro-imperialist and racist sentiments. He was later to become the somewhat autocratic leader of the Social Democratic Federation, the UK's first 'Marxist' party.

[6] Henry Champion was from a well-off Scottish family background. He was an ex-army officer, who resigned over British actions in Egypt in 1882. He became successively, a Christian Socialist, a friend then enemy of Henry Hyndman in the SDF, and a committed promoter of independent Labour representation, before migrating to Australia. He still retained his superior and racist attitudes.

conference support for universal suffrage. Land nationalisation and legislative independence for Ireland (Home Rule) were also passed. The only major dissension arose from the refusal of the Chair, Hyndman, to allow a debate on the abolition of the monarchy (17).

Engels, however, did not think the DF had much future. He gave his support instead to an initiative of the London Trades Council, which had offered him the pages of its *Labour Standard* to argue the case for an independent Labour party[7] (18). He misjudged the situation, as is shown by his supporters' later decision to join the DF's successor organisation, the Social Democratic Federation (SDF).

At this stage, though, the DF was still, in effect, a Radical united front. In opposing coercion, Radicals drew upon the longstanding Liberal tradition of hatred towards

Democratic Federation - set up in 1881 by 'real Radicals' to oppose 'sham Radicals' after Liberal imposition of coercion in Ireland

authoritarian states, which were associated with continental reaction. They thought that coercion in Ireland was preparing the way for coercion in Britain (19). Two HRL/IIP MPs, Justin McCarthy and James Lysaght Finigan, and a National Committee member of the INLL, Harold Rylett, attended the founding Conference of the DF (20). They gained a favourable impression.

Hyndman was brought on to the executive of the National Land League of Great Britain (21), joining Davitt's ally Ferguson, and Barry, as well as Jim Connell. Rylett invited the DF to send delegates to Ireland as guests of the League. Six representatives were sent, including Dr. G. B. Clarke, a member of the Democratic Federation and Land Nationalisation Society (22), who had been in the Boer camp at the Battle of Majuba Hill (23). Jessie Craigen[8]

---

[7] This reflected Engels' (and Marx's) longstanding policy of supporting Labour organisations. They thought that workers' involvement would make them more politically aware through their own experiences, instead of their joining Radical middle class led organisations. There were, however, occasions when Marx and Engels were prepared to work in united fronts of Labour representatives and Radicals, such as the First International.

[8] Jessie Craigen had been active, in 1874, in trying to recruit jute workers in Dundee to the Womens Protective and Provident League, a women's trade union.

Ladies Land League - launched by Fanny and Anna Parnell, with Davitt's backing to take charge when INLL was suppressed

(24), an active trade unionist and delegate from the TUC, made an impassioned and well-received speech in County Clare on internationalism, class solidarity and a call for women's suffrage (25). The Ladies Land League (LLL) took responsibility for her trip to Ireland (26). Helen Taylor was soon to work closely with the LLL too (27), whilst also taking the campaign for women's suffrage to Ireland, along with Jessie Craigen.

The DF threw itself wholeheartedly into anti-coercion work, seeing this as the best weapon to create a 'real Radical' alternative to the Liberal government's and the 'sham Radicals'' moves to the Right. The DF's first open air meeting was to be held later on 23rd October 1881, in Hyde Park, to protest at the imprisonment of Parnell and other INLL leaders (28). Furthermore, the DF had already actively sided with the INLL leadership, when it put up Harold Rylett against the Ulster Liberals, as the Land League candidate in the County Tyrone by-election in September. The DL even issued its own *Address to the Electors of Tyrone* (29).

What was not so clear at the time was that Parnell was opposed to the Liberal Party in Ireland, not because he wanted to build a 'real Radical' alternative, but because he wanted to completely displace the Liberal Party with his own populist party in Ireland. The DF was only useful in so far as it helped him with this aim. The last thing Parnell wanted was 'outside interference'. Known once as somebody who enjoyed close links with British parliamentary Radical Liberals, he became increasingly 'Whig' in the next phase of his politics, which was designed to make a quite different class appeal. To disguise this, Parnell would get his acolytes to stir up Irish chauvinist feeling, whenever he felt politically threatened. He was now strongly opposed to any all-UK Radical and social republican alliance, preferring to look for influential establishment support amongst the Liberals, or even the Conservatives in Britain, and increasingly from the Catholic hierarchy in Ireland.

When Gladstone's government finally passed its Land Act (30), in August 1881, Parnell abstained. It was a landlord/tenant not a peasant proprietor settlement. Davitt's ally and successor as INLL national organiser, John Dillon (31), clearly stated that, "Fixity of tenure meant fixity of landlordism" (32). This expressed the view of most Land League activists. They saw the government as being on the retreat in the face of a massive and still growing campaign. They wanted a 'No Rents' campaign.

Parnell did not go along with this clear-cut opposition though. He was already making moves to base himself upon the better-off tenant farmers. He had recently acquired a weekly newspaper, *United Ireland*, which was to remain under his personal control (33). This was Parnell's first step in building up his own alliance to bring about a 'counter-revolution within the revolution' (34). He realised that, "The large farmers, who had been late in joining the movement and whom alone the bill might be expected to benefit, were preparing to support {the new land act} and leave their impoverished brethren to their fate" (35).

Therefore, instead of stepping up the campaign, with the 'No Rents' policy, desired by the activists, Parnell suggested a tactic of 'testing the Act' (36), in a few trial cases, to see whether rents would be substantially decreased. "But of course, a breach having been made in the tenants' front, rot set in. A section of Ulster farmers secured reductions of about twenty-five per cent, and soon there was a rush to the courts" (37)

However, the plight of the poorest tenants worsened. This ensured their continued resistance. Many Land League national organisers had already been arrested - Davitt in February 1881, John Dillon and Thomas Brennan in May (38), along with lots of area organisers - but all this did was to leave things to local initiative. There was an increased resort to violent tactics. Meanwhile, disgruntled physical force Fenians, with backing in the USA, saw their chance, and began to implement their own 'Dynamite Campaign' (39).

The whole leadership, including Parnell, realised that it could not be long before the INLL was itself banned (40). Preparations had already been made. Davitt had ensured that the Ladies Land League, headed by Anna Parnell, was in place to take over the organisation, a job they were to undertake with great enthusiasm and effectiveness. Egan, the INLL's National Treasurer, had already moved himself to Paris. Other key leaders were also able to escape. However, Parnell was arrested between October 13th-15th (41), and sent to Kilmainham Jail in Dublin. The INLL, itself, was proscribed when it finally issued a *No Rents Manifesto* in response to this clampdown (42).

No Rents poster issued after the arrest of Land League leaders

The social republican wing of the INLL had wanted to launch the rent strike at the height of the campaign earlier in the year. Now, the jailing of Davitt and other key activists, and the divisive effects of Gladstone's Land Act, were having their effect. However, although rent strike action was not at the level hoped for, small tenants attacked property, livestock, landlords and their agents, as evictions were stepped up.

In response, Forster continued to pursue his policy of coercion. He authorised the use of more 'humanitarian' buckshot, rather than cartridges, to deal with those resisting evictions. On October 28th, 1881, at Grawhill in County Mayo, a widowed woman was shot dead, whilst a young girl was bayoneted (43). From then on, 'Buckshot Forster' was the name by which he was known to Irish Nationalists.

Joseph Cowen's *Newcastle Chronicle* highlighted the embarrassment of Radical Liberals, and their indignation over the hypocrisy of the Nonconformist anti-slavery, Irish Secretary. "Nothing can surpass the withering sarcasm which Continental politicians of every class cast upon this new phase of 'nationality interest', as they call it, developed in Her Majesty's Government. The men that have so often stood before Europe as the friends of every slave shivering in his chains, are now themselves putting in force as remorseless a despotism as is operating in Moscow." (44)

Back in Ireland though, 'Captain Moonlight' began to take over from the INLL (45).

References

(1)   **see** Vatican controversy and the Midlothian campaign **on** http://en.wikipedia.org/wiki/William_Gladstone

(2)   **see** http://en.wikipedia.org/wiki/William_Edward_Forster

(3)   **see** T. W. Moody, *Davitt and Irish Revolution, 1846-82 (DatIR)*, p. 455, (Oxford University Press, 1990, Oxford)

(4)   ibid., pp. 567-8.

(5)   ibid., p. 391.

(6)   Fintan Lane, *The Origins of Modern Irish Socialism, 1881-1896 (TOoMIS)* p. 36 (Cork Univesity Press, 1997, Cork)

(7)   **see** T. W. Moody, *DatIR*, op. cit., p. 455.

(8)   **see** http://en.wikipedia.org/wiki/John_Bright

(9)   **see** http://en.wikipedia.org/wiki/Joseph_Chamberlain

(10   **see** Fintan Lane, *TOoMIS*, op. cit., p. 51.

(11)   **see** http://en.wikipedia.org/wiki/Joseph_Cowen

(12)   **see** Martin Crick, *The History of the Social Democratic Federation*, *(THotSDF)* p. 25 (Ryburn Publishing, 1994, Keele University)

(13)   **see** http://en.wikipedia.org/wiki/H._M._Hyndman

(14)   **see** http://www.spartacus.schoolnet.co.uk/TUchampion.htm

(15)   **see** Martin Crick, *THotSDF*, op. cit., p. 26.

(16)   ibid., p. 25-26.

(17)   ibid., p. 26.

(18)   ibid., p. 26.

(19)   ibid., p. 27.

(20)   **see** Fintan Lane, *TOoMIS*, op. cit., p . 36.

(21)   **see** Martin Crick, *THotSDF*, op. cit., p. 26.

(22)   **see** Fintan Lane, *TOoMIS*, op. cit., p . 41 and Chapter 4, footnote 6.

(23)   ibid., p. 38

(24)   **see** D.W. Crowley, *The Crofters' Party - 1885 to 1892 - The first British independent common people's party in The Scottish Historical Review*, Volume 35 (Edinburgh University Press, 1956, Edinburgh)

(25)   **see** Fintan Lane, *TOoMIS*, op. cit., p . 39-40.

(26)   ibid., p. 38.

(27)   ibid., p. 70.

(28)   **see** Martin Crick, *THotSDF*, op. cit., p. 30.

(29)   **see** Fintan Lane, *TOoMIS*, op. cit., p. 51.

(30)   **see** T. W. Moody, *DatIR,* op, cit., p. 485.

(31)   http://en.wikipedia.org/wiki/John_Dillon

(32)   **see** T. W. Moody, *DatIR*, op. cit., p. 484.

(33)   ibid., p. 485.

(34)   **see** F. Sheehy-Skeffington, *The Counter-Revolution* in *Michael Davitt, Revolutionary Agitator and Labour Leader* (*MDRAaLL*) (MacGibbon & Kee, 1967, London)

(35)   **see** T. W. Moody, *DatIR*, op. cit., p. 484.

(36)   **see** F. Sheehy-Skeffington, *MDRAaLL,* op. cit., p. 293.

(37)   Brian O'Neill, *The War for Land in Ireland*, p. 79 (Martin Lawrence, 1933, London)

(38)   **see** T. W. Moody, *DatIR,* op. cit., p. 482.

(39)   **see** F. Sheehy-Skeffington, *MDRAaLL,* op. cit., pp. 105-6.

(40)   **see** T. W. Moody, *DatIR,* op. cit., p. 483.

(41)   ibid., p. 494.

(42)   ibid., p. 495.

(43)   **see** http://www.generalmichaelcollins.com/The_land_League/Michael_Davitt.html

(44)   ibid.

(45)   **see** T. W. Moody, *DatIR,* op. cit., p. 496.

6. 1882 - Parnell's 'counter-revolution within the revolution'

The government put all this mayhem down to local Land League leaders and the INLL leadership's *No Rents Manifesto* declaration of war. Parnell saw how he could take advantage of the situation. Perhaps the *No Rents Manifesto* could be useful after all, but not as a strategy for overthrowing landlord rule, but as a bargaining chip to force the government to come to a deal with himself. Parnell used his fortnight's parole to enter into secret negotiations with the government (1). He came to an arrangement with Gladstone, known as the 'Kilmainham Treaty' (2), which ensured the release of the jailed INLL MPs, including Davitt[1] (albeit still on a ticket-of-leave basis). Furthermore, tenants' rent arrears were to be annulled.

Charles Parnell - An atypical Protestant landlord and Home Rule supporter

However, there was another clause in the 'Kilmainham Treaty'. Parnell would "cooperate cordially for the future with the liberal party in forwarding liberal principles" (3). Furthermore, those 'liberal principles' would soon be modified to fit the Liberal Party's increasing acceptance of imperial realities, and many Irish Nationalists' acceptance of the Catholic hierarchy's social conservatism.

Parnell and the other MPs were freed on May 2nd 1882. Parnell met Davitt upon his release two days later. A "wild and angry" Parnell denounced, "the Ladies Land League {which} had... taken the country out of his hands and should be suppressed. 'I am out now and I don't want them to keep the ball rolling any more. The league must be suppressed, or I will leave public life'"

---

[1] Davitt had himself been elected as MP for County Meath to Westminster in a by-election in 1882, but was disqualified because he was in jail.

(4). What Davitt probably did not realise was that Parnell did not just mean the Ladies Land League but the whole INLL.

Davitt and many of his allies were uneasy about the 'Kilmainham Treaty'. However, Parnell was able to turn an event that threatened to overwhelm him to his advantage. Within hours of Davitt's release, the new Irish Secretary of State, Lord Cavendish, and the Under-Secretary, Thomas Burke, were murdered in Phoenix Park in Dublin by the Invincibles (5), a splinter group of physical force Fenians.

If the 'discrete charm of the bourgeoisie' was seducing Parnell and the middle class element of the INLL, then the individual terrorist activities of a number of small Fenian physical force groups began to disorientate and disorganise the INLL's more social republican wing. Furthermore, these Fenians came under the influence of the British too, but in this case it was the intrigues of the state security services. They manipulated these groups to bring discredit upon the Irish national democratic movement[2] (6).

A shocked Parnell quickly rallied, ensuring that an equally dismayed Davitt (7) was brought on board, to condemn the Phoenix Park murders. Davitt was reluctantly persuaded to withdraw the *No Rents Manifesto* too. However, Davitt was already looking for new ways to restart the campaign. Yet, the need to maintain unity in the face of the new, more draconian Coercion Act (8) helped Parnell to keep Davitt silent in public.

Furthermore, Davitt had turned his back on Fenian armed provocations, having been persuaded of the superiority of mass action[3]. Given his recent IRB membership, and the continued Fenian 'outrages', he was acutely aware that the British government would use these as a stick to beat him with. Both Parnell and Davitt were looking for new allies to advance their projects. Davitt's continued recognition of Parnell as the movement's leader, however, gave Parnell a decided advantage. Parnell was also a master of political manoeuvring.

Davitt could see that Parnell was in an increasingly strong position in Ireland,

---

[2] This seems to be a continued practice of the British security services. The state appears to have acted as an obstacle in the way of the victims' families of the Omagh Bombing (15th August, 1998) when they sought the full disclosure of information held by the security services. A possible explanation is that state agents operating inside the Real IRA had to be protected.

[3] Davitt probably still upheld the legitimacy of armed resistance when it had a chance of success, arising out of a strong mass movement. He was to support the Boers in 1899 in their challenge to British rule. Davitt also carried a revolver, a reflection of the more 'robust' way politics were often conducted in Ireland.

now that he had received Gladstone's 'blessing'. The larger tenant farmers, and their supporters in the Catholic hierarchy and the press, also wanted an end to mass campaigning. They were looking to build a new purely political movement. Parnell's main concern now was to create a constitutional nationalist party. Its principal job would be to advance Irish business and better-off tenant farmer interests. The prime political aim was to win Irish Home Rule.

Therefore, Parnell had to create a party, which could become acceptable enough to Gladstone that he would make Irish Home Rule a Liberal Party cause too. Any links such a demand might have had with Fenianism and social republicanism would have to be buried to make it compatible with a new political settlement for the UK. The INLL had to be killed off.

Davitt realised that the concerns of the smaller tenants, the landless and the rural and urban workers would be largely disregarded under such an arrangement. The issue of land nationalisation was therefore important (9), if new land and revenues were to be made available to meet their needs. He passionately believed that the better-off tenant farmers, and their urban business allies, should not be the sole beneficiaries of the 'Irish Revolution'.

However, Davitt faced a conundrum through his new support for land nationalisation. He had come to a position of reluctantly conceding the need for the UK state to take over the land and to compensate the landlords (10). Thus, both physical force Fenians and Parnell supporters could accuse him of wanting to hand Irish land over to the British state. This did not please many in Clan-na-Gael in the USA. Davitt's policy of land nationalisation would have presented less of a problem, if it had been linked with the original 'New Departure' policy of declaring an Irish provisional government at the height of the Land League struggle.

Parnell's supporters could also argue that their own promotion of peasant proprietorship actually took Irish land out of the hands of the 'English'[4] Ascendancy landlords. Davitt somewhat weakly, if ultimately correctly, pointed out that private ownership of the land would not end the collection of rents, rent inflation through speculation, indebtedness, or the further sale of land (11). In other words, over a long period of time, Irish land would be reconsolidated into larger units through market competition, forcing many smaller tenants into debt peonage, and then dispossession.

---

[4] Irish Nationalists usually concentrated on 'English' or Anglo-Irish landlords (there were Scottish landlords too). They largely disregarded the fact that, since the Great Famine, Irish Catholic farmers had bought an increasing number of indebted landed estates, after they had been divided and sold off in separate lots. Some of the worst rack-renting occurred when better-off farmers sublet their land at extortionate rates.

A decade later, Engels highlighted a similar problem in Germany. To deal with it, he advocated community control of land (12), and the promotion of agricultural cooperation, to win over the majority of small peasants, who could not otherwise hope to compete against the big farmers. Such a solution would have got round Parnell's Irish nationalist objection, although not, of course, the real class reasons which would have led him, and those he represented, to oppose such a measure[5].

Davitt was aware of his own growing political marginalisation in Ireland. Therefore, he looked to reinforce and develop the all-UK Radical and Irish social republican alliance, which had been built up in opposition to coercion. Only the more advanced or 'real Radicals', especially those in the DF, campaigned against coercion. The DF had even called a demonstration on June 11th, soon after the Phoenix Park murders (13). This was a brave act in the face of the public hysteria whipped up by the British press.

Davitt also gave his support to the Land Nationalisation Society in England (14). He realised though that any success in achieving this aim, could only be brought about by pursuing a wider 'internationalism from below' strategy. This meant creating independent Land League-type national bodies in Scotland, England, and later, in Wales too. These could join together to mount campaigns, which would not be confined to the activities of MPs.

Davitt started with a tour of Britain, planned with his allies, Ferguson and Rylett. This was headed by radical American land campaigner, Henry George. It commenced in Glasgow on March 17th (15), took in other places, including Liverpool on June 6th (16), and finished successfully in Dublin, on June 10th (17). The speakers attacked peasant proprietorship[6].

On April 19th, 1882, in the Battle of the Braes and later at Glendale, Skye crofters physically resisted the Glasgow police force sent to impose eviction notices (18). Highlanders, who had migrated to Glasgow and Liverpool (19), were strongly influenced by the INLL, which had branches in both cities. Donald

---

[5] Indeed, when the Irish farmers' cooperative distribution movement was launched in 1890s, it was to be opposed by exactly those small merchants, or 'gombeen men', who gained most from the Parnell inspired land reforms.

[6] Despite the accepted version of Irish history, which holds that land nationalisation had little support in the country, it proved popular whenever a city audience, with a large working class presence, was addressed. Parnell well knew this. When most Catholic tenant farmers abandoned him, in 1891, at the prompting of the Catholic hierarchy, after the Kitty O'Shea divorce scandal, Parnell cynically began to appeal to a working class audience in Dublin, claiming to support the very land nationalisation that he had previously strongly opposed.

MacFarlane, a Highlander, held an Irish seat in Westminster, which he used to highlight the crofters' cause (20). Furthermore, John Murdoch, the veteran campaigner and recent INLL member, campaigned amongst the Skye crofters, alongside Edward McHugh, an INLL organiser (21). Soon local branches on the model of the Irish Land

Battle of the Braes on Skye

League were operating. They became known as the Highland Land League. Davitt had opened up a second front in the struggle.

However, Parnell now launched a counter-offensive with the help of his moderate allies. Land nationalistion was lambasted in the press and pulpit, with only Bishop Nulty supporting it (22). The Irish Catholic hierarchy knew its firmest support lay amongst the better-off tenant farmers. The Irish-American Catholic hierarchy also faced the problem that American Labour and Radical movements were influencing many amongst its largely urban flock. Therefore, the hierarchy there virulently attacked land nationalisation too (23), when Davitt had made a tour of the USA, in June and July 1881 (24).

Parnell's supporters and the physical force Fenians both confronted Davitt on his USA tour. His previous social republican, Clan-na-Gael allies, such as Carroll, Devoy and Ford, were under increasing pressure from physical force Fenians[7]. Although as bitterly hostile to the constitutional nationalists as to the social republicans, the physical force Fenians shared the constitutional nationalists' opposition to any engagement with non-Irish issues and figures. This hostility was directed at the prominence given by Davitt to Henry George (25). Parnell and the physical force Fenians emphasised George's non-Irish origins. Davitt buckled under the assault.

Yet Parnell could not yet afford a public break with Davitt. He was still held in great regard by the poorer tenant farmers, the landless and the rural and

---

[7] This situation developed because of the failed promise of Carroll, Devoy and Ford's version of the 'New Departure'. This strategy had originally envisaged an Irish Parliamentary Party walk-out from Westminster, leading to a declaration of an Irish Republic in Dublin, as the culmination of the land struggle. This had not happened and the physical force Fenians regained their influence, taking over Clan-na-Gael in 1882. They gave their support to the 'Dynamite Campaign' in England.

urban workers in Ireland, as well as enjoying the powerful support within the Land Leagues of Great Britain and even from Archbishop Croke. They all thought that the land struggle was only half won (26). Parnell covered his back, though, by putting up a strong parliamentary opposition to landlord MPs and to continued coercion, and by helping to organise relief for evicted tenants (27).

Furthermore, in a move designed to dish Davitt, Parnell helped to set up the Irish Labour and Industrial Union[8]. However, this merely turned out to be a variation of Parnell's longstanding policy of asking labourers to "avoid conflict with farmers" and to "show moderation in pressing their claims {and} to keep within the law" (28). This body was meant to be subordinate to the new completely constitutional nationalist political party, the National League (NL) (29), which Parnell was about to launch[9].

The Land League had to be killed off. The first stage was to deal with the Ladies Land League. Parnell knew that its continued existence divided Davitt's supporters. He was able to close that body down in August, much to the disgust of Anna Parnell[10] (30). The next thing was to take advantage of Davitt's main political weakness – his overriding concern to maintain public unity. Parnell came to an understanding with Davitt, which has been named the 'Avondale Treaty', after Parnell's country house residence in County Wicklow (31). In the name of unity, Davitt agreed not to raise the issue of land nationalisation at the founding conference.

The launch of the NL was held in Dublin on October 18th 1882. Whilst some of Davitt's other policy proposals were taken on board, his wish to have NL support for the Irish language was ignored (32). Although a lot of the interest in the Irish language came from city-dwelling cultural nationalists[11], it was still the

---

[8] In creating the Irish Labour and Industrial Union, Parnell anticipated the politics of many twentieth century nationalist parties to ensure that they had politically subordinate trade unions under their control. However, Parnell did little to build this organisation since, once Davitt had been marginalised, it had largely served his immediate purposes.

[9] Organisationally independent trade unions were to develop further in Ireland over the next three decades, but just as many of their British counterparts accepted Liberal Party leadership in political affairs, so most Irish trade unions accepted Irish Parliamentary Party political leadership.

[10] Anna Parnell broke completely with her brother. Her history of the Land League, *The Tale of a Great Sham*, was unable to get a publisher, when it was written in 1907. The manuscript was preserved by Helen Maloney, an Irish socialist feminist and Republican, and was only finally published in 1986.

[11] The Society for the Preservation of the Irish Language was set up in 1876. Some of its members were later to take a leading part in the more widely based Gaelic League, formed in 1893, as well as joining the struggle for Ireland's national independence.

main, and sometimes the only, language of many of the poorest tenant farmers, labourers and the landless in the West. Parnell was just not interested in the issue. It also probably reflected the low priority that he gave to the plight of the worst-off tenant farmers, landless and agricultural labourers, who were more concentrated in the Gaelic speaking West.

Davitt decided to make his stand on the creation of democratic structures for the NL. However, he suddenly found himself confronted by Parnell's new clique of acolytes. They attacked Davitt for not believing in the leader, and they resorted to cutting anti-Ulster remarks[12] (33). Parnell was able to get his way, and the effective control of the new party rested with him and a small group of his parliamentary supporters. This parliamentary group soon constituted itself as the Irish Parliamentary Party (IPP) (34), and Parnell took responsibility for ensuring that his favoured candidates were approved (35).

Later, Davitt was to come to the following verdict on the Conference. It represented "the complete eclipse, by a purely parliamentary substitute, of what had been a semi-revolutionary organisation. It was, in a sense, the overthrow of a movement and the enthronement of a man" (36). The era of the 'Uncrowned King of Ireland' and his court clique of sycophants had arrived (37). Revolutionary democracy receded before populism.

---

[12] The political significance of this was that it been Davitt and his allies who had undertaken the hard work of trying to win support for the INLL in Ulster, with a degree of success. The Parnellites' attack also demonstrated a barely disguised sectarian anti-Protestant sentiment, which would grow considerably within the NL and particularly some of its successor organisations, as the Catholic hierarchy's influence was increasingly courted.

References

(1)   see T. W. Moody, *Davitt and Irish Revolution, 1846-82* (*DatIR*), p. 529, (Oxford University Press, 1990, Oxford)

(2)   see *Kilmainham crossroads* on http://en.wikipedia.org/wiki/Charles_Stewart_Parnell

(3)   see T. W. Moody, *DatIR*, op. cit., pp. 529-30.

(4)   ibid., p. 533.

(5)   see http://en.wikipedia.org/wiki/Phoenix_Park_Murders

(6)   see Christy Campbell, *Fenian Fire – The British Government Plot to Assassinate Queen Victoria* (Harper Collins, 2002, London)

(7) **see** T. W. Moody, *DatIR,* op. cit., p. 536.

(8) ibid., p. 538.

(9) ibid., p. 536.

(10) ibid., pp. 519-20.

(11) ibid., p. 520.

(12) **see** http://www.pinn.net/~sunshine/whm2003/js_mill4.html

(13) **see** Martin Crick, *The History of the Social Democratic Federation,* (*THotSDF*) p. 31 (Ryburn Publishing, 1994, Keele University)

(14) **see** Roy Douglas, *Land, People & Politics, A History of the Land Question in the United Kingdom, 1878-1952 (LPaP)* pp. 45-46 (Allison & Busby, 1976, London)

(15) **see** Henry George, Jr, *The Life of Henry George (TLoHG)* p. 389 (Double Day, Doran & Company Inc, 1930, Garden City)

(16) **see** T. W. Moody, *DatIR,* p. 539.

(17) **see** Henry George, Jr, *TLoHG,* op. cit., p. 383.

(18) **see** Roy Douglas, *LPaP,* op. cit., pp. 63-4.

(19) **see** Iain Fraser Grigor, *Highland Resistance, The Radical Tradition in the Scottish North,* pp. 57-8 (Mainstream Publishing, 2000, Edinburgh)

(20) Ewan A. Cameron, *Land for the People, The British Government and the Scottish Highlands, 1880-1925,* p. 18 (Tuckwell Press, 1996, East Linton)

(21) **see** Roy Douglas, *LPaP,* op. cit., p. 65.

(22) **see** T. W. Moody, *DatIR,* op. cit., p. 523.

(23) **see** http://en.wikipedia.org/wiki/John_Bruce_Glasier

(24) **see** Henry George, Jr, *TLoHG,* op. cit., pp. 384-7.

(25) **see** T. W. Moody, *DatIR,* op. cit., p. 540.

(26) **see** Henry George, Jr, *TLoHG,* op. cit., p. 387 **and** T. W. Moody, *DatIR,* op. cit., p. 527.

(27) **see** Michael Davitt, *The Fall of Feudalism - or the Story of the Land League Revolution (TFoF)* pp. 369-70 (Harpers & Brothers Publishers, 1904, London)

(28) ibid., pp. 541-2.

(29) ibid., p. 542.

(30) **see** http://en.wikipedia.org/wiki/Irish_National_League

(31) **see** Anna Parnell, *The Tale of the Great Sham,* edited by Dana Hearn (Arleen House, 1986, Dublin)

(32) **see** T. W. Moody, *DatIR,* op. cit., p. 542.

(33) ibid., p. 543.

(34) **see** http://en.wikipedia.org/wiki/Irish_Parliamentary_Party

(35) **see** T. W. Moody, *DatIR,* op. cit., p. 544.

(36) Michael Davitt, *TFoF,* op. cit., pp. 377-8.

(37) **see** *Trivia* on http://en.wikipedia.org/wiki/Charles_Stewart_Parnell

7. Shifting the main focus of the 'Internationalism from below' alliance to Scotland

Davitt was to remain a member of the NL and its principal successor organisations. However, his main work was now directed at trying to build a wider movement in the UK on 'internationalism from below' principles. He was aware that the 1884 Reform Act, which extended the franchise, particularly to male rural dwellers, would open up new prospects for the forthcoming General Election. He also realised that the hopes of many Radicals in a future Gladstone government had been shattered.

In a daring proposal, he put forward a plan to be implemented by the increased number of MPs, which he correctly thought the NL would gain in 1885. He thought that they should take the lead in establishing a wider cross-national Radical opposition in Westminster.

"His proposals contained the germs of Workmen's Compensation, Old Age Pensions, Taxation of Land Values... Local Government... the abolition of the House of Lords and the democratisation of the House of Commons. With this, he linked a proposal that an Irish seat should be provided for the veteran Indian reformer, Mr. Dabaddhai Naoroji[1] (1), so that India's voice might for the first time be directly heard in the assembly, and the solidarity of the two races[2] strikingly manifested" (2).

Davitt's social republican and internationalist beliefs stand out. Parnell soon dismissed this proposal. He stoked up Irish chauvinist prejudice by claiming these would tie the Party's hands with non-national demands (3). This marked a retreat from Parnell's parliamentary tactics of seeking support from Radical-Liberal MPs before the 1880 General Election.

---

[1] Dabaddhai Naoroji later became the first Asian MP in Westminster, representing Finsbury Central for the Liberal Party, between 1892-5.

[2] The use of the word 'race' seems incongruous nowadays. Davitt and other revolutionary or radical nationalists used it in the same sense as we would use the word 'nationality' today. In their view, the Irish 'race' had developed from the cultural mixing of many peoples. However, when British imperialists invoked an Irish 'race', they usually thought of distinct biological 'races', placing the Irish/Celtic 'race' at some point on their evolutionary ladder below their favoured Anglo-Saxon/Teutonic 'race'.

Dabadai Naoroji - Davitt suggested Irish National League seat for campaigner for Indian self-determination

However, there were problems with Davitt's orientation upon the Radicals. Radicals represented an ever more heterogeneous grouping, stretching from the old anti-Corn Law League 'free traders', like Bright; through the newer, more social Radicals, like Joseph Chamberlain and Sir Charles Dilke[3]; to advanced Radicals like Joseph Cowen and Charles Bradlaugh[4] (4). All but the most advanced Radicals were deeply entrenched in the Liberal Party. Some of these Radical Liberals were even represented in Gladstone's Cabinet, and thus shared responsibility for the Liberals' coercion of Ireland, and for their latest imperial exploits in Egypt.

But Davitt went beyond Radical MPs in his appeals for wider support. He switched his main attention to the new economic and social movements across the Irish Sea. With his allies, he threw his support behind the Land Reform Union, formed in 1882, but reconstituted as the English Land Restoration League (ELRL) in 1883 (5). With Davitt's assistance, a new tour of England, Scotland, and Wales was organised in early 1884, headed by Henry George.

Unlike George, most of the leading members of the ELRL, including Henry Champion (6), were Socialists. Champion called upon George to proclaim his support for the nationalisation of capital on the tour. George refused to make

---

[3] Sir Charles Dilke was a leading Radical Liberal MP, who had briefly championed the English republican cause in response to the declaration of a French Republic in the Franco-Prussian War. He soon withdrew himself from making public attacks on the monarchy, and became an ardent British imperialist, without ever losing the support of Radicals, or even Socialists like Keir Hardie.

[4] Charles Bradlaugh was an avowed supporter of atheism, republicanism, women's suffrage and trade unions. He upheld the most advanced Radical positions, but always remained opposed to Socialism. He strongly attacked the Paris Commune, and supported Adolphe Thier's Third French Republic. Although Davitt was personally opposed to atheism, he recognised Bradlaugh's right to take his Northampton seat, after the 1880 General Election, when this was denied to him because he refused to take Westminster's religious oath. Davitt's support was given on the grounds that Bradlaugh had been democratically elected.

this undertaking. This was consistent with his view that the owners of capital earned their profits, not through the exploitation of labour, but through their own efforts. Champion relented, and continued to help in the organisation of the tour, although Henry Hyndman tried to undermine it. This was the first hint of the later public divide between George's advanced Radicalism and the new Social Democratic and Socialist organisations (7).

The opportunity was also taken to launch the Scottish Land Restoration League (SLRL) in Glasgow (8). It was chaired by John Murdoch (9) and addressed by Henry George. William Forsyth was elected President, whilst Davitt's ally, Edward McHugh, formerly of the Irish National Land League, and executive member of the Glasgow (Irish) Home Rule Association, became its Secretary. This represented a substantial new gain for Davitt's wider alliance.

George went on to visit Caithness and Skye with McHugh (10). It was felt that the SLRL should emphasise the link with the Irish Land League struggle and methods. Just as George was returning to the USA, he became the subject of a personalised attack, *The Prophet of San Francisco*, by the Duke of Argyll. The SLRL persuaded George to make a reply, *The Peer and the Prophet*. This was used to great effect amongst a Scottish anti-landlord audience (11). However, landlords decided to oppose this new cross-nation alliance by forming their own Liberty and Property Defence League. It soon had branches in England, Scotland and Ireland (12). As well as providing supportive press releases, this organisation pushed to ensure that the government provided police and troops to enforce evictions.

Such was George's success that he was invited back by the SLRL for a second tour at the end of 1884 and the beginning of 1885. He kicked off his tour with a meeting in London also addressed by Davitt, the SLRL president, William Forsyth, and Helen Taylor (13). George then toured Scotland, including a visit once more to Skye, where Glasgow police and Royal Naval marines had been deployed to put down recent crofters' actions. John Macpherson, the Gaelic speaking 'Glendale Martyr', acted as George's interpreter (14). He called for, "The withdrawal of the army of invasion, the suspension, at least as to crofter holdings, of all laws for the collection of rent; the suspension of all laws for the preservation of game, and of the law requiring gun licenses[5]" (15).

George finished off his tour in Belfast, at the invitation of the Irish Land

---

[5] Now that deer stalking was developing as a commercial enterprise, the landlords' laws pressed even harder upon the semi-subsistence poaching activities of the Highland crofters and cottars.

Restoration Society[6] (16). Here he had to contend with the arch Orange bigot, the Reverend Hugh 'Roaring' Hanna[7]. Nevertheless, it was in Belfast, under the leadership of Protestant Radical Liberals, like the trade unionist, Alexander Bowman[8] and the Reverend Bruce Wallace, that an organisation supporting land nationalisation was established in Ireland. Wallace produced two papers, *Brotherhood*[9] and the *Belfast Weekly Star* which both promoted the cause (17).

Meanwhile, in Scotland, a conference of the Highland Land Law Reform Association (HLLRA) (later to be popularly called the Highland Land League) was organised in Dingwall in Ross-shire in 1884. It was much influenced by events in Ireland. However, a moderate Edinburgh-based, Liberal Party and Free Church leadership competed with a militant émigré Highlander, London-

---

[6] The Irish Land Restoration Society had been formed in Belfast, as early as 1876. Its demand that the land be restored to its rightful owners was based on the idea that the land was God's free gift to each successive generation. However, the impact of Henry George pushed the ILRS into the adoption of more secular and economic arguments. The ILRS began to see itself as part of a wider international campaign to ensure that ground rents were utilised for the benefit of the people.

[7] The Rev. Hugh 'Roaring' Hanna, was from the ultra-sectarian Presbyterian street preacher tradition. He took a leading part in the Belfast Riots, which had been provoked by the Orange Order marches of 1857. He was also to take a leading part in the even more violent 1886 Belfast anti-Home Rule riots. He was a forerunner of the Rev. Ian Paisley. Both Hanna and Paisley saw their roles as trying to deny the opportunity for any religious, political or social opposition to gain a foothold in north east Ulster, whether they be based on non-Protestant religions, Irish nationalism, Socialism, or just unconventional life-styles (e.g. gays today).

[8] Alexander Bowman was a member of the Flaxdressers Trade and Benevolent Union. He was Belfast Trades Council delegate to the TUC Conferences in 1882 and 1883. Bowman was a member of the Liberal Party, and after Gladstone came out for Irish Home Rule, he helped to form the Irish Protestant Home Rule Association in 1886, to counter the mass desertion of Ulster Liberals to Liberal Unionism and their alliance with the Conservatives. He moved later to Glasgow, and then to London, where he joined the SDF. Upon returning to Belfast, though, he began cooperating with his former adversaries, the local Conservative trade unionists, to become one of six elected Labour councillors in 1897. Whilst Radical Liberalism was to continue to exert its pull upon British Socialists and trade unionists, it was only in north east Ulster that the Tory Democrat tradition survived. Bowman, however, was still to become President of the Irish Trade Union Congress in 1901.

[9] The Reverend Bruce Wallace's paper, *Brotherhood* was a paper directed at workers, which circulated in both Ulster and Clydeside. Wallace later became a member of the Fabian Society, before moving to London, where he also spoke at SDF meetings with his longstanding friend, Alexander Bowman.

based, Radical and more secular leadership[10] (18). The moderates wanted to improve the relationship with the landlords, opposed 'Irish methods', focussed on religious denominational differences and grievances, and supported the Liberal Party. The militants wanted to abolish landlordism altogether, valued the Irish connection, adopted a secular approach to overcome religious differences[10], and challenged both Conservatives and Liberals.

The poetry and songs of Mary Macpherson, or Mairi Mhor nan Oran, (Big Mary of the Songs), who became the bardess of the Highland Land League, expressed the feelings of many Gaelic speaking crofters and cottars (19). Like Murdoch, she was able to draw on oppositional religious feelings which had developed since the split between the largely landlord supported Church of Scotland and the crofter and cottar supported Free Church.

John Murdoch managed to get the moderate Gaelic Society of Inverness[11] to take up the call for a government commission to look into the crofters' plight (20). However, it was the crofters' and cottars' militant actions that prompted a worried Gladstone government to set up the Napier Commission, in 1883, to look into the crofters' concerns (21). Although meant to dampen down their militant action, many crofters saw the Commission as legitimising their grievances and their hostility to the landlords. Their actions continued. In 1884, the Napier Commission reported, but its recommendations were not immediately implemented. Furthermore, Napier's proposals did not begin to address the problem of land shortage, caused by the previous expansion of sheep farming and deer forests[12] during the Clearances.

---

[10] The Radicals' ranks included many Christians, prepared to accept a more secular approach. John Murdoch adhered to an early version of 'liberation theology'. In 1883, he published *Iubile nan Gaidheal, Fuasgladh an Fhearainn a–rair a' Bhiubuill* (*'The Highlanders' Jubilee - The Land Question answered from the Bible'*) which invoked the radical early *Old Testament* tradition, with its opposition to slavery and landlordism. Significantly, this 'Jubilee tradition' was also adopted by black slaves in their struggle for emancipation.

[11] The Gaelic Society of Inverness was established in 1871. It remained under moderate leadership, mainly confining itself to cultural activities, such as the establishment of a Chair of Celtic Studies at Edinburgh University. When Scotland's main Gaelic organisation, An Comunn Gaidhealach, was formed in 1892, it sought aristocratic and royal patronage, making no attempt to highlight the economic and social conditions of the large majority of Gaelic speakers, who were crofters, cottars, or agricultural labourers. Its main task was to organise the annual Mod, which was modelled upon the Welsh National Eisteddfod.

[12] The development of deer hunting as a commercial sport very visibly highlighted the increasingly parasitic nature of the new industrial 'aristocracy', as more of their number used their wealth to ape the behaviour of the traditional landed aristocrats.

Helen Taylor - Davitt campaigned in support of her candidacy as a female parliamentary candidate for Camberwell in the 1885 General Election

This delay and neglect led to what has been called the Crofters' War (22). A Highland Land League conference (23) was held in Portree, on the Isle of Skye, in September 1885. It had delegates from its own expanding network of branches, from the Scottish Land League of America, the SLRL, and its fraternal English organisation, as well as from the Land Nationalisation League.

The conference delegates took the momentous decision to contest the Highlands and Islands crofting constituencies in the forthcoming General Election. They could take advantage of the recent extension of the franchise to the majority of the male rural population. Furthermore, to complement this initiative, the SLRL decided to stand six candidates, in Scotland's urban and mining areas (24).

The SLRL linked the issue of land nationalisation with ending the payment of mining royalties to the coalowners. The SLRL specifically sought labour support. These campaigns brought together, not just Scottish Radicals, like John Murdoch, John Shaw Maxwell and Bruce Glasier[13] (25), who had been inspired by the Irish Land League's struggle, but Davitt's former INLL and current National League of Great Britain (NLGB) allies, John Ferguson and Edward McHugh.

Following the earlier precedent of aspiring Lib-Lab candidates, they looked to the Liberal Party to adopt them as official candidates. However, they then broke from this Lib-Lab tradition, by standing independently, when not so adopted. This decision was soon to have big implications for independent Labour political organisation.

When the General Election was held in August 1885, the Crofters Party won four of the seats they contested. However, the moderate Edinburgh-based

---

[13] Bruce Glasier, very much inspired by the Irish Land League, became a member of the SDF and then the SL. He later became a member of the Independent Labour Party, becoming its Chair after Keir Hardie.

HLLRA, with its strong support from the Free Church leadership, helped to defeat Angus Sutherland, the Scottish Radical HLLRA Crofter candidate in Sutherland (26). However, a Crofter candidate was elected in Ross in the face of strong official Free Church opposition (27); whilst in Argyll, a Catholic Crofter candidate was elected (the first Catholic MP in Westminster from Scotland) in an overwhelmingly Protestant county (28). Another successful candidate was Dr. G. B. Clark, former member of the First International and the Democratic Federation, and founder member of the Land Nationalisation League, who won the Caithness seat.

Furthermore, Davitt was to be true to his promise to use the 1885 General Election to develop a wider Radical alliance. In London, Camberwell Radicals decided to put forward Helen Taylor as an unofficial candidate to make the case for women's suffrage. She faced the disruption of her meetings and physical attacks before being officially prevented from standing. Taylor was a founder member of the Democratic Federation (and the SDF) and had campaigned for the Ladies Land League with Anna Parnell and Jessie Craigen. Davitt spoke in support of Taylor (29).

References

(1)   **see** http://en.wikipedia.org/wiki/Dadabhai_Naoroji

(2)   F. Sheehy-Skeffington, *The Counter-Revolution* in *Michael Davitt, Revolutionary Agitator and Labour Leader*, p. 114 (MacGibbon & Kee, 1967, London)

(3)   ibid., p. 114.

(4)   see http://en.wikipedia.org/wiki/Charles_Bradlaugh

(5)   **see** Roy Douglas, *Land, People & Politics, A History of the Land Question in the United Kingdom, 1878-1952*, *(LPaP)* pp. 46 (Allison & Busby, 1976, London)

(6)   **see** http://www.spartacus.schoolnet.co.uk/TUchampion.htm

(7)   **see** Henry George, Jr, *The Life of Henry George* (*TLoHG*) pp. 423, 497-503 (Double Day, Doran & Company Inc, 1930, Garden City)

(8)   **see** http://en.wikipedia.org/wiki/Scottish_Land_Restoration_League

(9)   **see** James Hunter, *For the People's Cause – From the Writings of John Murdoch*, p. 37 (HMSO, 1986, Edinburgh)

(10)   **see** Henry George, Jr, *TLoHG*, op. cit., p. 433.

(11)   ibid., pp. 445-7.

(12)   **see** Edward P. Lawrence, *Henry George in the British Isles*, p. 31 (Michigan State University Press, 1953, East Lansing)

(13)   **see** Henry George, Jr, *TLoHG*, op. cit., p. 450.

(14)   **see** John D. Wood, *Henry George's Influence on Scottish Land Reform*, in *The Scottish Historical Review (Edinburgh University Press*, April 1984, Edinburgh) **and** http://www.cooperativeindividualism.org/wood-john_henry-george-and-scots.html

(15)   ibid., p. 451.

(16)   Terence Bowman, *People's Champion, The Life of Alexander Bowman, Pioneer of Labour Politics in Ireland*, pp. 28-9 (Ulster Historical Foundation, 1997, Belfast)

(17)   **see** Fintan Lane, *The Origins of Modern Irish Socialism, 1881-1896*, p. 89 (Cork Univesity Press, 1997, Cork)

(18)   *see* Allan W. MacColl, *Land, Faith and the Crofting Communities: Christianity and Social Criticism in the Highlands of Scotland (1843-93)* (*LFatCC*), pp. 136 and 159 (Scottish Historical Review Monographs, Edinburgh University Press, 2006, Edinburgh)

(19)   **see** Sorley Maclean, *Mhairi Mhor nan Oran* **in** *Calgacus,* pp. 49-52 (West Highland Publishing Co. Ltd., 1975, Breakish, Isle of Skye) **and** http://www.ambaile.org.uk/en/item/item_photograph.jsp?item_id=39855

(20)   **see** http://www.gsi.org.uk/centhist.htm

(21)   **see** Iain Fraser Grigor, *Braes and the Napier Commission* in *Highland Resistance, The Radical Tradition in the Scottish North,* (*HR*) pp. 67-81 (Mainstream Publishing, 2000, Edinburgh) **and** http://en.wikipedia.org/wiki/Napier_Commission

(22)   ibid., p. 99.

(23)   ibid., p. 111.

(24)   **see** Michael Keating & David Bleiman, *Labour and Scottish Nationalism,* p. 47 (The Macmillan Press Ltd, 1979, London)

(25)   **see** http://en.wikipedia.org/wiki/John_Bruce_Glasier

(26)   **see** Allan W. McColl, *LFatCC*, op. cit., pp. 163-4.

(27)   ibid., p. 134.

(28)   ibid., p. 152.

(29)   **see** *Helen Taylor* in *Biographical Dictionary of Modern British Radicals*, Vol. 3, 1830-1914, L-Z, edit. Joseph O. Baylen and Norbert J. Gossman, p. 802 (Harvester Wheatsheaf, 1988, Hemel Hempstead)

8. 1885 - The ending of the Liberal consensus in the face of the rise of the 'new imperialism'

By 1885, Parnell could see that continuing coercion and evictions made public support for the Liberal government near impossible. The last straw was the judicial murder of Myles Joyce, a Gaelic speaking, small tenant farmer who had been wrongly hanged for the killing of two bailiffs at Maamtrasna in County Mayo (1). Parnell, who had, and who would continue to overestimate his influence over the Liberal Party, now made a much greater mistake concerning a section of the Conservatives led by Lord Carnarvon and Lord Randolph Churchill (2).

These two individuals suggested that Conservative support might be forthcoming for a government enquiry into the Maamtrasna convictions. Seeking NL support in the forthcoming 1885 General Election, the Conservatives also dangled the prospects of an enhanced local government settlement and peasant proprietorship for Ireland. Carnarvon and Churchill, however, were unable to deliver on the Maamtrasna enquiry such was the hostility of the ultra-imperialist Conservative leader, Lord Salisbury (3).

Lord Salisbury - ultra-imperialist Conservative leader

After Gladstone's Liberal government had been forced to resign, with Irish Parliamentary Party help, Parnell began to make overtures to the new Conservative government under Lord Salisbury. The government suspended coercion and put in place the first stage of what was later to become peasant proprietorship – Ashbourne's Purchase of Land Act (4). Irish landlords feared that any possible future Home Rule administration might not give them full compensation, so this act ensured that the precedent was set for their guaranteed payment by the British government. However, this Westminster-initiated opening of the road to individual proprietorship also cemented the moderate middle class and better-off tenant farmer alliance in Ireland that Parnell desired.

Buoyed by this victory, Parnell now argued that Irish voters in Britain should switch their support to the Conservatives in the forthcoming General Election, whilst standing against Conservative, Liberal[1] and renegade former IPP candidates in Ireland. As political cover, Parnell claimed that the likely substantial increase in the number NL MPs[2] would allow them to hold the balance of power at Westminster. However, what probably most attracted Parnell's attention was the Conservatives' growing support for peasant proprietorship[3]. What this indicated more than anything else, was that Irish landlords knew the game was up. They would increasingly be looking to the UK state to buy them out on favourable terms.

In one of his poorer political judgements, Engels praised the NL's use of tactical voting for the Conservatives in the 1885 General Election (5). Whilst it was certainly true that the Liberal government had abandoned any pretence of liberalism with its continuous resort to coercion (and its armed invasion of Egypt in 1881), and also true that many Radicals had shown themselves to be 'sham Radicals'; there were also 'real Radicals', who had shown by their actions that they supported the Irish struggle. These included John Murdoch, Highland Land League and former INLL member, who stood as one of the SLRL candidates in the Central Belt.

Yet, Parnell demanded a disciplined Irish vote for all Conservatives, except in

---

[1] One of two exceptions to this was the Liberal Party member, and Labour candidate for North Belfast, Alexander Bowman, who also happened to be a member of the Irish Land Restoration Society. However, in this case, the NL gave Bowman backing in a seat it was not itself contesting. Bowman stood as a 'non-political' Labour candidate to try and win Protestant Conservative workers' votes. Although Bowman was himself a Presbyterian, Conservative workers were not taken in by this tactic, and they often disrupted his election meetings, although he bravely continued to campaign publicly.

[2] Both Davitt and Parnell were right in their belief that the NL would do well in the 1885 General Election. It increased its number of MPs from 60 to 86. However, in the absence of any NL poor tenant or working class candidates, this just consolidated the moderate middle class element. One MP, to take his seat for the first time, was the Dublin businessman, William Martin Murphy. He was to become infamous as the man who tried to destroy the Irish Transport and General Workers Union, led by James Larkin and James Connolly, in the Dublin Lock Out of 1913.

[3] The Conservatives' additional hope that peasant proprietorship might encourage social conservatism was well founded. Their other belief that this would open up a new era of Irish contentment with continued British rule proved to be fundamentally misplaced.

Liverpool Exchange, where he asked for a vote for a certain renegade Irish Nationalist, Captain O'Shea, for reasons that would only become clear later[4] (6). Furthermore, amongst those Conservatives, supported by Parnell, were sectarian reactionaries, including one member of the Orange Order in Glasgow (7).

In contrast, Davitt and allies like John Ferguson, with the backing of Glasgow's Home Government Branch of the NLGB, pursued a strategy of trying to peel off as many 'real Radicals' as possible, from supporting Gladstone's Liberals (8). They wanted to create a parliamentary alliance of 'real Radicals' with Irish Nationalists, to complement his land and labour alliance on the ground. Therefore they broke with Parnell's official NL pro-Conservative line, and backed the SLRL candidate, Shaw Maxwell, for the Glasgow Blackfriars seat (9).

What Davitt and his allies were facing were the consequences of Parnell's ongoing 'counter-revolution within the revolution'. In Ireland, Parnell had already ensured that Catholic priests had a guaranteed position on the NL parliamentary selection committees to minimise the number of independently minded and Radical Nationalist candidates there (10). They also made their presence increasingly felt in the NLGB bodies. Parnell's idea of 'internationalism' was to corral the overseas Irish into Irish-only organisations, with all links to external bodies through his own safe centrally approved channels.

Later, James Connolly was to accurately analyse what had happened. "English and Scottish socialists… {had} for years {been} the principal exponents and interpreters of Land League principles to the British masses, and they performed their task unflinchingly at a time when the 'respectable' moneyed men of the Irish communities in Great Britain cowered in dread of the displeasure of their wealthy British neighbours. Afterwards, when the rising tide of victorious revolt in Ireland compelled the Liberal Party to give half-hearted acquiescence to the demands of the Irish peasantry, and the Home Rule-Liberal alliance was consummated, the Irish businessmen in Great Britain came to the front and succeeded in worming themselves into all the places of trust and leadership in Irish organisations. One of the first and most bitter

---

[4] This was an exception to the general support for Conservatives in Britain, which Parnell ordered. This was because Parnell was involved in an affair with Captain O' Shea's wife, Kitty O'Shea failed to get elected to Westminster, so a worried Parnell imposed him, against the wishes of the local NL branch, as their candidate in the Galway City by-election in 1886. In order to appease O'Shea, Parnell continued to give his political backing to this highly disreputable character, at eventual very high cost, both to himself and the wider Irish national movement.

Lord Randolph Churchill - former 'Tory Democrat' with government colonial experience- made links with Liberal Unionists and sectarian Orange Order to defeat Irish Home Rule

fruits of that alliance was the use of the Irish vote against the candidates of the {Radicals and the} Socialist and Labour Parties... In so manoeuvring... the Irish bourgeois politicians were astutely following their own class interests, even while they cloaked their action under the name of patriotism" (11).

Yet, when the results of the 1885 General Election came in April, it initially looked as if Parnell's 'balance of power' tactic had paid off. There were 335 Liberals and supporters and 249 Conservatives and supporters elected in the 1885 General Election – a difference of 86, exactly the number of Irish Nationalists elected (12). Parnell and the NL's intervention amongst the Irish communities in Britain made a difference in many marginal constituencies (13), increasing Conservative representation at Westminster. Gladstone's Liberals still emerged as the largest party, but Parnell's IPP continued to prop up Lord Salisbury's minority Conservative administration.

Gladstone was now persuaded that the best way to defend the unity of the UK was through its liberal reform by means of Irish Home Rule. Gladstone issued the 'Hawarden Kite' (14) - a calculated press leak – to let his new support for Irish Home Rule be known. He hoped that Lord Salisbury's government would give such a measure cross-party support. This could overcome the opposition of the reactionary landlord-dominated House of Lords[5].

However, under the impact of the 'New Imperialism', the class base of opposition to any possible liberal constitutional reforms was widening. Opposition was no longer confined to the landlord Anglo-Irish Ascendancy. There were now also growing business interests, particularly in Ulster, which feared any Home Rule in Ireland. A Dublin parliament might levy extra taxes

---

[5] In the earlier more liberal days, before the rise of 'New Imperialism', Gladstone had been able, in 1869, to get such Conservative support in the House of Commons to overcome the hostility of the House of Lords to the disestablishment of the Church of Ireland.

and impose selected tariffs. Old sectarian fears were also stirred up in attempt to extend the oppositional alliance further. The Orange Order and Presbyterian bigots, like Hugh 'Roaring Hanna', told Protestant workers that 'Home Rule' meant 'Rome Rule'.

The Conservatives saw the opportunity to divide the Liberals, so they opposed Irish Home Rule vehemently, none more so than Tory Democrat, Randolph Churchill (15). During the Conservatives' short spell in office, between June 1885 and February 1886, he became the Secretary of State for India. Soon after ordering the latest imperial conquest in Burma (16), he visited Belfast in a pretty gung-ho mood, at the invitation of the newly formed Ulster Loyalist Anti-Repeal Union[6] (17). He invoked "the Orange card" (18).

With Gladstone's change of heart, Parnell switched back to supporting the Liberals. The IPP helped the Liberals turf the Conservatives out of office, when they refused to back a Liberal amendment[7] (19). Gladstone was returned in February 1886 (19). Gladstone then revealed his ill thought out First Irish Home Rule Bill. The effect of the bill would have been to place Ireland outside of the Westminster parliamentary union, making it another white colony with its own assembly, in a similar manner to the Canadian Confederation[8]. This met the traditional Irish nationalist demand to break the 1801 parliamentary Union. Therefore, it could be considered an anti-unionist measure, although of course, Gladstone never intended any threat to the Crown or Empire.

Colonel Waring, Conservative MP for North Down, declared that, "They were now part and parcel of one of the greatest Empires of the world that the sun ever shone upon, and were utterly determined that they would not be changed into Colonials, and made a Dependency" (20). Unionists wanted to ensure that they would remain part of the ruling imperial group, and not be relegated to a similar position to those in the white colonial assemblies.

---

[6] Just as the formation of Parnell's National League represented the triumph of Irish business and better-off farmer interests over the older landlord-led Home Rulers, so the formation of a distinctive Ulster Loyalist Anti-Repeal Union marked the rise of northern Protestant business interests. They soon gained considerably more political influence amongst Unionists than the southern landlord-based Irish Loyal and Patriotic Union.

[7] This proposal by Chamberlain's Birmingham colleague, Jesse Collings, called upon local authorities to buy land for the landless poor. It was nicknamed 'Three Acres and a Cow'. Collings soon joined Chamberlain as a Liberal Unionist.

[8] The former Irish Confederate, Thomas D'Arcy McGee, had fled to Canada after the abortive 1848 Rising. Here, he had accommodated himself to the British colonial regime and been heavily involved in the creation of the Canadian Confederation, in 1867, before being assassinated by Fenians.

However, Waring knew that his appeal had to be wider than to his own class's immediate concerns, so he also added that Loyalists "would be at the mercy of those from whom they differ politically" (21), i.e. Catholics. This was a clarion call to all Protestants, who feared an end to their relatively privileged position, whether in national or local administration, land ownership, business, or access to skilled jobs.

The proposed Irish parliament would also have had two houses, the upper of which was designed to be the domain of Irish peers and the wealthy. It is possible that Parnell thought that any immediate loss of an Irish parliamentary presence at Westminster could be compensated, in the long run, by the possible slow accumulation of more powers for the Irish parliament. However, Parnell would also have his own Irish 'house of lords' to act as a supplementary brake on any domestic Radicalism.

Support for such a measure constituted another breach with many British Radicals, after Parnell's earlier recommendation that the Irish vote Conservative in Britain. However, the vehemence with which the proposed Bill was attacked by British and Irish Conservatives helped to disguise its conservative and anti-democratic nature. Even Davitt gave Parnell his support in backing this particular measure.

The Conservatives built up their ultra-Unionist oppositional alliance, uniting with the darkest forces of reaction. Churchill attended another anti-Home Rule rally in the city and gave the reactionary Unionists a free hand – "Ulster will fight, and Ulster will be right" (22). The previously sidelined Orange Order and its leaders, Colonel Saunderson[9] (23), and William Johnston[10] (24), newly elected Irish Conservative MPs for North Armagh and South Belfast, were brought into the centre of politics. Saunderson helped to found a new Irish Unionist Party in Dublin, in 1886. In public, this party put forward a respectable face. It drew support from the breakaway Irish Liberal Unionists, but was dominated by the Irish Conservatives.

When it came to a vote on the Home Rule Bill, Gladstone found that those Radical Liberals, led by Joseph Chamberlain (25), and those aristocratic Whigs,

---

[9] Colonel Saunderson was an officer in the Royal Irish Fusiliers.

[10] William Johnston, a County Down landlord, had taken the lead of the plebian Orange Order opposition to the government's 1850 banning of Orange demonstrations. With the help of the Rev. Hugh Hanna and the Protestant Working Mens Association of Ulster, he successfully stood against the official Conservative candidate to become a Belfast MP. He was adopted as the Conservatives' official candidate in 1874 and served until 1878.

led by Lord Hartington[11], had defected. Chamberlain also revealed the flaw in many Radicals' thinking[12], when he said, "I have cared for the honour and the influence and the integrity of the Empire" (26). Such Radicals saw both the British Union and the Empire as progressive gains within which to pursue their reforms. Chamberlain and Hartington joined together to form the Liberal Unionists, and voted with the Conservatives to defeat Irish Home Rule. The Bill fell in the House of Commons by 30 votes, a fact that put a different complexion upon Parnell's earlier urging of the Irish in Britain to vote Conservative.

Joseph Chamberlain - one time Radical formed Liberal Unionists and joined the Conservatives to defeat Irish Home Rule. He became a prominent supporter of British imperialism

The Conservative leader, Lord Salisbury, showed that he had taken on board the latest 'scientific racist' thinking. "You would not confide free representative institutions to the Hottentots for instance... self government... works admirably when it is confided to people who are of the Teutonic race" (27). The ugly new mood created was highlighted in the Belfast anti-Home Rule Riots, which occurred after the Bill was defeated in August. Over fifty people were killed (28).

However, before the Liberal government was swept away in the 1886 General Election, it rushed through the Crofters Holdings Act (29) to try and stem the challenge represented by the crofters' continued militant action, and the emergence of independent Radical MPs outside its own ranks. With the defeat of the Irish Home Rule Bill another General Election was looming.

It was now clear to all that Conservative reaction would be a real factor in the forthcoming election. This had the effect of pulling Davitt and his allies in the NL behind Parnell. The Belfast Protestant land reform activists, Bowman and Wallace, became heavily involved in the Irish Protestant Home Rule Association

---

[11] Nor was Lord Hartington's support mere landlord class solidarity. He held extensive lands in County Waterford.

[12] Other Radical MPs, such as Joseph Cowen and Charles Bradlaugh, did give their support to Irish Home Rule. [13] The Conservatives held 316 seats and the Liberal Unionists 77.

(IPHRA), which campaigned vigorously, particularly in Ulster, for support for Irish Home Rule and the Gladstone/Parnell electoral alliance (30). The NLGB, the Highland Land League and the Crofter Party MPs were drawn back into the Liberals' ranks for the General Election of 1886. Even the SLRL swung behind Gladstone's Liberals (31).

After the election, the Liberal Party only held 192 seats, whilst the Conservative and Liberal Unionist alliance held 393 (32). Chamberlain and Churchill tried to form a Radical Liberal/Tory Democrat imperial alliance[13], but were dropped by the Liberal Unionist leader, Hartington, and the Conservative leader, Salisbury, who joined together to set up a Conservative and Liberal Unionist government (33).

Although the NL retained its number of seats[14], it no longer had much influence at Westminster. The number of Crofter MPs (now standing on a Liberal ticket) also fell by one to 3. However, this loss came about due to the defection of their own former Crofter Liberal MP, in Inverness-shire, to the Liberal Unionists. Although they also lost the Argyll seat[15], they gained the Sutherland seat. Here, Angus Sutherland, the longstanding campaigner and former member of the Glasgow branch of the Irish Land League, managed to take the seat on his second try. He campaigned as an advanced Radical against the limitations of the 1886 Crofters Holdings Act, for land nationalisation, Home Rule for Ireland and Scotland, women's suffrage and reform of the House of Lords (34).

In Ireland and the Highlands, the NL and Liberal Party undoubtedly put up a better show due the continued actions taken by tenant farmers and others, and their organisations' strong concern about future prospects under a Conservative government.

---

[13] Initially, Chamberlain attempted to maintain a separate National Radical Union, which he thought might attract Tory Democrats such as Randolph Churchill. This prospect proved to be short-lived. However, if it had been able to continue, it would possibly have developed similar political characteristics to the Social Christians in Austria, only with anti-Catholicism replacing anti-Semitism as the party's main prejudice.

[14] The Irish Parliamentary Party held 86 seats in both elections (one of these was in Liverpool). In Ireland, the IPP held 85 seats to the Irish Conservatives and Liberal Unionists 18 (including the Dublin University seat), whilst even in Ulster, the IPP held 17 seats to the Irish Unionists 16. The IPHRA's campaigning amongst Protestants possibly helped the IPP in two marginal seats.

[15] Argyll had been taken for the Crofter Party, in the 1885 General Election by Donald MacFarlane. He had previously sat as an Irish Nationalist in County Carlow.

References

(1)   **See** Michael Davitt, *The Fall of Feudalism - or the Story of the Land League Revolution* (*TFoF*) p. 381 (Harpers & Brothers Publishers, 1904, London) **and** Jarlath Waldron, *Maamtrasna, the Murders and the Mystery* (*MtMatM*) (Edmund Burke Publisher, 1992, Blackrock)

(2)   ibid., p. 290.

(3)   ibid., p. 290.

(4)   **see** *Irish Land Purchase Acts, 1885 and 1903* **on** http://en.wikipedia.org/wiki/Irish_Land_Acts

(5)   **see** Liz Curtis, *The Cause of Ireland, From the United Irishmen to Partition*, (*TCoI*) p. 126 (Beyond the Pale Publications, 1994, Belfast)

(6)   ibid., p. 126.

(7)   **see** Elaine McFarland, *John Ferguson, 1836-1906, Irish Issues in Scottish Politics* (*JF*), p. 173   (Tuckwell Press, 2001, East Linton)

(8)   ibid., pp. 162-174.

(9)   **see** David Howell, *British Workers and the Independent Labour Party, 1888-1906*, p. 141 (Manchester University Press, 1984, Manchester)

(10)   **see** Michael Davitt, *The Fall of Feudalism - or the Story of the Land League Revolution,* pp. 468-9 (Harpers & Brothers Publishers, 1904, London)

(11)   **see** James Connolly, *Labour in Irish History*, pp. 164-5 (Bookmarks, 1987, London)

(12)   **see** Liz Curtis, *TCoI*, op. cit., p. 127.

(13)   **see** Jarlath Waldron, *MtMatM*, op. cit., pp. 297-8.

(14)   **see** http://en.wikipedia.org/wiki/Hawarden_Kite

(15)   **see** http://en.wikipedia.org/wiki/Lord_Randolph_Churchill

(16)   **see** http://en.wikipedia.org/wiki/Third_Anglo-Burmese_War

(17)   **see** Liz Curtis, *TCoI*, op. cit., p. 130.

(18)   ibid., p. 129.

(19)   **see** Michael Davitt, *TFoF*, p. 486 **and** http://en.wikipedia.org/wiki/Jesse_Collings

(20)   **see** Liz Curtis, *TCoI*, op. cit. p. 137.

(21)   ibid., p. 137.

(22)   ibid., p. 139.

(23)   **see** http://en.wikipedia.org/wiki/Edward_James_Saunderson

(24)   **see** http://en.wikipedia.org/wiki/William_Johnston_of_Ballykilbeg

(25)   **see** *Liberal unionist* **on** http://en.wikipedia.org/wiki/Joseph_Chamberlain

(26)   **see** Liz Curtis, *TCoI*, op. cit., p. 138.

(27)   ibid., p. 140.

(28)   ibid., p. 141-3 **and** http://www.bbc.co.uk/northernireland/ashorthistory/archive/intro200.shtml.

(29)   **see** Iain Fraser Grigor, *Highland Resistance, The Radical Tradition in the Scottish North,* p. 115 (Mainstream Publishing, 2000, Edinburgh) **and** http://en.wikipedia.org/wiki/Crofters'_Holdings_(Scotland)_Act,_1886

(30)   **see** Terence Bowman, *People's Champion, The Life of Alexander Bowman, Pioneer of Labour Politics in Ireland*, pp. 62-72, 100 (Ulster Historical Foundation, 1997, Belfast)

(31)   **see** Elaine McFarland, *JF,* op. cit., pp. 180, 183-4.

(32)   **see** http://en.wikipedia.org/wiki/United_Kingdom_general_election,_1886

(33)   **see** *Liberal unionist* **on** http://en.wikipedia.org/wiki/Joseph_Chamberlain

(34)   **see** Andrew Newby, *Landlordism Is Going Skye-High - Michael Davitt and Scotland, 1882-1887*, **in** *History Scotland*, Vol.3. No. 4, p. 49 (History Scotland, 2003, Edinburgh)

9. Davitt widens his 'Internationalism from below' alliance and brings in Wales

The extent of the Conservative and Liberal Unionist victory, in August 1886, highlighted the increased domination of politics by 'New Imperialism'. This made its effect felt on the remnant Liberal Party, the Radicals, and even upon the new Socialists. Gladstone's Liberals had seen Irish Home Rule as part of a new political settlement, which left the running of the British Empire largely untouched. Radicals were divided. Many Socialists were confused.

When it came to Irish Unionism and Irish Nationalism's 'mainland' allies - the Conservative Party and Gladstone's Liberal Party respectively - the conservative unionist alliance was far more solid and hence coherent. In contrast, the Liberals, frightened of independent movements from below, had continually compromised and pursued policies, such as coercion in Ireland and intervention in Egypt, which had more benefited their Conservative political opponents.

The Conservatives realised that if Irish Home Rule was ever to be introduced, then the landlords' Anglo-Irish Ascendancy would come to an end. The Liberal Unionists feared that any resultant diminishment of their business representation in Westminster could undermine their economic interests in the wider British Empire.

Therefore, the Conservatives further developed their all-UK reactionary block. This now consisted of the House of Lords (with its veto on new Bills), the Liberal Unionist Party, the Irish Unionist Party[1], the Orange Order, army officers, local magistrates, Protestant church leaders and Presbyterian street corner preachers, all under the jingoistic, racist and sectarian banners of Union and Empire. From now on, it was clear that the demand for Home Rule would lead to a major political confrontation, and hence a constitutional crisis.

The new Conservative government was quick to clamp down on any opposition. Arthur Balfour (1) became the Secretary of State for Scotland. He sent the police and marines to the Highlands and Islands to deal with the continued crofters and cottars' struggles. Then, in 1887, his 'skills' were turned to coercion in Ireland, when he was made Secretary of State there. He soon earned the

---

[1] The Irish Unionist Party was overwhelmingly Conservative, but retained a subordinate space for the Irish Liberal Unionists.

nickname 'Bloody Balfour'[2]. Socialists like Eleanor Marx[3] (2) and Edward Aveling[4] (3), Radicals like Davitt, the dissident former Tory, William Scawen Blunt[5] (4), and even Gladstone, the recent the Liberal Prime Minister, joined the demonstration in Trafalgar Square, against the proposed new coercion bill (5). When their protests were ignored it was quite clear that the road for Gladstone's liberal unionist and Parnell's constitutional nationalist politics was now blocked. The only possible way forward lay in social republican and anti-imperialist politics, based on mobilising popular forces from below.

In response to this rapidly changing situation, Davitt further developed his 'internationalism from below' strategy. He brought Wales into the alliance. The South Wales valleys had undergone hothouse industrial and urban development, in the nineteenth century, based on the coalmining and iron industries, and upon a major influx of labour. The new workforce had been sucked in from all over the UK, including from both England and Ireland. However, the western valleys and their northern fringes, particularly around Merthyr Tydfil, had taken in many Welsh speakers from Mid Wales, where the old woollen industry had declined, and where agricultural depression now hit the tenant farmers and farm labourers. Furthermore, even in what superficially

---

[2] Arthur Balfour's early experience in defending British Unionism was later used to advance British imperialism, during the First World War. In 1917, he put forward the Balfour Declaration promising former Ottoman-controlled Palestine to the Zionists. Balfour's Conservative Government also passed the Aliens Act in 1905, directed against Jewish asylum seekers and economic migrants. Zionists have a long history of making deals with prominent anti-Semitic leaders.

[3] Eleanor Marx was Karl Marx's second-born daughter. She was highly active in the Socialist and trade union movements. She was a prominent advocate of independent working class women's organisation, and also a very strong supporter of the 'Irish cause'. After her father's death, in 1883, she along with her partner, Edward Aveling, and Engels constituted what has been called the 'Marx Party', to defend and advance his ideas within the Socialist and Labour movements.

[4] Edward Aveling enjoyed a simultaneous reputation as a talented Socialist and as a somewhat disreputable person in his personal relationships with women. His callous treatment of Eleanor Marx probably contributed to her suicide in 1898.

[5] William Scawen Blunt is a very interesting individual. He came from a traditional well-established English Catholic family and stood for Parliament as a Tory Democrat in 1884 and 1885. Unlike some of those who joined the infant Socialist movement, after they broke with the Tory Democrats, Blunt never did so. He completely rejected British imperialism, jingoism and racism. Blunt had already supported the Egyptian opposition to the British invasion in 1881, and had written a sympathetic book about the Irish Land League. He was arrested in Ireland, in 1887, for his part in supporting the NL-led 'Plan of Campaign' against landlordism. Blunt was the first person to refuse to wear prison clothing and begin a blanket protest. He became a friend of Robert Cunninghame-Graham, and also had an affair with Jane Morris, the wife of William Morris, so Blunt did move in Socialist circles.

appeared to be rural North and Mid Wales, the impact of the Industrial Revolution was also felt (6). Here, slate quarrying employed many workers, some of whom held smallholdings (7). Therefore, the links between land and labour soon became apparent.

Davitt was invited by Michael Jones (8) and Dr. Evan Pan Jones (9) to speak at Flint, Blaenau Ffestiniog and Llandudno, in February 1886. Michael Jones had been the founder of the Welsh 'Zionist' colony in the Chubut Valley in Patagonia[6] (10).

In 1883, Pan Jones had founded the Cymdeithas y Ddaear i'r Bobl, which was the Welsh version of the Land Nationalisation Society (11). He had had assistance from Helen Taylor (12) of the DF/SDF in his campaign (13). Pan Jones was

Blaenau Ffestiniog - centre of Radicalism in the slate quarrying area of North Wales

also editor of *Y Celt*, which he used to advocate the land nationalisation cause (14). Furthermore, both Pan Jones and Michael Jones attended the Highland Land League conference in Bonar Bridge, in Sutherland, in 1886, where a motion for 'Home Rule-all-round' was passed (15).

Pan Jones finally met Davitt at Chester and they agreed to organise the aforementioned series of meetings (16). Dr. G. B. Clark, former member of the First International and now the Crofter MP for Caithness, also addressed the Flint meeting, where many Irish were in attendance. The Blaenau meeting was attended mainly by slate quarrymen. It was here that a certain David Lloyd George also made his first public speech (17).

---

[6] This Welsh colony, set up, in the 1860's, was just one response to the widespread disillusionment felt after the defeat of the Chartism, which had attained its most revolutionary form in Wales.

Davitt and Parnell also campaigned in Wales in May 1886, on behalf of the Liberal Party, ousted from office after the defeat of the Irish Home Rule Bill (18). They spoke for the NL/Liberal alliance in the July 1886 General Election. Davitt took the opportunity to address the coalminers of Rhondda. He spoke alongside William 'Mabon' Abraham[7] (19), the Lib-Lab MP, condemning, "A phase of landlordism...particularly oppressive to all mining districts {where} a small body of favoured idlers exact large sums in the shape of royalties" (20). Davitt was further strengthening the link between land and labour.

In most of the UK, the Liberal Party made a poor showing, in the face of the Conservative and Liberal Unionist alliance. However, in Wales, only two defecting Liberal Unionists were returned, one an unopposed sitting MP (21). Although the overwhelming majority of Liberals in Wales stayed with the official Party, this did not mean they were all necessarily keen supporters of Irish Home Rule, nor the methods that had been used by the Irish National Land League.

Thomas Gee, a Calvinist Methodist preacher-publisher (22), who held conservative unionist sentiments, whilst still remaining in the official Liberal Party, set up the Welsh Land League in Rhyl, largely in order to head off the growing protest (23). He was helped by the judicious decision of many Welsh landlords, worried at the prospect of growing class conflict, to reduce their tenants' rents. However, Lord Penrhyn[8], a staunch old-style Conservative and Anglican, adopted a more confrontational approach. He had set up the North Wales Property Defence League. Gee was a Liberal and a Nonconformist, so he saw this as a provocation. Gee's Welsh Land League was organised more along the lines of the moderate Edinburgh-based Free Church and Liberal dominated right wing of the HLLRA (24).

Gee strongly opposed 'Irish methods' and used his influence to concentrate

---

[7] William Abraham, better known as 'Mabon' became the Lib-Lab MP for Rhondda in 1885. He was a biligual leader of the Cambrian Miners Association, and later became President of the South Wales Miners Federation in 1898. Along with other former Mining Federation-backed Lib-Lab MPs, he joined the Labour Party after the 1910 General Election.

[8] The Penrhyns had owned estates in Ireland and North Wales and a plantation in Jamaica. They had victimised tenants after the 1868 General Election for daring to vote against their approved Conservative candidate. By setting up the North Wales Property Defence League, Penrhyn was following the precedent of the already established landlord body, the Liberty and Property Defence League. He was a former Conservative MP and upholder of the interests of the Anglican Church of Wales. He raised more income from slate quarries than from land rents. Between 1900-3 he became involved in a three year lock-out of his workers, who were trying to defend the North Wales Quarrymens Union.

rural discontent in Wales upon the tithes issue[9]. Nevertheless, 'Irish methods' appeared in a full-scale anti-tithes riot at Mochdre, Flintshire, in June 1886, where 50 civilians and 34 policemen were injured (25). This threat had to be contained too, so Gee formed an Anti-Tithe League in September (26).

In May 1887, the Welsh Land and Anti-Tithe Leagues were merged as the Welsh Land, Commercial and Labour League (WLC&LL). This organisation also included amongst its aims, "limitation of mining royalties... the abolition of all game laws and the throwing open of rivers to all fishermen" (27). Gee was trying to contain all the new challenges. However, it was only in 1890, that the WLC&LL was finally absorbed into the North Wales Liberal Federation (28). In the meantime, Pan Jones took his land nationalisation campaign into South Wales, addressing meetings at Llandysul, Clydach, Seven Sisters, Glyncorrwg, Pontycymmer and Bargoed (29).

In 1887, Davitt visited Scotland again. He spoke to a St. Patrick's Day meeting in Glasgow, in March, where he said that the "triumph in Ireland over landlordism and Castle Rule would herald a victory for the crofters of Scotland and the artisans of Great Britain" (30). Angus Sutherland, the recently elected Crofter Liberal MP for Sutherland, had just toured Ireland over the winter of 1886/7,

Monument to the Pairc/Park Raiders of 1887

lecturing on Home Rule for Ireland and Scotland (31). In May, Davitt returned

---

[9] The majority of Welsh were Nonconformists, but still had to pay tithes to the (Anglican) Church of Wales.

the compliment and visited the crofting areas for the first time. Speaking in Bonar Bridge, Davitt claimed that the "Celts of Scotland, Ireland and Wales will soon succeed in completing the overthrow of landlordism" (32). He then addressed a large meeting in Portree. The crowds carried banners in English and Gaelic calling for 'Land for the People'. Sutherland and Murdoch also addressed this meeting (33).

Later that year, the landless cottars of Lewis organised a major raid on the Pairc/Park Deer Forest. There were lurid "reports circulating of rifles imported from Ireland and vast numbers of deer slaughtered" (34). The organisers justified the killing of the deer on the grounds that the meat was needed to feed the destitute parishioners of Lochs (35). Davitt sent £25 towards the costs of the trial in Edinburgh of Donald MacRae, a leading Lewis land raider (36).

Just as the Catholic Davitt had earlier demonstrated his ability to win over Protestant, including Orange, tenant farmers in Ulster, so he now showed his ability to win over crofter and cottar members of the Free Church. Davitt then went south to speak to miners in Kirkintilloch, linking the issue of rents and mining royalties (37). He had already made contact with the Lanarkshire miners' leader, William Small and suggested the formation of a Miners National Labour League in Scotland. A meeting in Hamilton, attended by Glasier and Shaw Maxwell, established the Scottish Miners Anti-{mining}Royalty and Labour League (38).

'Internationalism from below' was beginning to overcome old religious and ethnic prejudices, and to link rural and urban labour.

References

(1)   **see** http://en.wikipedia.org/wiki/Arthur_Balfour

(2)   **see** http://en.wikipedia.org/wiki/Eleanor_Marx

(3)   **see** http://en.wikipedia.org/wiki/Edward_Aveling

(4)   **see** http://www.pgil-eirdata.org/html/pgil_datasets/authors/b/Blunt,WilfridS/life.htm

(5)   **see** Liz Curtis, *The Cause of Ireland, From the United Irishmen to Partition*, (*TCoI*) pp. 146 (Beyond the Pale Publications, 1994, Belfast) **and** Fintan Lane, *The Origins of Modern Irish Socialism, 1881-1896*, p. 169 (Cork University Press, 1997, Cork)

(6)   Kenneth Morgan, *The Rebirth of a Nation, Wales, 1880-1980*, pp. 65-6. (University of Wales Press, 1981, Oxford)

(7)   **see** Cyril Parry, *The Radical Tradition in Welsh Politics – a study of Liberal and*

Labour politics in Gwynedd, 1900-1920, pp. 3-5 (University of Hull Publications, 1970, Hull)

(8)   **see** http://en.wikipedia.org/wiki/Michael_D._Jones

(9)   **see** Peris Jones Evans, *Euan Pan Jones – Land Reformer (EPJ-LR)* in *Welsh History Review*, Vol. 4, No. 2, (University of Wales, June 1968, Cardiff)

(10)   **see** http://www.historic-uk.com/HistoryUK/Wales-History/Patagonia.htm

(11)   **see** Peris Jones Evans, *EP -LR*, op. cit., p. 149.

(12)   **see** http://www.pinn.net/~sunshine/whm2003/js_mill4.html

(13)   **see** Peris Jones Evans, *EPJ-LR*, op. cit., p. 150.

(14)   ibid., pp 151-2.

(15)   ibid., p. 153.

(16)   ibid., p. 151.

(17)   J. Graham Jones, *Michael Davitt, David Lloyd George and T. E. Ellis – The Welsh Experience, 1886,* in *Welsh Historical Review*, Vol 18, No. 3, pp. 458-9 (University of Wales, June 1997, Cardiff)

(18)   ibid., p. 459.

(19)   **see** http://en.wikipedia.org/wiki/William_Abraham_(Welsh_politician)

(20)   J. Graham Jones, *MD, DLG TEE – TWE* op. cit., p. 477.

(21)   **see** Peris Jones Evans, *EPJ-LR*, op. cit., p. 152.

(22)   **see** http://en.wikipedia.org/wiki/Thomas_Gee

(23)   **see** Peris Jones Evans, *EPJ-LR*, op. cit., p. 153.

(24)   **see** Chapter 5, reference 18.

(25)   **see** Roy Douglas, *Land, People & Politics, A History of the Land Question in the United Kingdom, 1878-1952*, p. 100 (Allison & Busby, 1976, London)

(26)   ibid., p. 100.

(27)   ibid., p. 101.

(28)   **see** Peris Jones Evans, *EPJ-LR*, op. cit., p. 153.

(29)   ibid., p. 153.

(30)   ibid., p. 147.

(31)   ibid., p. 146.

(32)   ibid., p. 150.

(33)   **see** http://drb.ie/dec07_cruelty.html

(34)   Ewan A. Cameron, *Land for the People, The British Government and the Scottish Highlands, 1880-1925*, p. 64 (Tuckwell Press, 1996, East Linton)

(35)   ibid., p. 65.

(36)   Laurence Marley, *Michael Davitt – Freelance Radical and Frondeur*, p. 181 (Four Courts Press, 2007, Dublin)

(37)   **see** Peris Jones Evans, *EPJ-LR*, op. cit., p. 149.

(38)   **see** Laurence Marley, *MD-FRaF*, op. cit., pp. 173-4.

10. 'Internationalism from below' and the limitations of Irish Nationalism and British Radicalism

Two major things held back the further development of this promising 'internationalism from below' alliance. First, Davitt remained a loyal member of the NL. He hoped to copy the tactics adopted by the Lib-Labs in Britain, in getting Labour candidates adopted in Ireland, only now as Nat-Labs. Davitt remained concerned that he should not to break the unity of the NL, particularly in the face of continued UK state and Conservative attacks. *The Times* had launched a new press offensive in March 1887. It published a forged document, alleging Parnell's support for the murder of Thomas Burke by the Invincibles, in 1882 (1). These pressures continued to tie Davitt to Parnell's Liberal/NL Party alliance.

Indeed, at Parnell's prompting, Davitt was even slow to give his support to the new 'Plan of Campaign' (2), which had been launched in October 1886, by Timothy Healy[1] (3), John Dillon[2] (4) and William O'Brien[3] (5), after the new

---

[1] Tim Healy represented the increased influence of conservative Catholicism within the Irish national movement. He became a disruptive influence in the IPP. Cardinal Logue and William Martin Murphy, the Catholic business magnate and owner of the *Irish Independent*, gave their backing to Healy. Healy's supporters were sometimes known as the 'Pope's Brass Band'.

[2] John Dillon was a classic example of someone whose Radical predilections were slowly watered down by increased adherence to parliamentary politics. One time republican and key organiser in the INLL, he ended up supporting the First World War, becoming the leader of the IPP in 1918, before losing his seat to Sinn Fein in the General Election that year.

[3] William O' Brien is an interesting character. He remained committed to Davitt's support for the poorer tenants, the landless and the agricultural labourers, but he also strongly supported peasant proprietorship. An IPP MP from 1883, he became leader of the United Irish League in 1898, and the All-for-Ireland League in 1909. He strongly opposed the Catholic sectarianism of Tim Healy (and later Joe Devlin's Ancient Order of Hibernians). He allied with more moderate Unionist landlords to help bring about the Conservative government's final Land Purchase Act, in 1903, effectively ending landlord rule in Ireland. He then allied with Arthur Griffith's then more cultural nationalist Sinn Fein to try to develop a non-sectarian Irish national movement. O' Brien was also strongly anti-partitionist, which led him to offering Irish Nationalist support to the British in the First World War, provided that a united Irish army division was created. When it became quite clear that the Irish Unionists under Sir Edward Carson had no intention of honouring the shelved 1913 Irish Home Rule Act, O'Brien gave his support to the new republican Sinn Fein, which emerged after the 1916 Easter Rising.

Conservative government's defeat in parliament of Parnell's Tenants Relief Bill (6). Parnell did not want to upset Gladstone and the Liberal Party, by backing direct action, which might conjure up the spectre of the Land League and the Land War once more. Davitt initially went along with this (7).

The 'Plan of Campaign' involved a rent strike by tenants, where their rents were considered excessive. A fair rent was established by the campaign organisers and paid into a campaign fund instead (8). This was supplemented by boycott actions. Unlike the earlier Land League campaign, the 'Plan of Campaign' gained the support of the majority of the Irish Catholic hierarchy and clergy, although it was strongly opposed by the Vatican.

However, Davitt was provoked out of his silence by the viciousness of the Bodyke Evictions in June 1887. Davitt's old Fenian social republican and anti-imperialist sentiments resurfaced. "I... wished that people here had equal weapons and we could have taught these exterminators a lesson that would have given an example which crushed humanity in other parts of the world would have profited" (9). When the Vatican later issued his statement of condemnation of the 'Plan of Campaign', Davitt gave his public support to the struggle (10).

Once committed to the 'Plan of Campaign', Davitt threw himself again into building international support. He addressed a meeting in Glasgow to raise money for the Bodyke Eviction Fund (11). Edinburgh's 'Little Ireland' NL branch held a mass demonstration in Queens Park in support of John Dillon, jailed for his part in leading the campaign (12).

At first the incoming Conservative government made concessions with a new Land Act. This introduced a judicial review of rents, and brought a further 100,000 tenants within the scope of Gladstone's 1881 Land Act (13). However,

Bodyke Evictions memorial

with Balfour installed as the new Irish Secretary, the new draconian Criminal Law and Procedure (Ireland) Act, popularly known in Ireland as the 1887 Jubilee Coercion Act, was introduced in July 1887 (14). This soon led to evictions, and the jailing of many, including 24 Irish MPs[4] and one English MP[5] (15).

Then the 'Mitchelstown Massacre' took place in County Cork, in August 1887, when the Royal Irish Constabulary shot down three tenants. This incident became notorious, with even Liberal MPs shouting "Remember Mitchelstown!" at Westminster conveniently forgetting the former Liberal Irish Secretary, 'Buckshot Forster's actions at Grawhill in County Mayo in 1881 (16).

However, under the continued Unionist and press onslaught, Parnell kept his distance from the 'Plan of Campaign', in order to maintain Gladstone and the Liberal Party's support for the NL.

A second factor, which held back the four nations alliance, was the political shortcomings of the British Left of the day, still mainly tied to the politics of Radicalism. Plebian Radicalism had arisen in opposition to industrial capitalism when it had first developed at the end of the eighteenth century. Once industrial capitalism was victorious though, working class Radicalism became mainly associated with setting limits upon, or establishing a 'fairer' capitalism, with employers and employees working together. However, when this capitalism did not bring the promised progress for all, a new 'scientific socialist' alternative developed. By 1885, the previously advanced Radical-led Democratic Federation had become the Social Democratic Federation (SDF) (17). Under Henry Hyndman's influence, the SDF was the first ostensibly Marxist party in the UK.

Whilst Hyndman invoked Marx's *Capital*, much to his and Engels' annoyance (18), he was probably more influenced in his politics by Lassalle's state socialism (19) and by the 'freeborn Englishman' tradition[6]. "He was still motivated by a conception of imperialism whereby the English speaking... peoples would lead the way to Socialism" (20). He retained his earlier hostility to Chinese labour immigration (21) and showed anti-Semitic prejudice (22).

Although Hyndman came from a Tory background, many from a Radical background also shared his support for the British Union and Empire. Like

---

[4] William O'Brien was the first MP arrested under the new Criminal Bill. He followed William Scawen Blunt in refusing to wear prison clothes in protest at this attempt at criminalisation.

[5] This was the Radical Liberal, Charles Conybeare, who represented the tin mining constituency of Camborne in Cornwall.

[6] The 'freeborn Englishman' tradition had its origins in the English Civil War (1642-51), and was taken up by eighteenth century oppositionists both in England and the American colonies. The titles of Hyndman's first attempted 'Marxist' books, *England for All and The Historical Basis of Socialism in England*, strongly suggest this influence.

these Radicals, Hyndman now also wanted certain domestic and imperial reforms, for example, in Ireland and India. Hyndman's very English/British Socialism, which he hoped would supersede Radicalism, was not equipped to deal with the ultra-unionism, racism and jingoism, which was the product of the 'New Imperialism'.

Nevertheless, the SDF attracted more people to the idea of Socialism, in the early 1880's, than any other organisation in the UK (23). Furthermore, the SDF fought valiantly for the right to hold public meetings. The SDF was thus the next stage, beyond Henry George's land reform campaigns, in helping many people move beyond Radicalism to Socialism.

With the closure of the National Land League of Great Britain, and Parnell's continued attempts to corral the Irish in Britain into Irish-only organisations, it was not long before Hyndman's enthusiasm shifted its focus. Like many Radicals, he had never been that enthused about Irish Home Rule (24), but was impressed instead by the Irish Land League's militant methods in pursuit of social reform. He probably also admired Parnell's domineering style inside the NL. It is possible Hyndman was even inspired by Parnell's wooing of the Tories, when he, and his then ally, Henry Champion, accepted 'Tory gold' in the 1885 elections, so the SDF could contest two London seats (25).

By 1886, the depression in industry led the SDF to redirect most of its efforts into organising mass demonstrations of the unemployed in London. The most spectacular of these took place on Monday, February 8th 1886, in Trafalgar Square[7] (26). The press labeled them, the 'West End Riots'[8]. Hyndman adopted the rhetoric of revolution, whilst pushing for social reform measures, which he hoped the ruling class could be frightened into conceding. This too had a hint of Parnell's politics about it. Hyndman also insisted upon his leading role in directing events, and over the SDF journal, *Justice*, again rather like Parnell's personal control over *United Ireland*.

However, the SDF had already split, with prominent members, William Morris[9]

---

[7] These riots took place just as Michael Davitt was beginning his tour of Wales.

[8] Hyndman characterised these as "The beginning of the great English Revolution of the Nineteenth Century."

[9] William Morris was a leading designer and writer involved with the Arts and Crafts Movement. He was an internationally known and respected Socialist. He ended up fighting a rearguard battle against the Anarchists in the Socialist League, leaving to form the Hammersmith Socialist Society, before finally rejoining the SDF near the end of his life.

(27), Eleanor Marx, Edward Aveling, Ernest Belfort Bax[10] (28), and Andreas Scheu[11] forming the Socialist League (SL) in 1885 (29). Bruce Glasier, who had been active in support of the Irish Land League and a founder member of the SLRL, also joined. The political grounds for the split, according to new SL organiser, John Mahon[12], were "because {SL} members are not State

Edward Aveling and Eleanor Marx - founder members of the Socialist League

socialists, and do not care to uphold jingoism" (30), a pointed dig at Hyndman.

Under the influence of Morris, the SL was also more consistently anti-imperialist (31). The SL was also scornful about the SDF's concern with 'palliatives' and participating in the parliamentary system. They upheld the tradition of the Paris Commune, but had little notion of how to bring such an order into being[13]. Therefore, the SL became largely a Socialist propagandist organisation, producing its own quite influential journal, *Commonweal*.

The SDF and SL both attempted to set up branches in Ireland, with only limited success (32). They came up against the 'National Question' and the hostility of the NL leadership. Michael Cusack (29), founder of the Gaelic Athletic Association (GAA) (30), was at the abortive meeting to set up a Dublin SDF

---

[10] Ernest Belfort Bax became a theoretician, both for the SL, and again for the SDF when he rejoined it, after the SL's collapse into Anarchism. He also gained notoriety for his male chauvinist opposition to women's suffrage.

[11] Andreas Scheu was a founder member of the Austrian Social Democratic Workers Party and an early mentor to Karl Kautsky. He was forced to leave Austria. When the DF became the Social Democratic Federation in 1883 he joined, but soon left in protest at Hyndman's authoritarianism and chauvinism. Along with William Morris, Eleanor Marx and Edward Aveling, he formed the Socialist League in 1885. He moved to Edinburgh helping to set up the Scottish Land and Labour League. He was later involved with the Scottish Socialist Federation with the young James Connolly.

[12] John Mahon was an ironmoulder. He had formed a Republican Club in Edinburgh which affiliated to the DF.

[13] Whereas the French Commune came out of a communal and republican club tradition found in the French Republic from 1793-5, the equivalent tradition in the UK came from the earlier United Irishmen, Friends of the People and Chartist Conventions, and was to come later from Councils of Action based on the local branches of trade unions.

branch in Dublin. "He implored the audience to leave such 'international business' alone"[14] (35). The SDF and SL also had a problem relating specifically to Catholic workers.

THE MANIFESTO

Socialist League Manifesto - the SL split from the Social Democratic Federation in 1886

Nevertheless, the SDF and SL still joined forces, on November 13th 1887, with the London Radical Clubs, to protest at continued Conservative government coercion in Ireland. In contrast to the year before, at the West End demonstrations of the unemployed, the police and army were well prepared this time. Sir Charles Warren, the Commissioner for Police, had prior colonial experience in Bechuanaland and the Sudan (36). 'Bloody Sunday' led to the death of two protestors, the hospitalisation of 200, with 150 arrested (37). In the aftermath of this setback, the SDF fell back upon Socialist propaganda, but now coupled this to contesting elections. The SL soon retreated into internal disputes, with Anarchists gaining the upper hand.

When it came to the 'Irish Question', there was a range of opinions held by British Socialists. Some continued in one old Radical tradition, which believed that, if social and economic problems were seriously addressed, the 'National Question' would then be rendered redundant. The non-English peoples could then assimilate into the English/'British' nation which, when suitably reformed, would continue to be the beacon of human progress in the world. Amongst their number were those against raising the issue of the 'National Question' at all, seeing it as diversionary and reactionary. However, others upheld another Radical tradition, which acknowledged that the Irish had the right to self-determination, and if that meant they desired Home Rule, this should be

---

[14] Michael Cusack's attitude can be seen as part of a wider Irish national exclusivism encouraged by both Parnell and the later IRB. The GAA was set up in Thurles, County Tipperary, in 1884, to promote Irish sports, such as hurling and Gaelic football. Michael Davitt was a patron. The GAA, after initially allowing in members who still played British sports like rugby, later banned them. This was because, under the influence of IRB members, the GAA was seen as a possible recruiting ground for a future Irish republican army. Interestingly though, other Irish nationalists in urban industrial Scotland took the decision to participate in the Scottish Football League, with the creation of teams like Edinburgh Hibernian (1875), Dundee Harp (1879) and Glasgow Celtic (1888). Davitt supported them. James Connolly was a fervent Hibernian supporter when he lived in Edinburgh.

supported. In practice, this led to the tailing of the NL over constitutional issues.

The most advanced thinking was found in the SL. Belfort Bax looked at the issue of Irish Home Rule through anti-imperialist spectacles. He clearly stated that, "Everything which makes for the disruption and disintegration of the empire to which he belongs must be welcomed by the socialist as an ally" (38). However, given the SL's hostility towards parliaments, there was still an air of British Left condescension in this. It was as if the Irish would have to experience their own parliament first, before they could see the error of their ways, and then rise to the 'true socialist' politics advocated by the SL.

Just as the SL would not call upon Socialists to join trade unions[15] to assist workers' political development in the course of their own struggles; so it was unable to call on Socialists to take a consistent lead in democratic[16] (including national democratic) struggles involving workers and others. Adopting such a stance could have put Socialists in a leading position, ready to push further, whenever Liberals and Radicals retreated in the face of 'New Imperialist' reaction.

---

[15] This was the time when conservative Lib-Lab trade unionism still dominated, so the SDF and SLs' shared hostility to trade unions was more understandable. Individual members in both parties did involve themselves in trade unions, particularly when strike action occurred.

[16] The SDF, in contrast, saw the need for political struggle, but understood this mainly in electoral terms, i.e. putting forward candidates in elections at all levels, from Westminster to School Boards and the Boards of Guardians.

References

(1)   **see** *The Times-Unionist Plot* in Michael Davitt, **in** *The Fall of Feudalism - or the Story of the Land League Revolution* (*TFoF*) pp. 531-41 (Harpers & Brothers Publishers, 1904, London) **and** *The Piggott forgeries* **on** http://en.wikipedia.org/wiki/Charles_Stewart_Parnell

(2)   **see** Laurence M. Geary, *The Plan of Campaign, 1886-1892* (*TPoC*) (Cork University Press, 1986, Cork) **and** http://en.wikipedia.org/wiki/Plan_of_Campaign

(3)   **see** http://en.wikipedia.org/wiki/Timothy_Michael_Healy

(4)   **see** http://en.wikipedia.org/wiki/John_Dillon

(5)   **see** http://en.wikipedia.org/wiki/William_O'Brien

(6)   **see** Liz Curtis, *The Cause of Ireland, From the United Irishmen to Partition*, (*TCoI*) pp. 144 (Beyond the Pale Publications, 1994, Belfast)

(7)   **see** Carla King, *Michael Davitt (MD) Life and Times*, no. 15, p.49 (Historical

Association of Ireland, Dundalgan Press, 1999, Dundalk)

(8)   see Liz Curtis, *TCoI*, op. cit., pp. 144-5.

(9)   John S. Kelly, *The Bodyke Evictions,* pp. 78-80 (Fossabeg Press, 1987, Scariff, Co. Clare)

(10)   Carla King, *MD*, op. cit., p. 50.

(11)   see Andrew Newby, *Landlordism Is Going Skye-High - Michael Davitt and Scotland, 1882-1887*, in *History Scotland*, Vol.3. No. 4, p. 46 (History Scotland,2003, Edinburgh)

(12)   see Alan Lugton, *The Making of Hibernian I*, p. 134 (John Donald Publishing Ltd, 1999, Edinburgh)

(13)   see Laurence M. Geary, *TPoC*, op. cit., p. 77.

(14)   ibid., p. 76.

(15)   ibid., p. 77.

(16)   see Chapter 5, reference 43.

(17)   see Martin Crick, *The History of the Social Democratic Federation* (*THoSDF*), p. 36 (Ryburn Publishing, 1994, Keele University)

(18)   ibid., pp. 24 and 64.

(19)   ibid., p. 33.

(20)   ibid., p. 33.

(21)   ibid., pp. 33, 38.

(22)   ibid., p. 38.

(23)   ibid., p.32.

(24)   see Fintan Lane, *The Origins of Modern Irish Socialism, 1881-1896*, p. 42 (*TOoMIS*) (Cork University Press, 1997, Cork)

(25)   see Martin Crick, *THoSDF*, op. cit., p. 45.

(26)   ibid., pp. 45-6.

(27)   see http://en.wikipedia.org/wiki/William_Morris

(28)   see http://en.wikipedia.org/wiki/Ernest_Belfort_Bax

(29)   see Fintan Lane, *TOoMIS*, op. cit., p. 108 and http://en.wikipedia.org/wiki/ Socialist_League_(UK,_1885)

(30)   ibid., p. 108.

(31)   see http://www.morrissociety.org/JWMS/SP91.9.2.Faulkner.pdf

(32)   see Fintan Lane, *TOoMIS*, op. cit., pp. 90-6 and pp. 109-136.

(33)   see http://en.wikipedia.org/wiki/Michael_Cusack

(34)   see http://en.wikipedia.org/wiki/Gaelic_Athletic_Association

(35)   Fintan Lane, *TOoMIS*, op. cit., p. 94.

(36)   see Liz Curtis, *TCoI*, op. cit., p. 150.

(37)   ibid., p. 150.

(38)   Fintan Lane, *TOoMIS*, op. cit., p. 111.

11. 1888 - From land and labour struggles to the beginning of independent Labour political organisation in Scotland

However, it was economic developments and the various struggles in Scotland, which paved the way for the next big leap forward - the creation of an independent Labour party. Some of the most advanced industrial production in the British Empire, in steelmaking, heavy engineering, railway locomotive and ship building, was located in Scotland's Central Belt. The modernised Port of Glasgow was taking traffic away from the antiquated Port of London (1).

The Clyde Valley industrial colossus lay very close to the Highlands and Islands and to Ireland where, in contrast, some of the most primitive agricultural conditions in Europe still prevailed. A link was provided by migrant workers, who formed a substantial part of the industrial workforce in Scotland's Central Belt, living either in company mining towns and villages, or in high-density tenements in the cities. As in north-east Ulster, some employers, deliberately cultivated 'racial'/sectarian divisions, particularly through the Orange Order. Yet some of these divisions were being overcome.

However, one indication that neither the SDF, nor possibly the new SL, was adequately relating to the opportunities provided by the ongoing struggles in Ireland and Scotland, was the decision taken by John Mahon and Andreas Sheu to form the Scottish Land and Labour League (SLLL) as an autonomous part of the SDF (2). Sheu felt that the SDF had "neglect{ed} local sympathy for crofter agitation and the Irish Land League" (3). Henry Hyndman had tried to stymie the SLLL by organising a new loyal SDF branch in Glasgow (4). So, when the SLLL "affiliated to the Socialist League... {it} sent a clear message that it would function as a fully autonomous and independent section of the SL and not merely a branch" (5). This decision was to serve it well.

Most of the SL/SLLL's Scottish working class members saw the need to be involved in trade unions and labour disputes. Some were also beginning to appreciate the need to contest elections. Mahon "led the 'Parliamentary faction' within the {SL}" (6) which contested the organisation's slide into Anarchism. He could point to the success of the Crofters Party in winning seats, and the respectable showing of SLRL candidates in the urban and industrial Central

Belt, in the 1885 elections. This contributed to the decision to set up the SLLL in Scotland.

William Small, the Lanarkshire miners' leader and member of the SLLL, "set up a branch based on the political organisation of Lanarkshire miners committed to his campaign for the nationalisation of mining royalties. From the middle of 1885 he was urging Lanarkshire miners to imitate Highland crofters and run their own candidate in the forthcoming general election" (7). Small was influential in weaning Keir Hardie, an Ayrshire miners' leader (8), away from Gladstonian Liberalism. Hardie was invited to SLLL meetings in Edinburgh. The meeting Small arranged between Hardie and Engels went badly. Hardie was nevertheless persuaded of the need for independent Labour political organisation (9).

A wider group of Scottish labour activists, including the Lanarkshire miners' leader, Bob Smillie[1] (10), also became involved. The Scottish Miners National Federation (SMNF) was formed in 1886 (11). Hardie was able to use his editorship of its paper, *The Miner*, to put forward his ideas on independent Labour representation[2] (12).

In 1886, Robert Cunninghame-Graham[3] (13) had been adopted by the Liberal Party and won the North West Lanarkshire seat on a Socialist local manifesto. This included the nationalisation not only of the land but of mines and other industries too. It also included the demand for an eight-hour day, free school meals, universal suffrage, the abolition of the House of Lords and Scottish

---

[1] Bob Smillie was born in Belfast but his family moved to Glasgow. He became a miner. Later he was President of the new Scottish Miners' Federation (1894) and the first chair of the STUC (1897). A founder member of the Independent Labour Party, Smillie was to play a key role in getting the Miners Federation of Great Britain, a bastion of Liberalism, affiliated to the Labour Party (1909).

[2] *The Miner* later changed, under Hardie's control and editorship, to the *Labour Leader*. It only became the official Independent Labour Party paper in 1904. It is perhaps not surprising that Hardie was also an admirer of Parnell. They both knew the importance of having a paper at their disposal, as well as how to come to accommodation with the Liberal Party, albeit from a position of strength with their own independent organisations.

[3] Robert Cunninghame-Graham was an unusual person to become a Socialist. He was a minor Perthshire laird who had travelled extensively. Nevertheless, when elected, he took part in many Radical and Socialist campaigns. He was injured and arrested on 'Bloody Sunday' in 1887; expelled from Westminster for protesting about the working conditions of West Midland chainmakers; campaigned in London with the New Unions; and led the parliamentary campaign for the eight hour day, first for miners, then as a general principle. He attended the foundation meeting of the Second International in 1889, and was expelled from France in 1890 for making a revolutionary speech.

Home Rule (14).

In 1888, a vacant seat occurred in Mid-Lanark, adjacent to that held by Cunninghame-Graham. Hardie, still under the influence of Lib-Labism, first offered himself as a workingman and official Liberal Party nominee. He "described himself as 'a Radical of a somewhat advanced type', and a supporter of Scottish and Irish Home Rule, votes for women, the regulation of the mining industry, and the eight hour day" (15).

Hardie withdrew when he was rejected as official Liberal Party candidate, but London SDF member, Henry Champion[4], offered a £400 contribution to an independent Labour campaign.

Robert Cunninghame-Graham

Hardie then got the backing of the SMNF, the Highland Land League, the SLRL, the Crofter MPs, and the Scottish Home Rule Association, of which Hardie was Vice-President (16). Davitt himself personally intervened trying to persuade both Parnell and national Liberal organiser, Schnadhorst, to back Hardie (17). Davitt's allies in Scotland, John Ferguson and Edward McHugh, campaigned for Hardie (18). Predictably, Parnell pressured the local NLGB organisation to back the official Liberal candidate, a London Welsh carpetbagger (19). He won the seat, helped by most of the local Irish vote.

Hardie came third and last gaining 617 votes (20). However, it is doubtful whether such a small percentage vote (8%) has ever had such a wide political resonance. Within months the decision was taken to form the Scottish Labour Party (SLP) (21). John Murdoch, the veteran Highlands and Irish campaigner, chaired the preparatory meeting, held on 19th May 1888. Hardie was elected interim Secretary. When the inaugural conference was held in Glasgow on August 25th, the first president was Cunninghame-Graham, the Socialist Liberal

---

[4] Henry Champion, however, subsequently made a deal with the Liberal Whips at Westminster by which Hardie should step aside, but receive a safe Lib-Lab candidature at the next General Election. Hardie declined this offer. The two were to remain in conflict, until Champion moved to Australia.

MP. J. Shaw Maxwell of the SLRL was also involved[5]. Two of the vice-presidents[6] were Dr. Clark, Crofter Liberal MP, and Davitt's ally, Ferguson. Richard McGhee, another member of the NLGB, also joined (22).

Under the influence of John Mahon and Bruce Glasier, the six branches of the SLLL affiliated, providing much of the SLP's initial membership (23). The SDF also participated, sending seven branch delegations to conference. The Glasgow and Edinburgh Christian Socialist Societies attended (24). Glasgow Trades Council recommended that its affiliated trade union branches should affiliate to the new SLP (25). Later, the Glasgow Jewish Tailors Union was to affiliate, showing the SLP's support amongst another, more recent, section of migrant workers (26).

Keir Hardie - Ayrshire miners' leader, former Radical stands as first first independent Labour candidate for mid-Lanark in the 1888

The conference decided upon seventeen demands, including "Adult suffrage... home rule for each separate nationality or country in the British Empire, with an Imperial Parliament for Imperial Affairs... Abolition of the House of Lords and the hereditary system... Nationalisation of Land and Minerals... 8 hour day, state insurance, arbitration courts and minimum wage... Prohibition of liquor traffic... No war without consent... Free education, free school meals... Disestablishment... {and} Nationalisation of railways, waterways and tramways" (27).

These demands highlight the SLP's political location at the point of transition from advanced Radicalism to Socialism. The political demands did not go beyond those of the most advanced Radicals. They accepted the continuation

---

[5] J. Shaw Maxwell had managed to win 1156 votes in Glasgow Bridgeton, in the 1885 General Election, with Ferguson's support, despite the opposition of Parnell and the NLGB, who called on Irish constituents to vote Tory.

of the British Empire, with an Imperial Parliament, albeit with Home Rule for each constituent country. A declaration for a republic is not specifically mentioned, although there is a call for the ending of the hereditary system. The call for the disestablishment of the Church of Scotland reflects a combination of secular and Nonconformist influences upon the SLP. The call for the abolition of the liquor trade shows the continued influence of the Christian inspired Temperance Movement. The importance given to education by both Radicals and Socialists is also highlighted. The emphasis placed on arbitration courts shows the continued influence of Liberal influenced trade unions, or of 'Old Unionism' as it was soon to be called.

However, the SLRL's championing of the linked demands for nationalisation of land and minerals were also taken up. This was acceptable to a few of the most advanced Radicals. Yet, the demand for state control was taken a stage further with the call for the nationalisation of railways, waterways and tramways. Here the SLP was taking up contemporary Social Democratic demands. The standard Liberal attack on nationalisation, that it buttressed traditional state authoritarian rule, was countered by Socialists of the day with the demand for the fullest democratisation of the state, to permit popular control.

Having participated in the setting up of the SLP, both the SL/SLLL and SDF realised that a Socialist pole of attraction was required, to counter the continuing influence of Lib-Labism and Radicalism and to "imbue {the SLP} with socialist principles" (28). The Scottish Socialist Federation was formed in December 1888. It involved members from the SDF and SL/SLLL (29). Although SSF members participated in the SLP in the Central Belt, it appears that the SSF-affiliated Aberdeen Socialist Society organised independently to unite the Socialists there. It worked directly with trade unionists, including the rural Ploughmans Union, without resort to the SLP (30). SL/SLLL member, James Leatham was prominent in this coordinating activity (31).

This contrasted with the situation in England, where political developments had pulled the SDF and SL further apart. Here, the SL was hopelessly split having fallen under the domination of Anarchists. As a consequence, the SDF, despite its political weaknesses, had regained some of the impetus lost in the initial split. In Scotland, however, SL/SLLL members such as Mahon, Glasier, Small and Leatham appreciated the need for an orientation towards trade union struggles and independent Labour organisations.

The Broxburn Shaleminers' Strike of 1887, in West Lothian, organised by the SMNF, (32), had brought SDF and SL/SLLL members closer together. Police and troops were used to evict striking miners from their tied cottages. The government's coercive approach to Ireland, under the 'Plan of Campaign', had come to Scotland. A local Socialist compositor, Fred Hamilton, saw the connection clearly. He pointed out that the employers "with the aid of the dragoons {evicted striking workers} just as the Irish landlord {did} with his tenants" (33).

This important dispute, over a shorter working day and trade union recognition, which involved a mixed Scottish and Irish-Scottish workforce, enjoyed widespread backing. This came not only from the two main Socialist organisations in Scotland, and from Cunninghame-Graham, but even from the local Liberal MP, R. B. Haldane[7] (34), trying at this early stage in his career to make a name for himself as a Radical. The Edinburgh Trades Council, previously a pretty moderate Lib-Lab body, was also involved (35).

Meanwhile, in the same year, the SNMF organised the Lanarkshire miners' strike, which led to the use of police to protect blacklegs and troops to attack rioters. Whilst its defeat had helped to prompt moves towards the formation of the SLP, support work in Glasgow had once more brought together both SDF and SL/SLLL members (36).

Thus, just as the series of struggles, beginning in solidarity with the Irish Land League, extending to those of the Highland Land League and SLRL, and on to the miners' strikes in West Lothian and Lanarkshire, had placed the issue of independent Labour political organisation and the creation of the SLP on the political agenda; so these same events appear to have drawn SL/SLLL and SDF members in Scotland closer together in the SSF.

John Leslie[8] (37), a member of the SDF, was the main person involved in forging this new unity. He became the SSF's first Secretary (38). Leslie was from a mixed Scottish and Irish background and had an influence on the Connolly brothers, James, who first joined the SL/SLLL in Dundee in 1889,

---

[6] Charles Conybeare, the Radical Liberal MP was jailed in Ireland for his support for the 'Plan of Campaign'. He was to be made an SLP vice-president too. It was only in and after the 1892 General Election, after the impact of 'New Unionism', that Radical Liberals had to make a choice between standing for the Liberals or independent Labour. Conybeare stayed with the Liberal Party, whilst Cunninghame-Graham stood as an independent Labour candidate.

[7] R. B. Haldane, later to become Viscount Haldane, was a prominent Liberal Imperialist, who was close to the Fabian Society. He became the Liberal War Minister in 1905, and was involved in the organisation of British forces in the First World War. He joined Ramsay Macdonald's Labour Government in 1923. The politics of liberal imperialism drew in quite a wide spectrum of opinion. He soon became deeply entrenched in the Labour Party.

[9] John Leslie lived in Edinburgh. Later, he was to write the first Marxist analysis of *The Irish Question*, and involve himself in gun-running to Russian revolutionaries.

and John, who joined the SDF in the same city. Leslie brought both branches together to fight for free speech for Socialists in the city (39).

Leatham and Mahon also had to fight for the right of free speech in Aberdeen, in the face of police arrests. The audience at their court case was well aware of the Irish parallels, shouting out "Mitchelstown noo, boys!" (40). There was also a joint campaign in Edinburgh to prevent a local Protestant bigot from disrupting open-air meetings (41). At this time Edinburgh was the main centre of organised Socialism in Scotland[9] (42).

So, by 1889, there was an independent Labour party, and a reunited Socialist organisation, in Scotland, just at the time two key events were about to occur. The first was the foundation of the Second International in Paris; the second was the birth of 'New (Trade) Unionism'.

The SDF, under Henry Hyndman, played a reactionary, anti-internationalist role over the setting up of the Second International. Hyndman forged an unprincipled alliance with the Possibilists, the right wing of the Socialist movement in France, and ensured that 15 SDF branches[10] were sent to their alternative Conference in Paris. He then organised to prevent the merger of the two conferences (43).

In contrast, the SLP sent John Ogilvy[11] to represent it at the founding conference of the Second International (44). Individual SLP members, Hardie and Cunninghame-Graham went too (45). From England, former SL members, Eleanor Marx, Edward Aveling and William Morris also attended, and the latter was elected as British representative on to the Executive (46). The most significant decision taken was to back an international campaign for an '8 Hour Day', to be launched by worldwide May Day demonstrations in 1890. This demand was central to the wave of strikes that marked the birth of the 'New Unionism'.

---

[9] Desmond Greaves highlights the fact that Socialism was more advanced in Edinburgh than Glasgow at this time. One reason he gives is the influence in the city of continental refugees like Andreu Scheu, and Leo Meillet, a former Paris Commune mayor. However, the Edinburgh SSF also had a talented group of workers, such as John Leslie, and the Connolly brothers, able to draw upon Ireland's social republican tradition. They were already conscious Socialists, so had moved well beyond the advanced Radicalism and Lib-Labism of people like John Ferguson in Glasgow. They were also directly involved in trade unions and labour disputes.

[10] John Burns, an SDF member, who was very active in the 'New Union' movement, did attend the Second International conference, but not as an SDF delegate.

[11] John Ogilvy had been the onetime Secretary of Dundee Radical Association. He became converted to Socialism when William Morris visited the city.

References

(1)   Frederick Engels, *The Abdication of the Bourgeoisie*, **in** Karl Marx & Frederick Engels, *Articles on Britain*, p. 395 (Progress Publishers, 1975, Moscow)

(2)   **see** Fintan Lane, *The Origins of Modern Irish Socialism, 1881-1896*, p. 107 (*TOoMIS*) (Cork University Press, 1997, Cork)

(3)   Martin Crick, *The History of the Social Democratic Federation* (*THoSDF*) p. 38 (Ryburn Publishing, 1994, Keele University)

(4)   **see** Fintan Lane, *TOoMIS*, op. cit., pp. 107-8.

(5)   William Kenefick, *Red Scotland! The Rise and Fall of the Radical Left, c. 1872-1932* (*RS*) p. 59 (Edinburgh University Press, 2007, Edinburgh

(6)   Michael Keating & David Bleiman, *Labour and Scottish Nationalism* (*LaSN*) p. 47 (The Macmillan Press Ltd, 1979, London)

(7)   ibid., pp. 47-8.

(8)   **see** http://en.wikipedia.org/wiki/Keir_Hardie

(9)   **see** Jonathan Hyslop, *The Notorious Syndicalist, J. T. Bain: A Scottish Rebel in Colonial South Africa*, p. 73 (Jacana Media (Pty) Ltd, 2004, Johannesburg)

(10)   **see** http://en.wikipedia.org/wiki/Robert_Smillie

(11)   **see** David Howell, *British Workers and the Independent Labour Party, 1888-1906* (*BWatILP*) p. 33 (Manchester University Press, 1983, Manchester)

(12)   **see** http://www.spartacus.schoolnet.co.uk/PRhardie.htm

(13)   **see** http://en.wikipedia.org/wiki/Robert_Cunninghame-Graham

(14)   ibid., *Liberal Party MP*

(15)   Robert Maclean, *Labour and Scottish Home Rule, Part 1, Mid-Lanark to Majority Government* (*LaSHR*) p. 11 (Scottish Labour Action, undated, Broxburn)

(16)   ibid., p. 11.

(17)   **see** Elaine McFarland, *John Ferguson, 1836-1906, Irish Issues in Scottish Politics* p. 201 (Tuckwell Press, 2001, East Linton)

(18)   ibid., p. 199-202.

(19)   Robert Maclean, *LaSHR*, p.11.

(20)   ibid., p. 11.

(21)   **see** D. Lowe, *Souvenirs of Scottish Labour* (*SoSL*) (W & R Holmes, 1919, Glasgow) **and** http://en.wikipedia.org/wiki/Scottish_Labour_Party_(1888-1893)

(22)   **see** David Howell, *BWatILP* op. cit., p. 148.

(23)   **see** D. Lowe, *SoSL*, op. cit., p. 24.

(24)   **see** William Kenefick, *RS*, op. cit., p. 66.

(25)   Robert Maclean, *LaSHR*, op, cit., p. 67.

(26)   **see** Michael Keating & David Bleiman, *LaSN*, op. cit., p. 51.

(27)   D. Lowe, *SoSL*, op. cit., p. 83.

(28) C. Desmond Greaves, *The Life and Times of James Connolly*, (*TLaToJC*) p. 39 (Lawrence & Wishart, 1986, London)

(29) **see** D. Lowe, *SoSL*, op. cit., p. 128 **and** http://en.wikipedia.org/wiki/Scottish_Socialist_Federation

(30) **see** William Kenefick, *RS*, op. cit., pp. 67.

(31) R. Duncan, *James Leatham, 1865-1945 – Portrait of a Socialist Pioneer* (*JL-PoaSP*) (Aberdeen Peoples Press, 1978, Aberdeen)

(32) **see** William Kenefick, *RS*, op. cit., pp. 63-5.

(33) ibid., p. 65.

(34) **see** http://en.wikipedia.org/wiki/Richard_Burdon_Haldane_1st_Viscount_Haldane

(35) **see** William Kenefick, *RS*, op. cit., p. 64.

(36) **see** David Howell, *BWatILP* op. cit., p. 33.

(37) **see** William Kenefick, *RS*, op. cit., pp. 15, 65, 72-3.

(38) **see** C. Desmond Greaves, *TLaToJC*, op. cit., p. 39.

(39) **see** Donal Levin, *James Connolly, A Full Life*, p. 32 (Gill & Macmillan, 2005, Dublin)

(40) R. Duncan, *JL-PoaSP*, op. cit., p.24.

(41) **see** C. Desmond Greaves, *TLaToJC*, op. cit., pp. 38-9.

(42) ibid., p. 36-7.

(43) **see** Martin Crick, *THoSDF*, op. cit., p. 59.

(44) **see** D. Lowe, *SoSL*, op. cit., p. 43.

(45) ibid., p. 38 **and** *Scottish independence and the Scottish Labour Party* **on** http://en.wikipedia.org/wiki/Robert_Cunninghame-Graham

(46) **see** Martin Crick, *THoSDF*, op. cit., p. 59.

12. From land nationalisation to the eight hour day

Both 'land nationalisation' and 'eight hour day' had been key demands of the First International (1). Up until 1889, it had been the issue of the land, or 'Land for the People', which had inspired the biggest struggles, particularly those of the Irish Land League and its emulators. However, due to the difficulties in dealing with the varied systems of land tenure found in the UK, the USA and Europe, and despite the international campaigns undertaken by Henry George and Michael Davitt, land nationalisation had not been implemented anywhere[1].

The demand for land nationalisation had meant much more to the 'lower orders' than this dry term seems to suggest. In the early days of industrial capitalism, the remaining yeomen freeholders and small tenant farmers, as well as artisans, faced the daunting prospect of being forced to work in the new 'dark satanic mills'. The rising bourgeoisie was determined to eliminate all alternative sources of livelihood, in order to create a class of wage slaves. This is why many of the early plebian Radicals, including many Chartists, placed a high priority on campaigning for land and against the game laws, the better to avoid this fate.

When the issues of land nationalisation and a reduced working week were raised within the First International, these demands were seen as an alternative to unemployment and colonial emigration. Nationalised land could be offered to workers so that they could become economically self-sufficient, thus removing them from the labour market, without being forced into the colonial frontline; whilst reduced hours of work could create new jobs for the unemployed.

However, by the 1880's, these earlier reasons for demanding access to land had largely receded. Industrial labour was now acknowledged to be a permanent feature of society. Jesse Collings' '3 Acres and a Cow' (2) was increasingly seen as utopian, at least for urban industrial workers. This meant that many workers now limited their demand for land to the small area needed to supplement food bought in shops, or for what was needed for gardening and other leisure purposes. Thus began the movement for urban allotments (3).

---

[1] In the USA, the new land, after being taken from the Native Americans, was owned first by the federal government, but was then sold off to private companies or individuals.

Henry George's proposed 'Single Tax' on all ground rents also became watered down to the rating of urban land to provide revenues for local councils (4). The relationship between land and labour was changing, even amongst those for whom the demand for land was still important. More crofters and cottars were undertaking additional jobs, either working seasonally elsewhere, such as at the fishing, or locally, on the large estates[2], and by undertaking manual work on the roads, ferries and the new railways.

Therefore, it was the demand for the '8 Hour Day' that was to trigger the first global labour campaign. It met with a marked degree of success. Until the late 1880's, the eight-hour working day was largely confined to some skilled craft and white collar workers. Furthermore, the unions representing these workers were often opposed to the passing of any legal limits on hours. This followed from their belief in the liberal Manchester School of political economy, and their desire to negotiate premium overtime rates.

Socialists and Anarchists, however, were able to inspire millions of other workers, particularly those in semi-skilled and unskilled jobs, with their vision of an 'eight hour day'. As with the earlier demand, 'land nationalisation', this represented far more in workers' minds than the mere slogan suggested. It conjured up the prospect of a more human life with '8 hours labour, 8 hours recreation and 8 hours rest' (5). Therefore, this was not just a traditional trade union 'improve the conditions of employment' demand, but was tied into the idea of a new society.

The wider political demand for the 'eight hour day' emerged most strongly in the USA. As in the UK, the leadership of the main union - in the American case, the Knights of Labour (6) under Terence Powderley (7) - refused to support the demand for a legally imposed eight-hour day. The Knights were predominantly a labour organisation, albeit one moulded by the traditions of the 'White Republic'. In a partial break from that tradition it did open its ranks to black workers, but soon slid into accepting segregationist practices in its branches in the South. It also strongly supported the exclusion of Chinese labour from the USA.

As in the case of Henry George, the Knights did not see the essential social divide as lying between employers and workers. The industrialists' profits were seen, like the workers' wage, as a just reward for their labour. However, the Knights did exclude a number of categories of people, such as bankers, stockholders, gamblers and liquor merchants, on grounds that theirs was unproductive labour.

---

[2] Of course, this did not prevent them doing a spot of unpaid 'out-of-hours' work there either, i.e. poaching.

The Knights were able to organise large numbers, inspiring them with a wider social vision of an ideal American Republic, and with its elaborate and secret membership rituals. Furthermore, despite its leadership's shunning of strikes, local branches still took such action, expelling non-worker members in the process, thereby becoming recognisable trade union bodies. The Knights attracted white migrant workers.

Indeed, when the American Fenians split, leaving Clan-na-Gael in the hands of the physical force wing, many working class Irish-American social republicans became involved in the Knights (8). Davitt and his ally, Richard McGhee even helped to create small Knights of Labour organisations in the West Midlands of England, and McGhee was contemplating their spread to Glasgow, before the new opportunities associated with the New (Trade) Unions arose (9).

The American Anarchists, Albert Parsons (10) and Lucy Parsons[3] (11) were involved in one of the Knights' strongest branches, in the major industrial city of Chicago. On May 1st, 1886, "they led 80,000 people down Michigan Avenue, Chicago, in what is regarded as the first-ever modern May Day Parade, in support of the eight-hour day. In the next

Lucy Parsons - a prominent Anarchist campaigner for the Haymarket Martyrs

few days they were joined nationwide by 350,000 workers who went on strike at 1,200 factories, including 70,000 in Chicago, 45,000 in New York, 32,000 in Cincinnati, and additional thousands in other cities. Some workers gained shorter hours (eight or nine) with no reduction in pay; others accepted pay cuts with the reduction in hours."

"On May 3, 1886, August, {Albert} Spies[4] spoke at a meeting of 6,000 workers, and afterwards many of them moved down the street to harass strikebreakers at the McCormick[5] plant in Chicago. The police arrived, opened fire, and killed four people, wounding many more. At a subsequent rally on May 4 to protest

---

[3] Lucy Parsons, probably born as a slave, was of mixed African-American, Native American and Mexican background. She was to become a highly effective organiser in a succession of organisations including the Industrial Workers of the World. This was to be the USA's first genuinely multi-racial union, which actively contested racist discrimination. Parsons remained very active up to her death in 1941

[4] Albert Spies was another Anarchist and a German immigrant worker.

[5] McCormicks was one of the largest companies producing agricultural machinery for the rapidly expanding wheat farms on the Great Plains, recently seized from the Native Americans.

this violence, a bomb exploded at the Haymarket Square. Hundreds of labour activists were rounded up and the prominent labour leaders arrested, tried, convicted, and executed giving the movement its first martyrs" (12). Amongst the eight executed were Albert Parsons and five German migrant workers.

"The American Federation of Labor[6] (13), meeting in St Louis in December 1888, set May 1, 1890 as the day that American workers should work no more than eight hours. The... Second International, meeting in Paris in 1889, endorsed this date for international demonstrations, thus starting the international tradition of May Day" (14).

Therefore, when the series of strikes, which gave birth to 'New Unionism' in the UK, broke out in 1889, it was in the wider context of the formation of the Second International, and the growing international campaign for the '8 Hour Day'.

---

[6] Initially, the AFL was open to women, black and migrant workers, to some semi-skilled and unskilled workers and to Socialists. Before long it was largely confined to white male skilled craft workers.

References

(1)   **see** Henry Collins & Chimen Abramsky, *Karl Marx and the British Labour Movement, Years of the First International*, pp. 118 and 154-6 Macmillan & Co. Ltd., 1965, London)

(2)   **see** Chapter 8, footnote 7.

(3)   **see** David Crouch & Colin Ward, *The Allotment, Its Landscape and Culture*, pp. 64-81 (Faber & Faber Ltd, 1988, London) **and** http://www.eynsham.org/allothist.html

(4)   **see** Roy Douglas, *Land, People & Politics, A History of the Land Question in the United Kingdom, 1878-1952*, pp. 118-9 (Allison & Busby, 1976, London)

(5)   **see** http://en.wikipedia.org/wiki/Eight_Hours_Day

(6)   **see** http://en.wikipedia.org/wiki/Knights_of_Labor

(7)   **see** http://en.wikipedia.org/wiki/Terence_V._Powderly

(8)   **see** *New Departure 1879* **on** http://en.wikipedia.org/wiki/Clan_na_Gael

(9)   **see** *Richard McGee* in *Dictionary of Labour Biography*, Vol. VII, p. 113, edited by Joyce M. Bellamy & John Saville, p. 113 (Macmillan Press, 1982, London & Basingstoke)

(10)   **see** http://en.wikipedia.org/wiki/Albert_Parsons

(11)   **see** http://en.wikipedia.org/wiki/Lucy_Parsons

(12)   *United States* **on** http://en.wikipedia.org/wiki/Eight_Hours_Day

(13)   **see** *Early years* **and** *Early membership and exclusion* **on** http:// en.wikipedia.org/wiki/American_Federation_of_Labor

(14)   *United States* **on** http://en.wikipedia.org/wiki/Eight_Hours_Day

13. Broadening the 'Internationalism from below' alliance around the political demand for home rule in Ireland, Scotland and Wales

The 'New (Trades) Unionism' also developed within the context of the political confrontation over the future of the multi-nation UK and the British Empire. On this front, Davitt and his allies' wider 'internationalism-from-below' movement had been trying to push further than the leadership of the NL/Liberal Home Rule alliance and the 'sham Radicals', in opposition to growing Conservative reaction.

Whenever the Conservatives' vision for the future of the UK and Empire clashed with that of the Liberals, it was the Conservatives who most often emerged as the victors. The Liberals either lost out directly to the Conservative-dominated Unionist alliance; or they further accommodated themselves to the dominant politics of 'New Imperialism', despite the desertion of the Liberal Unionists from their party. The days of the old Cobden and Bright Radical Liberal pacifism and anti-colonialism were fast receding.

Several influential Liberals had schemes in mind, which were every bit as grandiose as those of the Conservatives when it came to the future of the Union and Empire. The gung-ho imperialist, Cecil Rhodes (1), was a Liberal Party supporter. He wanted to create an Imperial Federation and Parliament, with direct representation in Westminster from the white colonies. He opposed the Conservatives because of their promotion of over-centralised control of the British Empire by Westminster.

The prominent Liberal, the Earl of Rosebery[1] (2) became President of the Imperial Federation League in 1886 (3). The Radical Liberal (and former English republican) Sir Charles Dilke thought along similar lines (4). One feature most Liberal Imperial Federalists shared with the Conservative and Liberal Unionists was their belief in the supremacy of the 'Anglo-Saxon' race[2].

---

[1] The Earl of Rosebery was later to form an open pro-Imperialist faction in the Liberal Party and became its leader after Gladstone's death.

[2] 'Anglo-Saxon' (and 'Teuton') was used in a wider sense than 'English'. It could also include the Lowland Scots, the Protestant Irish, white British colonial settlers, the Boers (if they accepted 'home rule' within the British Empire), the White Anglo-Saxon Protestant elite of the USA, and the Germans (until German imperial interests clashed fundamentally with those of the British).

What was unusual about Rhodes, amongst gung-ho British Imperialists, was his support for Parnell. He demonstrated this as soon as Parnell retreated from his earlier advocacy of a complete withdrawal of Irish MPs from Westminster, and his acceptance of their continued role in the British Imperial Parliament at Westminster. Rhodes now saw Parnell as a supporter of Imperial Federation, and provided him with generous funding (5). Such was Rhodes' undying belief in the natural superiority of white Anglo-Saxon Protestants that he probably thought that people like Parnell would still dominate any future Irish Home Rule parliament.

Liberal Imperial Federalists envisaged the British Empire as a future English, Scottish, Irish and Welsh, British imperial 'joint-stock holding company' with 'share issues' also reserved for the white British colonies. The various colonial assemblies found in Canada, Australia and New Zealand probably informed Liberals Imperial Federalists' thinking about the possible Home Rule arrangements they wanted in the UK, just as they had earlier inspired some Irish constitutional nationalists.

The majority of the Liberal Party, though, officially stuck to its more limited policy of Irish Home Rule or, sometimes, 'Home Rule-all-round'[3] (including Scotland and Wales) for the UK only. Like the Imperial Federalists, the Liberal Home Rulers still wanted to maintain the over-arching British Imperial Parliament at Westminster, but were not so keen on the complications that direct white colonial representation at Westminster would bring. Both wings of liberal unionism, however, shared the idea of a division of labour between a strong Imperial Parliament and subordinate assemblies.

In contrast, the Conservative and Liberal Unionists remained focused on the defence of a unitary Westminster, with only administrative mechanisms permitted to deal with distinctive national issues in Ireland, Scotland, Wales and the colonies. Conservative unionism was not very keen about self-determination for the white colonies. When it came to the non-white parts of the Empire, they promoted either direct rule for the Crown Colonies, or indirect rule in the Protectorates, through traditional princes and favoured tribal leaders.

Therefore, due to both official Conservative and Liberal opposition, the British Empire was not politically reformed into an Imperial Federation in the later nineteenth or early twentieth centuries. This followed from the failure to

---

[3] 'Home rule-all-round' was to be a continuing theme for imperially minded liberal unionists. However, whenever the UK has faced the greatest political challenges, federalism emerged as the unionists' last-ditch tactic to hold the UK state together, e.g. when the Irish national struggle really took off after Sinn Fein's victory in the 1918 Westminster General Election.

transform the UK into a unitary British state and single nation in the earlier nineteenth century.

Davitt and his closest allies had realised early on that the issue of Irish Home Rule had produced a faultline through British politics. They had decided to open this up further, by giving their support to Home Rule for Scotland and Wales too. However, in order to ensure that the issue was not completely dominated by hostile class forces, such as those now ranged behind Parnell in Ireland, the issue of Home Rule was linked to land and labour struggles in Scotland and Wales.

In effect, Davitt widened Engels' earlier insight that Home Rule was the best political banner, under which to initiate a wider political struggle, when less heady political conditions prevailed. This fitted the situation Davitt found himself in, after the Gladstone/Parnell pact had successfully derailed the earlier revolutionary challenge represented by the Irish National Land League in 1882, and after the defeat of the first Irish Home Rule Bill in 1886.

The Scottish Home Rule Association (SHRA) had been formed in 1886 (6). Its membership included the Crofter Liberal MP, Dr. G. B. Clark, the Socialist Liberal MP, Robert Cunninghame-Graham, the veteran land campaigner and SLRL member, John Murdoch, the miners' leaders, Keir Hardie and Robert Smillie. Davitt's close ally, John Ferguson, gave his support too (7).

John Ferguson, based in Glasgow, outlined the new Liberal Radical understanding of the wider significance of Home Rule. "Give England, Scotland, Ireland and Wales national Parliaments for purely 'national' purposes. Call into existence an Imperial Parliament for purely Imperial purposes" (8). Thus, even Ferguson, a former IRB member, was being drawn away from Fenianism's anti-imperialist legacy, by his increasing adherence to the politics of 'mainland' Radicalism. With the old social republicanism unable to move towards a new socialist republicanism, its political limitations also would become more apparent as the impact of 'New Imperialism' made itself felt.

John Morrison Davidson[4] held perhaps the most advanced conception of the relationship between 'Home Rule-all-round' and future society. He had walked out of the first Democratic Federation meeting in protest at Hyndman's opposition to republicanism (9). He had been an organiser of the earliest anti-coercion demonstration in Hyde Park, and an SLRL candidate for Greenock in 1885 (10). He was one of those advanced Radicals who made the leap to

---

[4] Although a Scot, J. Morrison Davidson's earlier Radicalism drew heavily upon the 'freeborn Englishman' tradition. It was only later that he drew more inspiration from the legacy of the communism of the Celtic clans. William Skene's influential three-volume history, *Celtic Scotland*, was only completed in 1890.

Socialism.

In arguing for a 'British Federal Republic' (England, Ireland, Scotland and Wales) he wrote, "Nay, I go further, and affirm that the day is approaching when the commune, township or parishes cooperatively organized for the purpose of production and distribution, will be recognised as of more consequence in the social and political world than the nation itself. In the 'process of the suns' the nation may wither, but the commune will be more and more the future" (11).

Yet, in the early SHRA, it was Radical rather than socialist republican politics that dominated. Scottish Home Rule, along with Irish Home Rule, won support from the infant Scottish Labour Party, when it was formed within 1888. However, neither the SDF nor the SL/SLLL, nor even the united Scottish Socialist Federation, was able to push beyond the political limitations of this Radicalism. Their best members appreciated that Irish Home Rule might weaken the British Empire, but did not see the need for Socialists to take the lead in the national democratic struggles in Ireland, Scotland and Wales.

Such a strategy would have formed part of a break-up of the British Union and Empire perspective, the better to prepare the grounds for Socialism itself. Thus, the continued influence of Radicalism often led Socialists into tail-ending Irish populist and constitutional nationalist, or Scottish and Welsh Liberal, versions of Home Rule[5].

This tendency was accentuated because the SHRA also involved a number of Liberals, once Gladstone gave his support to Scottish Home Rule. As a consequence, the Radical SHRA leadership increasingly fell under the sway of liberal unionism. Support for Home Rule was seen in the context of maintaining an over-arching Imperial Parliament at Westminster. Ferguson had already shown this political slippage.

Keir Hardie's own political legacy of Radical Liberalism led him to be very much influenced by Liberal Home Rule thinking. He settled for a liberal unionist version of Home Rule within the UK and Empire. He also held to his own Left vision of Imperial Federation, which was based on the advances he saw being made by white workers in Australia, Canada and South Africa.

However, in contrast to the main advocates of Imperial Federation, Hardie

---

[5] The main reason for this was the continued Liberal domination of the issue of Scotland's self-determination by means of a Home Rule policy, which supported both Union and Empire. It took both the shock of the First World War, the impact of the renewal of the Irish Revolution in 1916, and the wider international revolutionary wave from 1916-21, before John Maclean arrived at a socialist republican 'Break up of the British Union and Empire' position.

also went on to support Home Rule for India. Thus, he did distinguish himself from the Anglo-Saxon/Teutonic racist politics of the Liberal Imperial Federalists. In a sense, Hardie was taking up the 'mantle' of those much earlier Radicals, James Mill, John Stuart Mill and Thomas Macauley[6]. Most Radicals, however, had cast off this liberal paternalist 'mantle', after the 1857 Indian Rebellion. It was from the Radicals and Nonconformists that Hardie also inherited his pacifism, now being jettisoned by many 'free trade' Liberals too.

Nevertheless, Hardie could still display pronounced racist characteristics when dealing with migrant workers in Scotland. He strongly opposed the use of Lithuanian labourers in the coalfields and ironworks of Ayrshire and Lanarkshire (12). This contrasted with the defence later offered by Davitt, to those Jewish migrants, also mainly from Tsarist Russian-ruled Lithuania, when subjected to the anti-Semitic Limerick Boycott in 1904 (13).

A young Lloyd George was a supporter of Cymru Fydd

The hold of Liberalism on the Welsh Home Rule movement was even stronger. When Cymru Fydd[7] (Young Wales) (14) had been formed in 1886, it remained an organisation within the Liberal Party. Initially it was mainly confined to the new group of Welsh Liberal MPs in London, along with the party officials and office bearers in their constituencies. Tom Ellis (15), the recently elected MP for Merionydd/Merioneth, was its principal spokesperson, whilst the young Lloyd George was also a supporter.

When Cymru Fydd members looked towards Ireland, it was not the political demand for Home Rule that provided the main inspiration for most, but Parnell's creation of a disciplined Irish Parliamentary Party. In effect, Cymru Fydd wanted a 'Welsh Parliamentary Party', not to challenge the UK state as such, but to achieve 'Welsh home rule' within the Liberal Party. The formation

---

[6] Thomas Macauley and other early Victorian Radicals had envisaged an enlightened native-born Indian political leadership emerging, guided by their more advanced mentors in England. Once they had thoroughly imbibed English/British liberal values, they could be entrusted with running India.

[7] It is interesting that those Liberal Party members, undoubtedly affected by political events in Ireland, chose to adopt, Cymru Fydd or Young Wales, as the name for their organisation. This older, by now largely sentimental, Mazzinian-style 'Young nation' label would have been more acceptable in traditional Liberal Party circles than say, the 'Welsh Home Rule Association'. This would have had too close an association for many Liberals with Ireland's recent troubled history.

of such a Welsh parliamentary grouping would make the party more effective in promoting the concerns of those Welsh recently enfranchised by the 1884 Reform Act.

The new plebian electors in Wales were much more consciously Welsh than those members of the middle class who already had the vote. Many of the new MPs were the product of a Welsh-speaking, Nonconformist, rural and small town society of tenant farmers, agricultural labourers, shopkeepers and artisans. Furthermore, a growing Welsh-speaking working class was to be found, not only amongst the slate quarriers of North and Mid Wales, but the miners in the north and west of the South Wales coalfield. As a consequence of these economic and social developments, the Welsh-speaking intelligentsia had become more confident. Its members addressed a wider range of political, social and economic issues in a vibrant national and local Welsh language secular and religious press (16).

An earlier generation of Welsh Radical Liberal MPs, such as Henry Richard[8] (17), had been very much part of the British Radical Liberal tradition - secularists who supported the separation of state and church as a principle, and also followers of the Manchester School in political economy. Whilst they might chafe at the earlier anti-Welsh prejudice shown by the UK state in the 'Blue Books' controversy[9] (18), they were quite at home in London, both amongst fellow Liberals and in the wider society they found there.

However, the new post-1885 wave of Welsh Liberal MPs expressed their Welshness in much more overt political terms than their predecessors. When they opposed the Anglican Church of Wales' control over education, they were more likely to highlight its 'alien' English nature, and its links with the Anglicised

---

[8] Henry Richard was a classic Welsh Radical supporter of the Liberal Party. He was a former Congregationalist Minister, an anti-slavery campaigner and Secretary of the Peace Society. He was elected MP for Merthyr Tydfil in 1868, soon after the 1867 Reform Act.

[9] The 'Blue Books' was the colloquial the name given to a Westminster commissioners' report into Welsh education, published in 1847, which placed its failings on the continued use of the Welsh language.

[10] Matthew Arnold, the influential English literary critic, had already developed an approach in his *Celtic Literature* by which he hoped to overcome both the earlier arrogant English ruling class dismissal of all things Celtic (Welsh and Gaelic), and the consequent resentments found amongst those living in the 'Celtic Fringe'. Arnold believed that the Celtic languages and societies were indeed dying, but had already contributed much to the dominant English language and literature. Furthermore, a scholarly study of these ancient languages and cultures was as valid as studying Latin and Greek, which then held high status in schools and universities. This way of thinking would have appealed more to the previous generation of Welsh Liberals, but could not win the support of the new wave, associated with Cymru Fydd, for whom Welsh was very much a living language.

landlord class. They thought that the Welsh language had a great future, not just a noble past[10]. The National Eisteddfod Association had been formed in 1880 (19). The Society for the Utilisation of the Welsh Language was founded in 1885 (20). Furthermore, this new generation of Welsh Liberal MPs believed that Westminster should step in and set fair rents for tenant farmers, something very much against the grain of the old Liberal Manchester School of political economy.

Nevertheless, Cymru Fydd's immediate practical concerns were more economic and cultural than political nationalist. Thus, the political situation in Wales contrasted with that in Ireland, where Gladstone was forced to put forward the First Irish Home Rule Bill; or in Scotland, where he conceded a greater measure of administrative devolution, through the appointment of a Scottish Secretary, sitting in the Cabinet (21). Disregard for Welsh political reform came about because the demand for Welsh Home Rule was initially more muted. Most members of Cymru Fydd believed that as long as Gladstone's Liberal Party controlled Westminster, this was enough to ensure their specific Welsh economic and cultural demands would be met.

Therefore, a major political weakness of the 'Home Rule-all-round' political demand, which Davitt and his Radical allies used to front his 'internationalism from below' land and labour alliance, was its inability to break free from the limitations imposed by dependence on Parnell's National League and Gladstone's Liberal Party. In this sense, Davitt's accommodation to the Liberal Party (like Hardie's) led to a slippage towards the acceptance of Gladstone's and Parnell's ever-weakening 'internationalism from above' alliance.

Certainly, the pressure of new class forces from below was a vital component of any 'internationalism from below' alliance, but this needed to be complemented by political demands, which went beyond the constitutional nationalism of Parnell, and the constitutional liberalism of Gladstone's admirers in England, Scotland, Wales and Ulster[11], and fully recognised the reactionary implications of the developing 'New Imperialism'. It also needed to go beyond the still dominant Lib-Labism found in England, Wales and Scotland, and the Nat-Labism found in Ireland (apart from north-east Ulster). These traditions held up the formation of politically independent Labour organisations.

Davitt had acted both as an Irish social republican and a British Radical. His social republicanism came from his Irish Fenian past, and a sentimental

---

[11] Despite the heroic efforts of Radical Liberals like Alexander Bowman, and the Irish Protestant Home Rule Association, Radical and Gladstonian Liberalism were virtually destroyed in Ireland by the defection of the Irish Liberal Unionists to the Conservative-led Irish Unionists.

attachment for an Irish Republic never left him. His Radicalism came more from his contact with British Radicals (and to a certain extent, with Socialists). As Davitt devoted more of his time to labour issues in England, Scotland and Wales (and later the British colonies), this sharpened the hazier class politics bequeathed to him by the IRB, but it also blunted the earlier keen republican political edge that Fenianism had provided him with.

Whilst often to the forefront of wider campaigns, in Ireland, England, Scotland and Wales, particularly over land and labour conditions, Davitt was still very much attached to the National League in Ireland, and Lib-Lab and Radical Liberal figures in Britain. Therefore, his political limitations played a part in holding back the development of independent Labour organisation, not only in Ireland, but throughout the UK.

Furthermore, the British Socialism, which Davitt came into contact with, did not offer a political perspective beyond that of Radical Liberalism[12] – Irish Home Rule or alternatively 'Home Rule-all-round'. The SDF largely accepted the UK state (whilst pushing for certain limited reforms) as the framework for its campaigning. In contrast, but also misguided, most SL members saw little need to conduct political work within the existing representative bodies. The SL began with a pro-Commune, anti-Parliamentary, anti-British imperial stance, before collapsing into more individualistic Anarchism.

Just at the time when the majority of the British ruling class was backing the Conservative and Liberal Unionists' resort to the full panoply of the anti-democratic powers of the UK state - the House of Lords, the judiciary and certain military officers - as well as building their own reactionary extra-parliamentary force, in order to face down the new challenge represented by the national democratic movement in Ireland, a clear socialist republican politics failed to develop. This weakness was soon to be highlighted, in 1893, when the Second Irish Home Rule Bill appeared before Westminster.

Moreover, between 1889-92, there was an excellent opportunity to develop socialist republican politics. Huge numbers of unskilled workers took their place on the historical arena, as birth was given to 'New (Trade) Unionism'. Furthermore, both Socialists and social republicans played key roles in this new movement. It coincided with the foundation of the Second International, the growing international campaign for 'the eight hour day', and the worldwide action taken on May Day, particularly in 1890 and 1891.

---

[12] This does not mean that all Radical Liberals supported Irish (or Scottish and Welsh) Home Rule, as Joseph Chamberlain had shown. Some Socialists shared his disdain for Irish self-determination, including individual members of the SDF and SL. This attitude was also common in the Fabian Society.

References

(1)   **see** http://en.wikipedia.org/wiki/Cecil_Rhodes

(2)   **see** http://en.wikipedia.org/wiki/Archibald_Primrose,_5th_Earl_of_Rosebery

(3)   Pat Walsh, *The Rise and Fall of Imperial Ireland*, p. 19 (Athol Books, 2003, Belfast)

(4)   ibid., p. 18-9.

(5)   Paul Bew, *C. S. Parnell*, p. 99 (Gill and Macmillan, 1980, Dublin)

(6)   **see** http://www.skyminds.net/politics/scottish-politics/scottish-home-rule

(7)   **see** Elaine McFarland, *John Ferguson, 1836-1906, Irish Issues in Scottish Politics* p. 196 (Tuckwell Press, 2001, East Linton)

(8)   ibid., p. 196.

(9)   **see** Martin Crick, *THoSDF*, op. cit., p. 26.

(10)   **see** Autopylus, *Grand Old Man of Fleet Street,* pages unnumbered, in J. Morrison Davidson, *Politics for the People* (William Reeves, 1892, London)

(11)   J. Morrison Davidson, *Scotia Rediviva – Home Rule for Scotland* (William Reeves, 1890, London)

(12)   **see** John Miller, *The Lithuanians in Scotland*, pp. 23-4 (House of Lochar, 1998, Isle of Colonsay)

(13)   **see** Manus O'Riordan, *Citizens of the Republic in an Independent Ireland* **on** http://www.drb.ie/june_citizens.html

(14)   **see** http://en.wikipedia.org/wiki/Cymru_Fydd

(15)   **see** http://en.wikipedia.org/wiki/T._E._Ellis

(16)   **see** Kenneth Morgan, *The Rebirth of a Nation, Wales, 1880-1980 (RoaN)* p. 21 (University of Wales Press, 1981, Oxford)

(17)   **see** http://en.wikipedia.org/wiki/Henry_Richard

(18)   **see** http://en.wikipedia.org/wiki/Treachery_of_the_Blue_Books

(19)   **see** Kenneth O. Morgan, *RoaN,* op, cit., p. 21.

(20)   ibid., p. 95.

(21)   **see** http://en.wikipedia.org/wiki/Secretary_of_State_for_Scotland

14. 1889-92 – The birth of 'New Unionism' and the new industrial offensive

The 'annus mirabilis' of 1889 had been preceded by significant events. Scotland had seen the formation of a Scottish National Miners Federation in 1886, and the widely supported Broxburn Shaleminers' Strike of 1887, followed by the formation of the Scottish Labour Party (SLP) and Scottish Socialist Federation in 1888.

Annie Besant - an SDF member and active in the Match girls' (1888) and Dockers' Strikes (1889)

In England, the successful London Matchgirls' Strike (1), led by SDF member, Annie Besant[1] (2), had also taken place in 1888. Eleanor Marx, active in the Women's Trade Union League, gave her support (3). A more unlikely figure in the initiation of the 'New Unionism' was Joseph Havelock Wilson[2] (4). He organised strike action to seek recognition for the National Amalgamated Sailors and Firemens Union (NAS&FU) (5). Launched in Sunderland, the union's main base soon became Glasgow, as successful secondary action by dockers led to a victory for union recognition in the 'Second City of the Empire'.

The NAS&FU then proceeded to extend its organisation to both sides of the Irish Sea, in

---

[1] Annie Besant, who was from an Irish background, was a consistent supporter of Irish (and later Indian) self-rule. She began her political life as a Radical Secularist and birth control advocate, alongside Henry Bradlaugh. However, after 'Bloody Sunday' in 1887, she soon became a Socialist, joining the SDF in 1888. As well as being a leader in the Matchgirls' Strike, she went on to play a prominent part in the London Dockers' Strike of 1889.

[2] Despite the NAS&FU's militant reputation and Joseph Havelock Wilson's success as an independent Labour candidate in 1892, he remained a Liberal Party member, and took the Liberal whip. Henceforth he strongly opposed independent Labour representation. The NAS&FU's resort to expensive litigation was probably more responsible for its early demise in 1893, than any costly post-1888 militant action.

Scotland, England, Wales and Ireland. The support action given by dockers soon led to the formation of the National Union of Dock Labourers[3] (NUDL) (6), initiated on Clydeside, and led by James Sexton[4] (7). The two biggest sections of the union were Irish Catholics followed by Highland Protestants (8).

Edward McHugh and Richard McGhee - two of Davitt's Irish lieutenants who became involved in the Highland Land League and the fight for 'New Unionism'

Key figures in building the union were Davitt's allies, Edward McHugh and Richard McGhee. Avoiding strike action, they used 'ca canny'[5] methods, and boycott actions[6] by carters and seamen to develop union organisation on the docks (9). The Glasgow Trades Council also helped organise the union locally, whilst the NUDL officers, Hugh Johnston (originally from Ireland) and Charles Kennedy (of the SLP) (10), helped to extend the union to Ireland and England. So successful was their recruiting on Merseyside, that the union headquarters were moved to Liverpool in September 1891 (11).

---

[3] The National Union of Dock Labourers preceded the formation of the London-based, Port, Wharf, Riverside and General Labourers Union (PWR&GLU). It joined the wider Transport & General Workers Union, one year after its foundation in 1922, formed at the initiative of the PWR&GLU.

[4] James Sexton, brought up in Newcastle-upon-Tyne, had a Fenian family background. Initially, he had tried unsuccessfully to organise a branch of the American Knights of Labour in Bootle. Like J. Havelock Wilson, once the heroic militant phase of 'New Unionism' was over, he too emerged as one of the first of the new generation of trade union bureaucrats, who marked the acceptance and consolidation of the new general unions within the existing British political order. Unlike Wilson, though, he joined the new Independent Labour Party.

[5] McHugh publicly attributed 'ca canny' or 'go slow' methods to downtrodden farm labourers, but both the phrase and the method were strongly associated with Lanarkshire miners, whom McHugh would certainly have come into contact with.

[6] Thus the boycott actions Davitt originally copied from his experience in the Lancashire cotton mills, and extended to the Irish Land League, were picked up in turn by the new industrial unionism on the Clyde and Mersey waterfronts.

117

A strike was launched on Merseyside, from December 20th 1888 to February 18th 1889, and again from June 6th to July 13th, 1889, over union control of labour (12). It involved both Protestant and Catholic workers[7]. Cunninghame-Graham provided McHugh with assistance (13). In contrast to Glasgow, the sailors on Merseyside did not reciprocate the dockers' supportive strike action, so the dispute, played for high stakes, became bitter. It was only ended, after growing privation amongst the dockers, by the arbitration of Davitt[8] himself (14). Union control of labour was not won, but members were successful in defending the union's existence, despite further attacks by the dock owners.

The two key disputes, which made many more people aware that something wider was stirring, were the London Gasworkers' Strike (15) for the '8 hour day' in May, 1889, soon followed by the London Dockers' Strike in August (16) for the 'dockers' tanner', or six pence per hour. 'New Unionism' was now a recognised phenomenon.

The Gasworkers' Strike was led by Will Thorne[9] (17) and Ben Tillet[10] (18). They were both members of the SDF. Another key figure was Peter Curran, a former member of both the Irish Land and Scottish Land and Labour Leagues, who moved south from Glasgow to join the SDF in Woolwich in south London and became a union organiser (19). The gasworkers also received strong

---

[7] The sectarian divisions encouraged by many employers and some politicians, in the 'Belfast-Glasgow-Liverpool Triangle' were highly visible in the latter city. This was highlighted by the city's large number of Conservative Unionist MPs on one hand, and on the other, by the fact that the Irish Nationalist MP, T. P. O'Connor, held the Liverpool Scotland constituency from 1885-1929.

[8] Davitt's role here is interesting. That he was acceptable to the Liverpool dock owners, as well as the dockers themselves, is probably due to his Radical and Lib-Lab influenced thinking. This upheld the view that conciliation and arbitration was the most civilised framework for conducting unresolved industrial disputes. With the development of the New Model trade unions in the 1850's, and the widening electoral franchise in 1867 and 1884, a number of employers had given their backing to trade unions to provide an alternative to unruly strikes and mass demonstrations. They also supported conciliation and arbitration. This can be seen as an early form of 'social partnership'. Davitt, however, often learned something new from the latest struggles. He did go on to accept aspects of 'New Unionism'. This highlights his transitional role in the wider Labour movement in the period when it moved from Radicalism to Socialism.

[9] Will Thorne was a member of the SDF. He became the first General Secretary of the NUG&GL, before being replaced by Ben Tillett. Thorne became an independent Labour councillor for West Ham, in east London, in 1891.

[10] Ben Tillett was a member of the Fabian Society, although he later joined the SDF, after a period in the ILP. He became General Secretary of the NUG&LU.

backing from two other SDF members, John Burns[11] (20) and Tom Mann[12] (21), as a well as from former SL member, Eleanor Marx (22). The immediate result of the Gasworkers' Strike was the formation of the National Union of Gasworkers and General Labourers[13] (NUG&GL) (23)

The Dockers' Strike had an even wider impact. It involved thousands of casually employed dock labourers and other workers who struck in solidarity. It led to rent strike action by the dockers' partners, and to large-scale international financial support, particularly from Australia. Many of the individual organisers in the Gasworkers' Strike became involved in the Dockers' Strike. The Port, Wharf, Riverside and General Labourers Union was formed[14] (PWR&GLU) (24). The organisation of the NUDL, which had been initiated in Scotland and then spread south to England and Ireland, also contributed to the wave of action that launched what first became known as 'New Unionism' in London. This in its turn spread back to Scotland, Wales and Ireland.

Stevedores' banner celebrating the help from Australia

---

[11] John Burns very much enjoyed a Radical reputation, particularly after taking part in the West End Riots of the unemployed in 1886, and being jailed for six weeks for his role in 'Bloody Sunday' in 1887. He joined the SDF. At the time of the Gasworkers' Strike, he was an independent Socialist and close friend of Tom Mann. He won the Battersea seat as an independent Labour candidate, in the 1892 General Election but, in a move that surprised most Socialists, ended up giving his support to the Liberals.

[12] Tom Mann was a member of the SDF, and acted as Keir Hardie's campaign manager during the Mid-Lanarkshire by-election. Mann had also helped to found the Eight Hour League and promoted independent Labour representation with Henry Champion. He was a member of the craft union, the Amalgamated Society of Engineers. He became a leading member of a group of New Union supporters, who contested the 'Old Unionist' and pro-Liberal sympathies in long established unions.

[13] The National Union of Gasworkers and General Labourers became the main component of one of the two largest general unions - the General and Municipal Workers Union in 1924.

[14] The Port, Wharf, Riverside and General Labourers Union became the main component of the other large general union, the Transport & General Workers Union.

In Wales, the PWR&GLU was able to extend beyond Cardiff docks to include metalworkers badly hit by the effect of McKinley Tariffs (25) introduced in the USA (26). The national economic protectionism, associated with the rise of 'New Imperialism', was making its effect felt. Elsewhere in Wales, Helen Taylor, inspired by the London Dockers' Strike, addressed a meeting of the pro-land nationalisation Cymdeithas y Ddaear i'r Bobl in Blaenau Ffestiniog (27), the stronghold of the slate quarriers.

Scotland had had few of the New Model-type unions[15]. These had formed the backbone of 'Old Unionism' in England. They tried to block the advance of 'New Unionism'. To compensate for the comparative weakness of trade union organisation in Scotland, trades councils were to the forefront in trying to extend the new England-based unions to gasworkers, seamen and brickworkers over the border (28).

It was at its annual conference in Dundee, in 1889, that the 'Old Unionism' dominated, all-UK, TUC voted down 'the eight hour day' and the formation of an all-UK independent Labour party (29). Liberal politics still had much influence amongst the supporters of 'Old Unionism' in the well-developed network of English-based craft and skilled workers' unions represented at the TUC[16]. However, even the TUC and some of the 'Old Unions' were to be nudged into modernity by the impact of 'New Unionism' over the next few years. In 1892, the all-UK TUC finally voted to support the 'eight hour day' at its conference in Glasgow.

The mood of the times was best captured by former Fenian and Land League activist, now SDF member, Jim Connell. He wrote the famous Labour anthem, *The Red Flag*, in response to the Dockers' Strike, and to an earlier visit to London by Lucy Parsons, wife of one of the Chicago Haymarket Martyrs (30).

---

[15] The thinking behind the New Model unions, which first developed in the 1850's, particularly amongst skilled craft workers, now became known as 'Old Unionism'.

[16] However, the larger and stronger unions, based on 'Old Unionism', in England did enjoy more purchase upon the Liberal Party, making it more likely that local Liberal organisations would adopt Lib-Lab candidates there, particularly in mining constituencies, where the working class vote was more concentrated. In Scotland and Wales, in contrast, the organisational weakness of local unions made this a more difficult task. In Scotland and Wales, the Liberal Party also enjoyed wider electoral support through being able to effectively present itself as a cross-class national party. Furthermore, in Scotland, sectarian divisions, particularly in mining communities, added to the difficulties in making workers' independent political influence felt. Thus, despite the earlier emergence of politically advanced Socialist and Labour organisations in Scotland, they took longer to make an electoral breakthrough compared to England, even after 'New Unionism' enhanced prospects for independent Labour politics.

References

(1)   **see** http://www.spartacus.schoolnet.co.uk/TUmatchgirls.htm

(2)   **see** http://en.wikipedia.org/wiki/Annie_Besant

(3)   **see** http://en.wikipedia.org/wiki/Eleanor_Marx

(4)   **see** http://en.wikipedia.org/wiki/Havelock_Wilson

(5)   **see** *National Amalgamated Sailors' and Firemen's Union*, 1887-93 **on** http://en.wikipedia.org/wiki/National_Union_of_Seamen

(6)   **see** http://en.wikipedia.org/wiki/National_Union_of_Dock_Labourers

(7)   **see** http://en.wikipedia.org/wiki/James_Sexton

(8)   **see** William Kenefick, *Red Scotland! The Rise and Fall of the Radical Left, c. 1872-1932 (RS)* p. 14 (Edinburgh University Press, 2007, Edinburgh)

(9)   ibid., p. 32.

(10)   ibid., p. 18.

(11)   ibid., p. 11.

(12)   **see** Eric Talpin, *Liverpool Dockers and Seamen, 1870-1890*, p. 64 (University of Hull, 1970, Hull)

(13)   ibid., p. 73.

(14)   ibid., p. 77.

(15)   Yvonne Kapp, *The Air of Freedom: The Birth of the New Unionism*, (Lawrence & Wishart, 1989, London)

(16)   **see** http://libcom.org/history/1889-the-great-london-dock-strike

(17)   **see** http://en.wikipedia.org/wiki/Will_Thorne

(18)   **see** http://en.wikipedia.org/wiki/Ben_Tillett

(19)   **see** David Howell, *British Workers and the Independent Labour Party, 1888-1906*, p.114 (Manchester University Press, 1984, Manchester)

(20)   **see** http://en.wikipedia.org/wiki/John_Burns

(21)   **see** http://en.wikipedia.org/wiki/Tom_Mann

(22)   **see** http://en.wikipedia.org/wiki/Eleanor_Marx

(23)   **see** http://www.unionancestors.co.uk/GMB.htm

(24)   **see** http://en.wikipedia.org/wiki/Dock,_Wharf,_Riverside_and_General_Labourers_Union

(25)   **see** http://en.wikipedia.org/wiki/McKinley_Tariff

(26)   **see** Kenneth O. Morgan, *Rebirth of A Nation, Wales, 1880-1980*, p. 30, (Oxford University Press, 1981, New York)

(27)   **see** Peris Jones Evans, *Euan Pan Jones – Land Reformer* in *Welsh History Review*, Vol. 4, No. 2, June 1968, p. 154. (University of Wales)

(28)   **see** William Kenefick, *RS*, op. cit., p. 11.

(29)   ibid., p. 20.

(30)   **see** Andrew Boyd, *Jim Connell – Author of the Red Flag*, pp. 7-8 (Donaldson Archives/Socialist Historian Society, 2001, Oxford)

15. The rise and wider effects of the 'New Unionism' in Ireland

As 'New (Trade) Unionism' spread to Ireland, the NUG&GL recruited so fast in Dublin that it held its second Conference in the city in May 1891 (1). The Socialist, Adolphus Shields, was the Dublin district secretary. Michael Canty, a future Nat-Lab[1] advocate, became a national organiser (2). Frederick Allan, a prominent Fenian, was a key activist (3). Herein, lay one of the problems faced by 'New Unionism' in Ireland.

In Scotland, at the time, there was a united Scottish Socialist Federation, and a Scottish Labour Party, as well as mainly supportive trades councils to promote the 'New Unionism'. In England, prominent Socialists, particularly individual SDF trade unionists, understood the significance of the 'New Unionism' and tried to develop it in a Socialist direction. This combined offensive even made its mark on the TUC, previously dominated by 'Old Unionism'.

In Ireland, however, 'New Unionism' was pulled in different directions by various versions of competing nationalist and unionist politics. Here, the socio-economic situation was different, and the ongoing political struggle over Irish Home Rule made the development of independent Labour politics much more fraught. A few of the skilled trades were organised in UK-wide unions such as the engineers, carpenters, printworkers and coachmakers (4). There was even an attempt to organise Knights of Labour branches in Ireland (5). However, as in Scotland, there were a few national trade unions, but many workers were in locally based trade unions, with trades councils playing a compensating coordinating role.

The Irish Socialist Union (ISU), confined to Dublin, which had been influenced by the politics of the SDF, was quite peripheral to the Labour upsurge in Ireland, despite the participation of individual members in the new trade unions (6). Indeed, the loss of the ISU's few Labour activists led to its collapse, and its short-lived replacement by a Fabian Society branch[2] (7)

---

[1] Nat-Labism was Ireland's equivalent to the Lib-Labism found in Britain. Nat-Lab supporters looked to the NL (and some, such as Davitt, later to the Irish National Federation) to adopt Labour candidates for Westminster and local elections.

[2] Although the early Fabian Society did attract a few workers, its overwhelmingly middle class character, and its continued flirtation with the Liberal Party, meant it did not hold on long to these members. It also advocated an 'enlightened' British unionism and imperialism, so its attractions were limited in Ireland. Even the Belfast branch only lasted a year, where ironically, however, its branch secretary was R. H. Feagan, an Irish nationalist.

Unlike Scotland, where most of the population had direct experience of the Industrial Revolution, in Ireland, this was only true of the Lagan Valley in northeast Ulster. Yet, it was precisely in this area that industrialisation failed to create longer term, favourable conditions for 'New Unionism'[3]. The highpoint was undoubtedly, the Linen Lappers' Strike in Belfast in 1892, accompanied by an impressive support demonstration, with both Orange and Green marching bands (8).

However, as on so many future occasions, whenever wider political and democratic issues arose, or whenever there was a serious threat to the existing Unionist-dominated set-up in the North, reaction quickly moved to the counter-attack, frightening most Protestant workers back into the Unionist fold. The short-lived unity of 1892 occurred only a year before the Second Irish Home Rule Bill was to be put to Westminster.

Most Protestant workers in Ulster were politically tied to a cross-class UK Unionism. They mainly supported the Conservatives. The minority of workers, who had previously supported the Liberal Party, had switched overwhelmingly to Liberal Unionism. Thus they soon ended up supporting the new Conservative-dominated Irish Unionist Party too. Belfast Trades Council adopted a public 'non-political' stance, which, when challenged, usually quickly revealed its members' Conservative and pro-Unionist views (9).

Although there were no major industrial centres in the rest of Ireland, there were railways, docks and, in Dublin, activities such as building, carting and gasworks labouring, which employed large numbers of workers. In these areas 'New Unionism' made a rapid impact and led to spin-offs, such as growing support for an eight-hour working day, and the demand for the political organisation of labour.

The first Dublin May Day parade in 1890 was a considerable success. Attended by thousands, it was addressed by Michael McKeown, one of the NUDL strike leaders in Liverpool, and by NUG&GL member, John Whelan, who called for working men to be elected to parliament (10). However, precisely what this meant became the subject of dispute. The idea of an independent Labour party soon withered before the onslaught of competing Nat-Lab organisations. It was also undermined by the lack of support from the 'non-political' (i.e. Unionist accepting) Belfast Trades Council.

---

[3] The only New Union to retain a small base in Belfast was the smallest of the general unions created during the post-1889 wave of action – the Tyneside-based, National Amalgamated Union of Labour (NAUL), which became one of the components of the National Union of General & Municipal Workers in 1924.

In 1888, the first steps had been taken to create a national trade union federation in Ireland. T. J. O'Reilly, a printer and the treasurer of Dublin Trades Council, was "impressed by the power of the Irish National League, the rank-and-file organisation of Parnell's parliamentary party" (11). He wanted 'home rule' within a wider organisation "of the trades throughout not only Ireland but the United Kingdom" (12). He also appealed to the example of "the Trades' {Union} Congress in England {Britain}... a power which was not only respected but feared" (13).

His timing had been auspicious. The Irish Federated Trade and Labour Union (IFT&LU) was launched in Dublin on 4th May 1889. There were delegates from all of Ireland's cities, including Belfast. There were messages of support from Britain, including London Trades Council. There was also a well-received visit from Havelock Wilson, Secretary of the NAS&FU, who was in the process of extending the union's organisation to Ireland (14).

A tentative suggestion was made that workmen should be taken on as candidates for Westminster and the local councils. However, there was a shared, if undeclared, understanding, that these would be adopted by the existing parties. This most obviously meant the National League in most Irish cities and towns, but also tacitly, the Irish Unionist Party in Belfast. Nevertheless, Belfast delegates soon had second thoughts about further participation in the IFT&LU, preferring to prepare a loyal address to the Lord Lieutenant on his visit to their city (15).

In 1890, 'New Unionism' was still advancing strongly in Ireland. The key NUG&GL organisers, Shields and Canty, gave their support to the Dublin United Building Labourers' Strike, launched in March (16). After facing continued employer intransigence, Davitt was once more appointed as arbitrator (17). The supporters of 'New Unionism' increasingly resented Davitt's adherence to the older trade union traditions of conciliation and arbitration.

Davitt refused to chair a mass meeting, initiated by the NUG&GL, of between 8-10,000 in Phoenix Park on March 30th, 1890 (18). At this meeting, Shields claimed that Irish workers "had as much claim upon Mr. Davitt as the labourers of England, Scotland and Wales" (19). There was some truth in this dig, since Davitt was preparing to launch his *Labour World* in London. This was primarily targeted at what he saw as the more advanced Labour consciousness in England and Scotland (20).

Davitt attacked the lack of 'home rule', or autonomy, to be found in the new general unions. "All I ask... - in the matter of international relationship with the labour cause outside Ireland – is, that we are not deprived of the principle of home rule in our Irish labour organizations" (21).

Davitt also feared that an unconsidered extension of British based general unions might lead "to a strike or similar action because it may seem expedient or necessary to men unacquainted with the peculiar economic conditions of Ireland to order a resort to such proceeding in Ireland"[4] (22). Here, Davitt, in looking to the past, was acting as a brake on the further development of an 'internationalism from below' alliance. However, some of Davitt's long time supporters, such as McHugh and McGhee, and others, such as Canty, were politically ahead of him in their recognition of the importance of the 'New Unionism'.

Edward Aveling also addressed the Dublin demonstration (23). In 1887, Davitt had refused to meet Aveling, after they had both addressed an anti-coercion rally in London. He was opposed to Aveling's openly declared atheism[5] (24). Yet, Aveling and Eleanor Marx were amongst the most sympathetic of all the non-Irish Socialists to the cause of Ireland. Aveling used his speech to attack arbitration, whilst also pointing out that British workers had supported Home Rule (25).

Engels was well aware of the importance of Davitt in recent struggles. He trod more carefully than Aveling. He praised Davitt and his allies' response to the "impetus {given} to the labour movement in Ireland. Many of their branches consist of agricultural labourers" (26). This was a recognition of Davitt's role in founding the Irish Democratic, Trade and Labour Federation (IDTLF) in Cork in January, 1890 (27).

The IDTLF consisted mainly of agricultural labourers and country town workers, and the Nat-Lab advocate, Michael Austin, became its co-Secretary (28). Engels claimed that "Davitt, too, who had at first wanted independent Irish Trade

---

[4] It is also ironic, that when the next political upturn occurred in the first decade of the twentieth century, James Larkin attacked the British-based NUDL for its lack of support for more militant Irish workers. Times had certainly changed since Davitt's original worries about the relative backwardness of Irish labour. To his credit, the old Radical, Davitt, was able to learn at least some of the lessons of the need for an independent Labour party, and later worked more closely with Socialists.

[5] Davitt felt that specific religious denominational (and anti-religious) opinions should be excluded from politics. Although, as a Catholic, he never attacked the clergy on religious grounds, in contrast to other Irish (and Scottish) Labour figures, he was quite prepared to publicly attack any unwarranted clerical interference in politics (until he became politically disorientated by the Kitty O'Shea Scandal in 1891 that is). In this attitude he anticipated James Connolly. Furthermore, like Connolly (and Eleanor Marx), Davitt was strongly supportive of independent women's trade unions.

125

Unions, has learned from them {the New Unions}: their constitution secures them perfectly free home rule"[6] (29). This was too optimistic an appraisal, as events were soon to show.

---

[6] Davitt had not argued for independent trade unions but for Irish 'home rule' within international Labour federations, although he had expressed conservative doubts about the ability of Irish labour to give supportive strike action to British workers. However, despite Engels' claim that 'home rule' existed within the New Unions, when the employers began their retaliatory counter-offensive, union leaders leaders usually responded by centralising control in the union HQ. This rendered redundant any national autonomy, and also undermined the sovereignty of the members in their workplaces and branches.

References

(1)   **see** Fintan Lane, *The Origins of Modern Irish Socialism, 1881-1896*, p. 177 (*TOoMIS*) (Cork University Press, 1997, Cork)

(2)   ibid., p. 166.

(3)   ibid., p. 173.

(4)   **see** John W. Boyle, *The Irish Labor Movement in the Nineteenth Century* (*TILM*) pp. 92-9(The Catholic University of America Press, 1988, Washington D.C.)

(5)   ibid., p. 106.

(6)   **see** Fintan Lane, *TOoMIS*, op. cit., p. 164.

(7)   ibid., p. 188.

(8)   **see** John W. Boyle, *TILM*, op. cit., p. 140.

(9)   ibid., pp. 158-62.

(10)   **see** Fintan Lane, *TOoMIS*, op. cit., p. 169

(11)   **see** John W. Boyle, *TILM*, op. cit., p. 131

(12)   ibid., p. 131.

(13)   ibid., p. 131

(14)   ibid., pp. 132-3.

(15)   ibid., p. 134

(16)   **see** Fintan Lane, *TOoMIS*, op. cit., p. 166.

(17)   ibid., p. 167.

(18)   ibid., p. 167.

(19)   ibid., p. 168

(20)   **see** F. Sheehy-Skeffington, *The Counter-Revolution* in *Michael Davitt, Revolutionary Agitator and Labour Leader* p. 148 (MacGibbon & Kee, 1967, London)

(21)   **see** Fintan Lane, *TOoMIS*, op. cit., p. 168.

(22)   ibid., p. 168.

(23)   ibid., p. 168.

(24)   ibid., p. 169.

(25)   ibid., p. 168.

(26)   *Frederick Engels to Friedrich Adolph Sorge, 2.11.1891* **in** Karl Marx & Frederick Engels, *Ireland and the Irish Question,* p. 470 (Lawrence & Wishart, 1978, London)

(27)   **see** John W. Boyle, *TILM*, op. cit., pp. 137-8.

(28)   ibid., p. 138.

(29)   Marx & Engels, *IIQ*, op. cit., p. 470.

16. The limits of Davitt's politics reached as the Irish Home Rule movement splits

In December 1890, in the middle of the surge of 'New (Trade) Unionism', Davitt's political bearings were shattered by Parnell's involvement in the Kitty O'Shea divorce scandal (1). As recently as February 1889, a Westminster Parliamentary Commission had eventually revealed that *The Times* letter of March 1887, attacking Parnell, was a forgery. As a result of these findings, Parnell probably reached the zenith of his popularity amongst British Liberals and Irish Nationalists (2). Opposition to the Conservatives was growing. The Gladstone/Parnell alliance seemed to promise Irish Home Rule in the near future.

Kitty O'Shea - Parnell's partner

Davitt began to address the issue of the political organisation of Irish Labour in readiness for this eventuality. However, what he envisaged was the promotion of Nat-Lab candidates, under the auspices of Parnell's National League, not an independent Labour party. Just as Davitt's conception of trade union organisation was still based upon his pre-1889 British experience, so his idea of Labour political organisation was inspired by the Lib-Labs backed by the Radicals.

Parnell had persuaded Davitt of the need for an alliance with the Liberal Party, if Home Rule was to be achieved. Parnell understood this alliance in mainly personal terms. It was between himself and Gladstone. Davitt, however, saw the need for a much more broadly based alliance, which linked the whole of the Irish National League (NL) with the English, Scottish and Welsh Radicals, in a joint Home Rule, land and labour campaign.

However, both men's strategies were blown apart, when details of Parnell's private life were revealed to the court in the O'Shea divorce case, which Parnell himself had declined to contest. Davitt felt betrayed, since Parnell had reassured him that he would emerge from the O'Shea case "without a stain on his name or reputation" (3). In other words, Parnell tried to dismiss the allegations as just another lying attack upon him following the exposure of *The Times* forgery. The court case publicly revealed what many (if not necessarily Davitt) had already privately known (4).

Davitt was the first to publicly break with Parnell over this betrayal of trust. The NL leadership was still prepared to back Parnell, however, and even the Catholic hierarchy initially remained aloof. It was the strong British Nonconformist element in Gladstone's Liberal Party that changed the political balance. They made it known that they could no longer uphold their party's alliance with the NL.

It was then that the majority of the NL leaders turned on Parnell (5). For, if there was one thing Parnell had drummed into their heads, over the past five years, it was the need to maintain the NL/Liberal alliance, at all costs. Now, only jettisoning Parnell himself could do that. Thus, the majority of the NL leadership unceremoniously dumped Parnell, although he retained enough support in Dublin to hold on to the party apparatus and paper (6).

Davitt joined the majority of the NL leadership, when it split and formed a breakaway party, the Irish National Federation (INF) (7). He still remained convinced of the need for a single national party, yet was now helping to create one led by his class enemies, backed by the Catholic hierarchy. They had been prepared to go along with Parnell, so long as the NL could advance their own interests under his umbrella. Now, though, the hierarchy took the opportunity to break with any need for a Protestant frontman, so that it could mould the new national party to better meet its needs.

Therefore, instead of the previous NL-Liberal alliance, with some Catholic hierarchy support, a much closer INF-Catholic hierarchy alliance was forged, which would look to whatever British party could best serve its interests. The INF was to become the political depository for those Catholic businessmen and better-off farmers, who had previously mainly given their support to Parnell and the NL. These were the people who had largely abandoned the poorer tenants, the landless and agricultural labourers, whom Davitt and his allies had represented within the Land League, and were still trying to organise.

Furthermore, one effect of the split in the NL was to kill off the 'Plan of

Campaign'. This had been smouldering on, with Balfour continuing his harsh line, after the 'Mitchelstown Massacre'. Both sides were preparing for a showdown. The Irish Tenants' Defence Association was formed in October 1889, to give more effective NL backing to the Campaign (8). The Conservatives introduced the Congested Districts Board (9) to alleviate the worst poverty in the West. Once this concession had been made, Balfour undertook further preparations to break the remaining resistance. However, the split in the NL achieved this particular aim for him, since it now proved impossible to raise money from demoralised supporters, particularly in the USA (10). In 1891, the new INF leaders took the opportunity to quietly drop the 'Plan of Campaign' (11).

Parnell, the consummate political opportunist, realised that his support base had now shifted dramatically from the Irish Catholic businessmen and the better-off farmers towards the artisans and workers of Dublin (12). Parnellism now seemed to equate with Nat-Labism, and even, sotto voce, with the Fenians. Thus, Parnell made a startling U-turn, and began to make appeals to the Labour movement and to the IRB.

Leading NUG&GL members, Shields, Canty and Allan, became involved in organising a Labour conference, which was held in Dublin on March 14th, 1891. Dr. P. J. Neilen, of Kanturk Democratic Labour Federation in County Cork, chaired the conference. It attracted delegates from sixty-nine labour bodies, mainly from around Dublin, but also including Belfast (13). It passed support for the eight-hour working day and land nationalisation. To these were now added the demand for state control of railways, canals, harbours, docks and other transport facilities. The conference also advocated payment of MPs and election expenses, thus paving the way for Labour candidates. However, the conference also displayed some of the conservative social attitudes and religious sectarianism still found in Ireland. It opted for adult male not universal suffrage, and dropped a motion advocating secular education (14).

Parnell addressed the conference, despite a cautionary note from the Belfast NUG&GL delegate, who wondered why the Irish Unionist and Orange Order MP, Colonel Saunderson, had not been invited as well! (15) Somewhat hypocritically, Parnell gave his support to his own bowdlerised version of land nationalisation, and to the eight hour working day (16).

The new organisation decided to call itself the Labour League (LL) (17). Although it failed to win the support of Dublin Trades Council, which mainly represented the skilled trades, the latter, nevertheless, took part in the joint 1891 May Day demonstration. This was an advance on the year before (18). The NUG&GL organised a further demonstration in Dublin, a few weeks later, to coincide with its own second conference being held in the city (19). Will Thorne, Eleanor Marx and Edward Aveling addressed the demonstrators. Eleanor Marx criticised the LL's failure to uphold universal suffrage. Aveling proclaimed his support for Irish Home Rule, whilst adding the need for Irish Nationalists to embrace internationalism (20).

Had Parnell lived on, it would have been interesting to see how he would have used the LL. He might have tried to make it into a subordinate arm of the rump NL, rather than abandoning it after it had served his immediate purposes, as he had with the short-lived Irish Labour and Industrial Union, which was created a decade before to dish Davitt (21). However, with many LL members having undergone the recent experience of 'New Unionism', there might have been stronger opposition to any moves Parnell might have made to limit the LL's aspirations.

Therefore, Davitt's decision to boycott the LL's founding conference represented another bad decision, following the precedent of his agreeing to the 'Avondale Treaty' in 1881 (22). Furthermore, Parnell only had a few more months to live, so the debate on genuine independent Labour political organisation could have had a wider audience; especially since Parnell's successor as NL leader was to be John Redmond (23) who "claimed that trade unions were dangerous to national unity" (24).

Sidelined into fighting for the INF, Davitt had to abandon his *Labour World* initiative in May 1891 (25). Instead he decided to promote a new Irish trade union congress (26). Whilst he had been contemplating this for some time, the split between the NL and INF changed the nature of the meeting, which was finally held in July 1891. Delegates attended from both skilled and unskilled unions, from the IDTLF and from several trades councils, but significantly not from Belfast (27). If the LL founding conference had appeared to many to be little more than a front for Parnell and the NL, others would no doubt have seen Davitt's proposed new congress as a front for the INF.

At the conference an argument was waged between Michael Austin, who supported Davitt's line of trying to get the INF to adopt Labour candidates, and Michael Canty, who suggested the need for independent Labour representation, after his experiences in the struggle for 'New Unionism' in Ireland (28). In the end it was decided to adopt Davitt's line and several Nat-Lab candidates were later put forward for the 1892 General Election.

In September, 1891, Engels briefly visited Dublin (29). Very much influenced by recent events throughout the UK, he had just written a private memo to the leaders of the German Social Democrats, in support of a federal republic for

England, Ireland, Scotland and Wales, "where the two islands are peopled by four nations" (30). This was the first time that Engels recognised the existence of the distinct nations of England, Scotland and Wales.

In the early 1880's, Engels had accepted the Irish Nationalists' policy of Home Rule to front their 'New Departure' campaign. However, in the late 1860's and early 70's, in response to the Fenian struggles, both he and Marx had moved towards support for an independent Ireland (31). As the 1879-82 'Irish Revolution' developed, Engels began to appreciate that the political conditions were returning, once more, to allow the raising of this more advanced demand (32).

However, after Parnell's successful reigning in of the full revolutionary potential

of the 'Irish Revolution', and after the recent acrimonious split amongst the Irish Nationalists, a politically astute Engels appreciated the weaker position the Irish people found themselves in. Irish Labour was also divided between the Parnellite LL and Davitt's anti-Parnellites. Yet Engels did learn from Davitt's 'internationalism from below' alliance. So, whilst Engels retreated from advocating an independent Irish Republic in the conditions prevailing in the early 1890's, he updated his earlier support for Irish Home Rule to include Scotland, Wales and England too. He now advocated a federal republic for the four nations[1]. It would take the rebirth of the Republican movement, and rising class struggles, in the 1900's, before the demand for an independent

Engels learnt from Davitt's 'internationalism from below'

---

[1] In the same advice to the German Social Democratic Party (SPD), which mentioned Engels' support for a federal republic in 'Britain', he was already criticising the more politically advanced SPD's apparent retreat from support for a German republic. Under the same growing pressures of 'New Imperialism' upon the Socialist and Labour movements, and with British leaders like Hyndman (SDF) and Hardie (SLP then ILP), Engels' advocacy of a British federal republic found little support. British federalism however was to emerge as the Unionists' last ditch defence when faced with the rise of Irish Republicanism after the First World War. Federalism remains in the UK state's armoury, as weapon of last resort, even if only held currently in the British Liberal Party's very rusty munitions box.

Irish Republic became part of the political agenda once more.

Meanwhile, in Ireland, a string of bitter by-elections occurred, in which the anti-Parnellite INF confronted the Parnellite NL. Davitt campaigned in Kilkenny and Sligo, where the INF was successful (33). He stood unsuccessfully in Waterford City against new NL leader, John Redmond (34), in December 1891.

When the 1892 General Election was held, Michael Austin and Eugene Crean, both on Cork Trades Council, were to be elected as anti-Parnellite Nat-Lab MPs. The LL put forward William Field in Dublin, and he was elected as a Parnellite Nat-Lab MP[2] (35). People like Michael Canty, and later Lawrence Strange from Waterford (36), tried to overcome the divisions caused by the split, but the damage was already done. This led to the wider setbacks, which soon followed the apparent 1892 General Election victories.

Sadly, Davitt, up until 1889, the foremost representative of the growing 'internationalism from below' alliance, must take a lot of the blame for the new situation, precisely because of his leading role up to this point. It was during the 1892 General Election campaign that Davitt reached his political nadir. He stood for the INF in North Meath. However, so brazen and virulent was the intervention of the Catholic hierarchy in its campaigning on behalf of the INF against the Parnellite candidates, that both Davitt and the INF candidate for the neighbouring South Meath, were unseated after a petition was successfully lodged (37).

Once Redmond became NL leader, after Parnell's death in December 1891, any pretence that the NL represented the interests of workers, artisans, poorer tenants and the landless, was soon abandoned[3]. Thus Davitt missed the chance to link up with those workers who had been so misled by Parnell. Thus, the political promise opened up by the meeting of Ireland's semi-revolutionary Land League tradition with the New Unions spreading from Scotland and England was never realised.

It is not surprising that the first Marxist analysis of the situation in Ireland, by the Edinburgh-based SDF/SSF member, John Leslie, in *The Irish Question* (38), written in 1891, was particularly scathing about Davitt's actions over the previous two years.

---

[2] In getting elected to the Dublin St Patrick's seat, Field defeated Dublin's biggest capitalist, the anti-Parnellite businessman, William Murphy.

[3] After the defeat of Gladstone's government in 1895, both the INF and the NL were to move closer to the Conservatives – the first to promote the Catholic hierarchy's interests in Irish education, the second to consolidate the proprietary interests of the better-off Irish Catholic farmers.

References

(1)   **see** *The divorce crisis* **on** http://en.wikipedia.org/wiki/Charles_Stewart_Parnell

(2)   **see** http://en.wikipedia.org/wiki/Parnell_Commission

(3)   **see** Liz Curtis, *The Cause of Ireland, From the United Irishmen to Partition*, (*TCoI*) p. 157 (Beyond the Pale Publications, 1994, Belfast)

(4)   **see** F. Sheehy-Skeffington, *The Counter-Revolution* in *Michael Davitt, Revolutionary Agitator and Labour Leader (MDRAaLL)* p. 150-1. (MacGibbon & Kee, 1967, London)

(5)   **see** Liz Curtis, *TCoI*, op. cit., p. 156.

(6)   **see** Paul Bew, *C.S. Parnell*, (*CSP*) pp. 118-9 (Gill & Macmillan, 1980. Dublin)

(7)   **see** http://en.wikipedia.org/wiki/Irish_National_Federation

(8)   **see** Laurence M. Geary, , *The Plan of Campaign, 1886-9* (*TPoC*) p. 125 (Cork University Press, 1986, Cork)

(9)   **see** http://en.wikipedia.org/wiki/Congested_Districts_Board_for_Ireland

(10)   **see** Laurence M. Geary, *TPoC*, op. cit., pp. 134.

(11)   ibid., pp. 135-6.

(12)   *see* Fintan Lane, *The Origins of Modern Irish Socialism, 1881-1896*, p. 173 (TOoMIS) (Cork University Press, 1997, Cork)

(13)   ibid., p.174.

(14)   ibid., p.174.

(15)   ibid., p. 174.

(16)   ibid., p. 174.

(17)   ibid., p. 174.

(18)   **see** John W. Boyle, *The Irish Labor Movement in the Nineteenth Century* (*TILM*) p. 136 (The Catholic University of America Press, 1988, Washington D.C.)

(19)   **see** Fintan Lane, *TOoMIS*, op. cit., p. 177.

(20)   ibid., pp. 178-9.

(21)   **see** Chapter 6, reference 28.

(22)   **see** Chapter 6, reference 31.

(23)   **see** Paul Bew, *CSP*, op. cit., pp. 118-9.

(24)   **see** http://en.wikipedia.org/wiki/John_Redmond

(25)   Laurence M. Geary, *TPoC*, op. cit., p. 128.

(26)   **see** John W. Boyle, *TILM*, op. cit., pp. 137-8.

(27)   ibid., p. 138.

(28)   ibid., pp. 138-9.

(29)   **see** Fintan Lane, *TOoMIS*, op. cit., p. 179.

(30)   Frederick Engels, *Critique of Draft S.D. {Erfurt} Programme of 1891*, **in** K.   Marx
         and F. Engels, *Selected Works*, Vol. 3, p. 436 (Lawrence & Wishart, 1985, London)
         and http://www.marxists.org/archive/marx/works/1891/06/29.htm

(31)   **see** Karl Marx and Federick Engels, *Ireland and the Irish Question*, Karl Marx,
         Letter to Frederick Engels, 30.11.1867, p. 158, **and** Frederick Engels, *Relations
         between the Irish Sections and the British Federal Council*, p. 419   (Lawrence &
         Wishart, 1978, London)

(32)   **see** Chapter 4, reference 25.

(33)   **see** F. Sheehy-Skeffington, *MDRAaLL*, op. cit., pp. 152-5.

(34)   ibid., p. 151.

(35)   see Fintan Lane, *TOoMIS*, op. cit., p. 190.

(36)   ibid., pp. 203-5.

(37)   **see** F. Sheehy-Skeffington, *MDRAaLL*, op. cit., pp. 152-5.

(38)   **see** John Leslie, *The Irish Question*, pp. 23-5 (The Cork Workers Club Historical
         Reprints no. 7, 1974, Cork)

17. The thwarted hopes of 'New Unionism' and the Home Rule movement after the 1892 general election

Whereas the 1892 General Election saw independent Labour candidates put forward in Scotland and England, Ireland only had Parnellite and anti-Parnellite Nat-Lab candidates. The election of three Nat-Lab candidates, in the 1892 General Election, showed the continued domination of Irish nationalism over Irish workers.

This split amongst the Irish Nationalists, between the Parnellite NL and the anti-Parnellite INF, led to an overall drop in the number of their MPs at Westminster from 85 to 81, despite the election, for the first time, of the three Nat-Lab MPs, and of Davitt himself. The Irish Unionist Party was the main beneficiary in Ireland of the Nationalists' setbacks. Ireland was the only nation in the UK that saw advances by both Liberal and Conservative Unionists. Liberal Unionists won three more seats - in West Belfast, South Londonderry and Dublin, St Stephens Green[1] (1). The Conservatives won their extra seats in the City of Londonderry, North Fermanagh and South Dublin[2].

However, in England, Scotland and Wales, the Irish Nationalists' Liberal allies made major gains, with an increase from 192 to 272 MPs (2). This was at the expense of both the Conservative and the Liberal Unionists. In the Highlands, Crofter Liberal candidates not only regained Argyll, but also ousted one of

---

[1] The successful Liberal Unionist candidate in Dublin St. Stephens was William Kenny, a 'Castle Catholic'. In 1885, he became a Queen's Counsel. He represented that shrinking strand in British Catholic politics, linked with figures such as the Duke of Norfolk, that looked to Vatican backing for the continuation of the Union, as the best defence for aristocratic landed property. Catholic Unionist candidates were extremely rare, and only confined to areas outside of Ulster, with a majority Catholic population. In Northern Ireland, even to this day, Unionism has never fielded a Catholic parliamentary candidate.

[2] The winning Unionist candidate in South Dublin was Sir Horace Plunkett. Ironically, he was to be, along with the Irish Nationalist, George Russell, one of the founders of the new Irish farmers' cooperative movement. However, the sustained attacks on this body were not to come from the reactionary Protestant Anglo-Irish Ascendancy landlords, now a rapidly declining political force, eager to be bought-off, but from the new better-off Irish Catholic farm owners and rural merchants, who feared any competition from the cooperative movement.

their renegade former members in Inverness-shire, who had deserted to the Liberal Unionists in 1886. His opposition to Irish Home Rule was the reason given for his defeat (3). In Wales, the Liberals further extended their domination of the political scene, by ousting the only Liberal Unionist, despite Joseph Chamberlain organising a counter challenge of eight Nonconformist Liberal Unionist candidates, who got nowhere (4). From the working class point of view, though, it was the fielding of 16 independent Labour candidates that marked the most positive development in the 1892 General Election.

In Scotland, there were two independent Labour party slates, both backed by the Scottish Socialist Federation[3] (SSF). Indeed, it was probably the SSF that was responsible for smoothing over the tensions that had already emerged between the Keir Hardie-led SLP, and the Henry Champion-led Scottish United Trades Council Labour Party (SUTCLP)[4] (5).

Radical Liberalism still heavily influenced the SLP (6), whereas key members of the SUTCLP, such as Champion and Chisholm Robertson[5], were more influenced by the Tory Democrat tradition[6] (7). Hardie and Robertson were often at loggerheads. Nevertheless, the strong push by the SSF led to the fielding of non-competing slates with three SLP candidates[7] (8), three SUTCLP candidates[8] (9), and one jointly sponsored candidate[9] (10). The SLP

---

[3] The Scottish Socialist Federation included Socialist League/Scottish Land & Labour League and Social Democratic Federation (SDF) members. Once the SL had collapsed, and the SSF no longer had a role in uniting the previously disunited parties, John Leslie, like James Connolly in Scotland, and Eleanor Marx, Edward Aveling and William Morris in England, (re)joined the SDF.

[4] The emergence of two parties also partly reflected differing local conditions, especially between Aberdeen and the other Scottish cities; and the slowness, from the points of view of Henry Champion, Tom Mann, Chisholm Robertson and John Mahon, of the SLP in getting a stronger base in the trade union movement.

[5] Chisholm Robertson was a leader of the Stirlingshire miners and Secretary of Glasgow Trades Council.

[6] In Henry Champion's case this went along with strong unionist, imperialist, and racist sentiments.

[7] The SLP's candidates were Robert Cunninghame-Graham in Glasgow Camlachie, Bennet Burleigh in Glasgow Tradeston, and James Macdonald in Dundee.

[8] The SUTCLP's candidates were Henry Champion in Aberdeen South, Chisholm Robertson in Stirlingshire, and R. Brodie in Glasgow College.

[9] John Wilson, the Broxburn miners' agent, stood for Edinburgh Central. The closer connection between the SLP and the local trades council, reflected a tradition of joint work going back to the Shaleworkers' Strike (1887) and the recent Scottish Railworkers' Strike (1891), coupled to the careful work of SSF members like John Leslie and James Connolly.

candidates[10] averaged 681 votes each (11), whilst the SUTCLP averaged 571[11] votes each (12). This represented modest progress.

The real electoral breakthrough occurred in England, where the average vote for 9 independent Labour candidates was 2355. 'New Unionism' had made a dramatic impact. James Havelock Wilson and John Burns were elected at Middlesborough and Battersea respectively, whilst Keir Hardie was elected in West Ham (13). Ben Tillett, someone else very much associated with 'New Unionism', polled well in the Bradford West in the aftermath of the Manningham Mills Strike (14). Clearly, the recent major labour struggles in England had created a wider stir.

Manningham Mills in Bradford

Despite the impact of 'New Unionism', Henry Hyndman still insisted on pushing an anti-trade union line in the SDF (15). However, the prestige of the trade union members in the SDF increased as a result of the events in 1889. This meant that Hyndman was challenged more effectively over his stance. Two distinct pro-trade union tendencies did emerge within the SDF (16). Furthermore, Ben Tillet and Tom Mann co-authored the pamphlet, *New Unionism,* linking it to the idea of a Socialist Commonwealth (17).

Nevertheless, the continued denigration of trade union work by such a prominent Socialist as Hyndman put many trade unionists off the SDF, who were attracted to the idea of independent Labour representation. Furthermore, Tillet and Mann's own pamphlet amounted to propaganda for an abstract Socialism. It did not provide an immediate advanced democratic programme,

---

[10] Robert Cunninghame-Graham, former Socialist Liberal MP for North West Lanarkshire, failed to get elected for Glasgow Camlachie. The Avelings were to remark that Labour had lost "something more than a head – their heart".

[11] In the website reference this figure is obtained by including John Wilson as a SUTCLP candidate, although he was backed by the SLP too. His individual vote is not given.

which could have helped combat the renewed Conservative and employers' offensives under the conditions of 'New Imperialism'.

Therefore, many trade unionists and Socialists became more attracted to the new Independent Labour Party (ILP) (18), when it was formed in Bradford between January 14th and 16th, 1893. Significantly, the party attracted Robert Smillie, Lanarkshire miners' leader and SLP member, as well as present and ex-SDF members, Tom Mann and Henry Champion, and ex-SL members, Bruce Glasier, Eleanor Marx and Edward Aveling (19). The SLP delegation, which included Robert Smillie, tried unsuccessfully to have the founding conference adopt the name, the 'Socialist Labour Party' (20).

Under the prevailing conditions of economic and political retreat, and British Socialist and Social Democratic political confusion, the ILP soon adopted a very British Labourist Socialism, more influenced by Radicalism, Christian Socialism (21) and Fabianism (22), than by contemporary European Social Democracy or the SLP's earlier social republican wing.

Keir Hardie was very influential in this respect. In 1894, he asked Sir Charles Dilke, a leading Liberal Imperial Federalist, if he would chair the second ILP Conference. Dilke declined, since he was looking to a possible alliance with the Conservatives at the time, in preparation for an imperial war with Russia! (23) Hardie's open acceptance of British imperialism was also highlighted by his view that Home Rule was only permissible "provided the supremacy of the Imperial parliament be maintained unimpaired" (24).

The loose structure of the ILP meant that it reflected local traditions in those parts of England, Scotland, Wales and Ireland where it was established[12]. However, it was unable to provide effective leadership to the wider national democratic movements. This contributed to the further undermining of the 'internationalism from below' alliance, already weakened by Davitt's political shortcomings.

Furthermore, Hardie still took inspiration from the political legacy of Parnell seeing him, "as the one man in politics, for whom, as a politician, I was ever to feel genuine respect" (25). Interestingly, following both Parnell and Hyndman, Hardie also ensured that the new ILP paper, *Labour Leader*, remained under his effective personal control (26).

Hardie, who was to make his own deals with the British Liberal Party, understood

---

[12] Despite some very different national and regional traditions, the ILP, due to its regional federal organisation, could encompass the Nonconformist traditions of Scotland, Wales, and Northern England, the Radical secular traditions of London and the East Midlands, and even the Loyalism of Belfast and the Irish Catholicism found in Glasgow and Clydeside.

Irish workers' attraction to Parnell and the NL. Even as Hardie attempted to organise ILP branches in Dublin and Waterford, he found he was up against the powerful influence of Parnellite Irish Nationalism over the Labour movement there. The ILP branches failed there partly because of their inability to campaign for a more vigorous policy of national self-determination, compared to the Home Rule policy of the NL-Liberal alliance (27). Furthermore, and from a very different angle, the ILP in Belfast, led by Alexander Bowman and a keen young agitator, William Walker (28), met concerted opposition from Loyalists because of leading ILPers' well-known support for Irish Home Rule, no matter how limited (29).

If Scotland had seen the most precocious developments in independent Labour representation in 1888, England the most successful in 1892, Ireland's attempt

was the most delayed and much more muted. It was largely confined to one province, Munster. Here in 1894, a new organisation, the Irish Land and Labour Association[13] (30), was formed, led by D. D. Sheehan (31). It was based on the Davitt principles of uniting poor tenants and agricultural labourers.

One consequence of the formation of the all-UK (in intent) ILP was the SLP's decision, at its final conference in 1894, to dissolve itself into the new party. This no doubt reflected a desire for wider class unity, following the success of independent Labour candidates in England in 1892. The ILP itself retained the earlier SLP commitment to Home Rule. In addition, many SLP members were no doubt reassured that the new ILP President was Keir Hardie, whilst Peter Curran, former member of the Glasgow-based Irish Land League and SLRL, was on the new Executive (32).

Robert Smillie - Lanarkshire miners' leader and SLP member

Furthermore, those SLP members most committed to Home Rule (whether for Ireland or Scotland or Wales) came from a Radical Liberal background, like Hardie, Smillie and Glasier. The ILP was in the process of separating itself

---

[13] In 1901, the Irish Land and Labour Association was successful first in getting Sheehan nominated as the official Irish Parliamentary Party candidate against the sitting member, and then elected as an independent Labour MP in 1906, thus breaking with the deeply entrenched Nat-Labism found in Ireland.

from Henry Champion (33), an increasingly manipulative crypto-Tory Democrat, who had committed his supporters to voting for Conservative against Liberal candidates (34), and to quietly taking 'Tory gold' to finance candidates who would split the Liberal vote. These included the former republican and SL/SLLL member, John Mahon, now seen as somewhat of a renegade[14] (35). Former Radical Liberal SLP members would have seen the ousting of 'Tory Socialism' (36) within the ILP as a welcome blow against any linkage with Conservative Unionism[15].

Nevertheless, the narrowness of the vote of SLP delegates - 28 to 22 - against the setting up of a specifically Scottish Council (37) within the new ILP, shows that a substantial minority held reservations. These reflected the earlier doubts that had led Scottish members of the SDF (then the SL) to form the Scottish Land & Labour League in 1884; and Scottish members of both the SDF and SL to form the Scottish Socialist Federation in 1888[16]. The SLP vote against a Scottish Council for the ILP further contributed to Socialists in Scotland's secession from the 'internationalism from below' alliance and their subsequent adherence to the British Left, and its 'British road to socialism'.

---

[14] A possible explanation for John Mahon's political trajectory from his initial republicanism and support for revolutionary principles, when he joined the SL/SLLL, was his realisation of the need for independent Labour political action. As a worker, he probably felt uncomfortable with the more middle class and anti-trade union Socialism, which dominated the all-UK SL, as reflected in the pages of *Commonweal*, and the similar attitude adopted by Hyndman's supporters in the SDF. Champion was always ready to finance independent Labour candidates, but was not choosy about who gave him the money to do so.

[15] The legacy of 'Tory Democracy', morphed into 'Labour Unionism', was nevertheless to maintain a foothold in the Belfast ILP, and in the person of William Walker was to return to Scotland when he stood as an ILP candidate in Leith in 1910.

[16] This issue of national autonomy within Socialist organisations was to be raised by John Maclean when he demanded the setting up of a Scottish National Council for the Social Democratic Party (formerly the SDF) in 1911.

References

(1)   **see** John Biggs-Davidson & George Chowdharay-Best, *The Cross of St. Patrick – The Catholic Unionist Tradition in Ireland*, p.254 (The Kensal Press, 1984, Bourne End)

(2)   **see** http://en.wikipedia.org/wiki/United_Kingdom_general_election,_1892

(3)   **see** Ewan A. Cameron, *Land for the People, The British Government and the Scottish Highlands, 1880-1925*, p. 76 (Tuckwell Press, 1996, East Linton)

(4)   **see** Kenneth O. Morgan, *Rebirth of A Nation, Wales, 1880-1980*, pp. 43-4, Oxford University Press, 1981, New York)

(5)   **see** David Howell, *British Workers and the Independent Labour Party, 1888-1906*

(*BWatILP*) p. 150-1 (Manchester University Press, 1983, Manchester) **and** http://en.wikipedia.org/wiki/Scottish_United_Trades_Councils_Labour_Party

(6)   **see** David Howell,*BWatILP*, op. cit., p. 152.

(7)   ibid., pp. 158-60, 288, 375-9.

(8)   ibid., p. 154.

(9)   ibid., p. 156.

(10)   ibid., p. 151.

(11)   ibid., p. 154.

(12)   **see**http://en.wikipedia.org/wiki/Scottish_United_Trades_Councils_Labour_Party

(13)   **see** *Foundation* **on** http://en.wikipedia.org/wiki/Independent_Labour_Party

(14)   **see** http://www.genuki.org.uk/big/eng/YKS/Misc/Transcriptions/WRY/BradfordTillettIndex.html

(15)   **see** Martin Crick, *The History of the Social Democratic Federation*, p. 77 (Ryburn Publishing, 1994, Keele University)

(16)   ibid., pp. 77-9.

(17)   **see** *Activist and leader* **on** http://en.wikipedia.org/wiki/Tom_Mann

(18)   **see** http://www.answers.com/topic/independent-labour-party

(19)   **see** Yvonne Kapp, *Eleanor Marx. Volume II – the Crowded Years, 1886-1898*, p. 527 (Virago Press, 1979, London)

(20)   **see** David Howell, *BWatILP*, op. cit., p. 293.

(21)   **see** http://www.answers.com/topic/christian-socialism

(22)   **see** http://en.wikipedia.org/wiki/Fabian_Society

(23)   **see** Roy Jenkins, *Dilke – A Victorian Tragedy*, p. 393 (Papermac, 1996, London)

(24)   Geoff Bell, *Troublesome Business – The Labour Party and the Irish Question*, p. 12 (Pluto Press, 1982, London)

(25)   ibid., p. 12.

(26)   **see** http://en.wikipedia.org/wiki/Labour_Leader

(27)   **see** Fintan Lane, *The Origins of Modern Irish Socialism, 1881-1896*, (*TOoMIS*) pp.197-209 (Cork University Press, 1997, Cork)

(28)   **see** Terence Bowman, *People's Champion, The Life of Alexander Bowman, Pioneer of Labour Politics in Ireland*, p. 122 (Ulster Historical Foundation, 1997, Belfast)

(29)   **see** Fintan Lane, *TOoMIS*, op. cit., p. 194.

(30)   **see** http://en.wikipedia.org/wiki/Irish_Land_and_Labour_Association

(31)   **see** http://en.wikipedia.org/wiki/D.D._Sheehan

(32)   **see** David Howell, *BWatILP*, op, cit., p. 305.

(33)   ibid., p. 303.

(34)   ibid., p. 289.

(35)   ibid., p. 378.

(36)   ibid., p. 373.

(37)   **see** D. Lowe, *Souvenirs of Scottish Labour, p. 176* (W & R Holmes, 1919, Glasgow)

18. The employers' counter-offensive and the retreat of 'New Unionism'

The boom of the late 1880's and early 1890's in industry and commerce soon peaked. The employers mounted a counter-offensive. A number of powerful new employers' organisations were founded, including the Shipping Federation (1890) (1) and the Engineering Employers Federation[1] (1896) (2). This was the bosses' response to the growth of 'New Unionism'. A key aim was to ensure the state provided police protection for strikebreakers. This followed the precedent set by the earlier landlords' Property Defence Leagues, formed in response to the Land Leagues. They had ensured that the state provided police (and troops, if necessary) to evict tenants.

The defeats of the 1890-1 Manningham Mills Strike in Bradford (3), and the Scottish Railworkers' Strike in 1890-1(4), were public indications of the employers' growing confidence. In Bradford, troops were used to help break the strike mainly of women mill workers (5), whilst in Motherwell troops evicted railworkers' families from their houses, provoking a workers' attack on the railway station (6).

The immediate responses to these two defeats are interesting. The large, closely packed millworkers' communities in Bradford allowed Tom Mann to make his significant electoral challenge as an independent Labour candidate in the 1892 election. In Scotland, however, the railway workers constituted a much more dispersed workforce. So, when John Wilson stood as joint trades council/SLP candidate in Central Edinburgh, his vote was quite small.

Nevertheless, it was the financial solidarity to Scottish strikers offered by the English-based Amalgamated Society of Railway Servants, which contributed to the Scottish union's amalgamation into the broader ASRS of England, Ireland, Scotland and Wales, when it formed in 1892 (7).

Yet, the problem, which Davitt had already highlighted about the curtailment of local autonomy within the New Unions, also arose within the new ASRS. A breakaway Scottish Railwaymens Union was formed as a result of the lack of

---

[1] This new wider organisation followed the precedent established, in 1895, by the alliance of Belfast and Clydeside engineering employers to break the action of the Amalgamated Society of Engineers attempting to win an eight-hour week.

Mob attack Motherwell railway station after striking railworkers are evicted from their tied homes.

effective local autonomy and democratic accountability of ASRS officials (8). Not being able to offer the prospect of wider solidarity, the SRU proved to be short lived. Nevertheless, the demand for greater democracy, and the desire to take independent industrial action was to resurface in both Scotland and Ireland in the first decade of the twentieth century, when workers regained their confidence.

In Ireland, the demise of the New Unions, with the partial exception of the NAUL in Belfast, was rapid. The Irish economy outside of Belfast and the Lagan Valley was much less developed. In particular, the previously very successful Gasworkers Union, the NUG&GL, collapsed after 1892 (9). Apart from the brief cooperation that led to the joint organisation of the 1891 May Day, there was considerable hostility from the skilled workers towards the New Unions. Dublin Trades Council remained largely a preserve of the skilled workers' unions. The NUG&GL faced a combination of employer intransigence, poaching by local unions, and the formation of a scab union (10).

Some of the skilled union and Dublin Trades Council leaders enjoyed a close relationship with William Martin Murphy, the pro-monarchist, Irish Nationalist, big businessman and newspaper proprietor. Murphy welcomed the subservience and flattery of the Nat-Lab skilled union leaders, just as certain businessmen and sections of the Unionist press in Belfast adopted Con-Lab or Labour Unionist trade unionists (11). Murphy even gave his support to the formation of the Irish TUC in 1894[2] (12). However, he resorted to the use of non-union labour on his own tramways, refusing to recognise the Dublin Trades Council-backed local Dublin and District Tramwaymens Union (13). Murphy's

---

[2] William Murphy was perhaps a forerunner of the pro-monarchist, homophobic and SNP-supporting owner of the Stagecoach transport group, Brian Souter. Shortly after giving a major contribution to the SNP, the party dropped its opposition to the deregulation of buses. He addressed the STUC in 1998.

hostility towards the semi-skilled and unskilled unions was to become notorious.

In England, and to a lesser extent Scotland (14), most of the New Unions survived the renewed employer onslaught. This was largely because they fell back on the methods of 'Old Unionism' – cautiousness in defending pay and conditions, calls for recognised conciliation and arbitration procedures, and the provision of services for members, but without the effective accountability of officials. The elementary mass participation, associated with 'New Unionism' when it surged forward, soon gave way to bureaucratic centralised control by general secretaries, opposed to any real independence shown by the branches[3], which might lead to costly and unwanted labour disputes (15).

One person who found the new situation uncongenial was Davitt's ally, Edward McHugh, a leader in the NUDL. He had turned down a nomination for the Liverpool Kirkdale parliamentary seat in the 1892 General Election, saying, "I'm not a politician I'm an agitator" (16). He did campaign in Middlesborough though, for Havelock Wilson. He was removed as a delegate from the 1893 TUC annual conference in Belfast, probably due to his role in having a scab union expelled at the previous conference in Glasgow (17). He left the NUDL, to be replaced by James Sexton, who, as the union's general secretary, became very much a product of the period of retreat (18). McHugh went abroad looking for new opportunities to agitate and helped to set up a longshoremen's union in New York (19).

Another one-time Davitt supporter, who had then thrown his lot in with the 'New Unionism' of the NUG&GL, and championed independent Labour representation, was Michael Canty. As workers retreated, he abandoned the idea of large amalgamated unions for, first Irish, then for Dublin-based, unions. He later became a supporter of Sinn Fein (20), when it was a pro-monarchist, largely cultural organisation led by Arthur Griffith. This was the same Canty who a few years before had argued that, "the labour question comes before so-called nationality" (21). Canty was not the only person desperately looking for a way out of the political impasse, but who became politically stranded in the process.

Irish social republicanism and British Radicalism had not been able to bridge the gap between the now politically-limited Home Rule movement and the

---

[3] The warning that Davitt and the Scottish Railwaymens Union had made from an 'Old Unionism' viewpoint about the lack of local autonomy in the New Unions, was to come to the fore again, only this time in the form of a socialist republican and syndicalist critique, when unions, such as Sexton's NUDL failed to support their Irish members' actions, after 1907, or their Scottish members in 1911.

political requirements of the new surge in working class activity represented by 'New (Trade) Unionism'. Neither had British, Scottish and (the very few) Irish Socialists been able to take Davitt's 'internationalism from below' alliance on to a higher political plane.

References

(1)   see Alastair Reid, *United We Stand – A History of Britain's Trade Unions* (*UWS*) p. 223 (Penguin Books, 2004, London)

(2)   ibid., p. 170.

(3)   ibid., pp. 234 **and see** http://www.bbc.co.uk/radio4/history/longview/longview_20021015_readings.shtml

(4)   **see** William Kenefick, *Red Scotland! The Rise and Fall of the Radical Left, c. 1872-1932* (*RS*) p. 41-5 (Edinburgh University Press, 2007, Edinburgh)

(5)   **see** http://www.bbc.co.uk/radio4/history/longview/longview_20021015_readings.shtml

(6)   **see** William Kenefick, *RS*, op. cit., pp. 42-3.

(7)   ibid., p. 44.

(8)   ibid., p. 44-5.

(9)   **see** John W. Boyle, *The Irish Labor Movement in the Nineteenth Century* (*TILM*) p. 114   (The Catholic University of America Press, 1988, Washington D.C.)

(10)   ibid., p. 114.

(11)   ibid., pp. 160-2.

(12)   ibid., pp. 145, 150.

(13)   ibid., p. 115.

(14)   **see** William Kenefick, *RS*, op. cit., pp. 37-9.

(15)   **see** Alastair Reid, *UWS,* pp. 224-5.

(16)   **see** Andrew C. Newby, *The Life and Times of Edward McHugh (1853-1913)* p. 136 (Edwen Mellen Press, 2004, Ceredigion)

(17)   ibid., p. 137.

(18)   ibid., p. 140.

(19)   ibid., p. 141.

(20)   **see** John W. Boyle, *TILM*, op. cit., p. 114.

(21)   ibid., p. 139.

19. 1892-95 - The final break-up of the 'Internationalism from below' alliance

In a sense, the 1892 General Election results represented the furthest advance of the incoming swash brought in by the waves of 'New Unionism' and the Home Rule movement. However, like breaking surf found at the highest point on a beach, the energy was already spent and the backwash was soon in retreat.

The Liberals' manifesto, for the 1892 General Election, agreed at their national conference the previous year in Newcastle-upon-Tyne, had recognised the threat represented by 'New Unionism'. The manifesto adopted the mimimum necessary policies the leadership thought would be needed to contain this challenge. It included a promise of the extension of employer liability for industrial accidents, a mention of the limitation of work hours (a calculatedly evasive formulation to avoid commitment to the eight hour day), and the payment of MPs (a reluctant recognition of the growing demand for independent Labour representation, which it was hoped could be headed off by a minimal increase in the number of Lib-Lab MPs) (1).

In the end, a Royal Commission on Labour was established which, according to one coalowner, "was meant to shelve the questions affecting the working class" (2). Locked out miners rioted in Featherstone, in South Yorkshire, on 7th September 1893. They were fired on by troops, with two people killed and another six injured. Robert Cunninghame-Graham spoke at the funeral, whilst Keir Hardie addressed a large meeting there soon afterwards. Herbert Asquith, the Liberal Home Minister, set up a parliamentary commission stacked with his friends. Amongst the miners, he earned the name 'Assassin Asquith', responsible for the 'Featherstone Massacre' (3). This nickname followed that of the earlier Conservative Home Minister, 'Bloody Balfour', after the 'Mitchelstown Massacre' in 1887 (4).

Workers' retreats on the industrial front were matched by setbacks on the political front. Although elected in opposition to the official Liberal candidates, both Wilson and Burns took the Liberal whip when they entered parliament. Thus, they collapsed into the Lib-Labism that had formed part of Westminster politics since 1874. The new Nat-Lab MPs in Ireland did not distinguish themselves either.

In Scotland, Davitt's ally, John Ferguson, was expelled from the SLP because of his backing for Liberal Party candidates in the 1892 General Election (5). Although Ferguson had a good record over trying to get Labour candidates adopted and voted for, often in

Liberal Asquith responsible for 'Featherstone Massacre'

opposition to the NL leadership, he too saw the election of a Liberal government pledged to Irish Home Rule as the number one priority this time.

Gladstone's attempt to introduce a liberal measure of Irish Home Rule was undermined by the Liberals' continued capitulation to jingoistic conservative imperialism. The private British East Africa Company had been forced to withdraw from Uganda, because of the mayhem caused by company officials and missionaries. The Liberal government stepped in and made the Kingdom of Buganda a British Protectorate, initiating several years of brutal war to buttress their ally[1] (6).

Meanwhile, Cecil Rhodes, now the Prime Minister of the Cape Colony, presided over the introduction of the Glen Grey Act, in 1894, which imposed a hut tax on Africans to force them to work in the new gold mines[2] (7). The penalties for failing to pay the tax were draconian. Thus, even under the Liberals, elements of what later became a fully-blown apartheid system were being put in place.

The first Land League leaflet had called on County Mayo tenants to compare their situation to the Africans living in the "kraals of Kaffirland" and to defy the British "tyrants" and "invaders" (8). However, the retreats of Davitt's

---

[1] Uganda became just one more territory where British divide-and-rule tactics left the toxic political legacy still found today.

[2] White settlers enjoyed Home Rule in the Cape Colony. However, their parliament more resembled the Ascendancy dominated, pre-1801 Irish Parliament, and ruled the interests of a small minority. Quick to claim its own right to make decisions, the leaders of these 'Home Rule' parliaments were even quicker to call on the aid of the imperial state when their interests were threatened by the indigenous populations.

'internationalism from below' alliance continued to narrow the political focus, and principled opposition to the 'New Imperialism' became increasingly diluted.

Gladstone's priority in government, after 1892, was the achievement of a measure of Irish Home Rule[3]. Therefore, Ireland became the real political cockpit with Westminster as the focus for a new Home Rule Bill. However, as the General Election results highlighted, it was in Ireland that the forces of Home Rule were most damaged, and where the forces of conservative unionism were best prepared. For, even before the 1892 General Election, the Irish Unionists had begun preparing (9), beginning with a convention in their stronghold of Ulster[4]. Lord Salisbury (10) and Joseph Chamberlain[5] (11) actively encouraged this.

The Ulster Unionist Convention, which met on June 17th in Belfast, drew together the forces of Ulster Conservative and Liberal Unionism, the Orange Order, and all the main Protestant denominations (12). The Duke of Abercorn was in the chair and the most specific targets mentioned in the conference resolution were the Land League and the 'Plan of Campaign' (13). However, a real attempt was made to broaden the social base, beyond the usual Conservative landlords and their plebian Orange Order followers, by bringing in Liberal Unionist businessmen and tenant farmers (14).

Clerical interference in favour of the INF, during recent by-elections, provided grist to the anti-Romanist mill (15), but attempts were made to restrain any grosser anti-Catholic diatribes at the Conference (16). The street preacher and Orange Order provoked riots of 1886 were not the image these Unionists wanted to convey. They were trying to persuade the wider British public of their respectable loyal, Protestant, Empire-supporting credentials, in the run-up to the Second Home Rule Bill.

Therefore, above the Convention's platform were displayed the Royal Arms and the verse, "One with Britain heart and soul. One life, one flag, one fleet, one throne" (17). There was no political contradiction in Unionist thinking. Their

---

[3] The disestablishment of the Churches of Scotland and Wales were also seen to be important policies to retain the support of the middle class-led Scottish Free and Welsh Nonconformist churches.

[4] Ulster Unionists then organised on the traditional basis of a nine county Ulster, although the conference delegates were most heavily represented by Belfast City and Counties Antrim and Down.

[5] The former Radical Liberal, Joseph Chamberlain had abandoned his attempt to split the Tory Democrats from the Conservative Party, after he had split the Radical Unionists from the Liberal Party. By 1895, he was prepared to directly join the ultra-Conservative Lord Salisbury government.

anti-Irish Nationalist conservative unionism was complemented by their jingoistic British conservative imperialism. A majority vote in the House of Commons had no validity in the delegates' thinking. This was a time when resort to the anti-democratic Crown Powers was required. The Unionists knew they could rely on the reactionary House of Lords. They also had the partisan backing of most of the local judiciary, and the locally resident army officers. The Loyalist organisations could also be depended upon to oppose and disrupt any public presentation of the Home Rule case, or any other ideas, such as land nationalisation and Socialism, which could be perceived as threatening to Unionist control.

The Ulster Unionists had the backing of the ever more jingoist British Conservative Party. However, it was not their intention to hive off Ulster and to partition Ireland[6]. Such thinking was even more marginal then, than that of those Loyalists today who advocate an independent 'Ulster'. Ulster Unionists saw themselves as the shock troops to prevent Home Rule being implemented anywhere in Ireland. Therefore, they gave their support to the much more narrowly-based Southern Unionist Convention held in Dublin on June 23rd, This was also organised to oppose Irish Home Rule (18).

Gladstone did manage to get a majority of House of Commons votes - 301 to 267 - for the Second Irish Home Rule Bill on September 1st 1893 (19). The Bill was then predictably voted down in the House of Lords. After this, there was no longer any necessity for the pretence of Unionist/Loyalist moderation. The annual conference of the TUC was being held in Belfast at the time. A large Labour demonstration was organised to follow this. The previous year had seen the highpoint of 'New (Trade) Unionism' in Ulster[7] (20). So it was agreed to follow this earlier precedent, with Protestant and Catholic bands marching together. However, in celebration of the House of Lords' defeat of the Irish Home Rule Bill, Orange mobs attacked and hospitalised some from the Nationalist flute band. Speakers, including Keir Hardie, were severely heckled, whilst John Burns' horse-drawn brake was attacked by 500 men armed with sticks (21).

---

[6] Before the 1892 General Election, Ulster Unionists only held 15 parliamentary seats in Ulster, compared to the Irish Nationalists 17 in the nine-county Ulster. A Unionist majority could not be guaranteed in Ulster. It took the partition of Ulster itself, in 1922, leaving three counties in the Irish Free State before that could be achieved.

[7] A mixed Protestant and Catholic march had taken place in Belfast, in 1892, in support of striking linen workers. As was to be shown on several future occasions, initial common action around economic issues was not enough to sustain wider labour unity in a society with systematically promoted sectarian division.

Just as the advance of 'New Unionism' had been largely contained, so now the Home Rule movement had been brought to a standstill. Not surprisingly, it was not long before the 'internationalism from above' alliance, represented by the rather weak official Liberal support for 'Home Rule-all-round', backed by the divided Irish Nationalist parties, fell apart too. Gladstone was replaced as Prime Minister by the Liberal Federal Imperialist, Lord Rosebery. Home Rule was ditched.

As a result of these events, Davitt's 'internationalism from below' alliance, already badly mauled, finally broke apart too. Davitt further contributed to this degeneration. This was highlighted by his acrimonious refusal to back Bob Smillie as an Independent Labour Party candidate in the Mid-Lanarkshire by-election in 1894 (22). The Liberal government had effectively dropped Irish Home Rule and the official Liberal candidate was a recent Liberal Unionist. Yet Davitt ended up holding a similar position towards Independent Labour Home-Rule supporting candidate in 1894, to that Parnell had held towards 'real Radical' Home Rule supporting candidates in 1885[8]. Thus, it was Davitt, himself, who was now delivering the final blows to his earlier Radical and social republican alliance. He continued to back the socially conservative INF/Liberal Imperialist alliance, from which little could now be expected.

The demand for Irish Home Rule had originally been seen by its social republican exponents, as part of a strategy to achieve an Irish Republic. However, the vast majority of Irish, English, Scottish and Welsh supporters of Irish Home Rule ended up giving their support to the specific measures advocated by the Liberal Party. The heroic days of the Irish struggle, associated most strongly with the Land League, had given way, under Parnell's National League, to political wheeler-dealing. As a consequence, those Scottish and Welsh Radicals, and later Socialists, who had first drawn their inspiration from Ireland, now tended to fall in behind Liberal formulations of Irish, Scottish and Welsh Home Rule.

The Scottish Home Rule Association (SHRA) came under increasing official Liberal Party influence. This could already be seen in an SHRA document published in 1890, when a criticism was made of the greater attention given

---

[8] There had been simmering resentment about the role of the NL in the past in undermining independent Labour candidates. However, Scottish Socialists and independent Labour leaders had usually understood the difference between the role of Parnell's NL who had opposed, and Davitt and his supporters, who had backed independent Labour candidates in the past. Davitt's own retreat from this stance, led both Hardie and Smillie to express public anti-Irish resentment, which bordered on racism. In the Scottish context this played to a strengthening Orange and Labour unionist gallery.

by the UK government to Ireland - It "appears to set a premium upon disorder"[9] (23).

The same creeping Liberal Party takeover had led to a split in the Highland Land League at its 1890 conference. This had been preceded by a conference of the Liberal Party-supporting Free Church, held in Inverness in 1888. " *The Scotsman...* viewed {this} as a belated attempt... to exercise control over its wayward crofter and cottar adherents" (24). It also worried about the Irish connection, wondering whether "the Free Church {might} be dragged at the hands of the Highland Land League, playing a more degraded part than the Catholic Church in Ireland in connection with the National League" (25). However, as in Ireland, it was the Church that was to emerge as the dominant force, as the land movement went into retreat. Only instead of the split between Parnellites and anti-Parnellites, many Highland crofters and cottars focused their attentions on the growing split in the Free Church. This led to the breakaway Free Presbyterian Church, or the 'Wee Frees' in 1893 (26).

Moreover, the government established Crofters Commission was tending to favour tenants by lowering rents (27) just as government action in Ireland was moving towards acceptance of peasant proprietorship. In Ireland, the poorest tenant farmers and landless labourers were left more isolated; in Scotland it was the cottars, although land hunger continued to be a grievance for many crofters too. Radical Liberal Crofter MP for Caithness, G.B. Clark led the breakaway reformed Highland Land Reform Association, but it only lasted three years (28).

Like the new Labour Movement, those without land in the Highlands and Islands faced much greater government resistance to their demands. The Deer Forest Commission (29), set up in 1890 by the Conservatives, was supposed to address the issue of land shortage. Its formation was no doubt prompted by the sweeping successes of Land League candidates in the local elections (30), which took place after the Local Government (Scotland) Act of 1889[10] (31). However, the Commission was really a delaying tactic, designed to curb crofters' militant actions, and did not report until the end of the succeeding

---

[9] This wheedling complaint was to reappear again amongst liberal devolution supporters in Scotland in the 1990's, when the Conservative Government began preparing for political devolution for Northern Ireland, whilst ignoring the demands coming from Scotland.

[10] The passing of the Local Government Act for England and Wales, in 1888, and the Local Government (Ireland) Act in 1898, also provided both Socialists and Irish Nationalists with a new arena for political advance, particularly at a time when this was not possible at the UK level because of the political climate prevailing under 'New Imperialism', and the increasing domination of the Conservatives and Liberal Unionists.

Liberal government in 1895. It achieved very little.

Meanwhile, in Wales, Thomas Ellis (32), the Cymru Fydd leader, had accepted the post of second Government Whip in the new Gladstone government. He felt that his earlier support for Welsh Home Rule was unnecessary, since he was now in a position to influence a sympathetic Gladstonian Liberal government in power at the all-UK level. Ellis was a social imperialist and admirer of Cecil Rhodes. He had friends amongst the Fabians (33). In reality, Ellis's notion of Welsh nationalism was more cultural than political (34).

Under Gladstone, the main concession gained by cultural nationalists was the creation of the federal University of Wales (Aberystwyth, Bangor and Cardiff) (35). When it came to social policies such as the land issue, Welsh tenants were fobbed off, in the same manner as workers in the New Unions – a Royal Commission on Land was set up. It achieved nothing (36). Even the moves to disestablish the (Anglican) Church of Wales petered out (37).

The disappointments felt at the inability of the Liberal government to address the main social and religious issues facing rural and Nonconformist Wales led to the setting up of a renewed, more political, Cymru Fydd League, under the leadership of David Lloyd George and Beriah Gwynfe Evans[11] (38). It was chaired by former moderate Welsh Land Leaguer, Thomas Gee (39). However, in as far as Lloyd George took inspiration from Ireland, it was not the demand for Irish Home Rule that really inspired him. Indeed, he had almost become a Liberal Unionist in 1886 (40). His immediate concern was 'Welsh home rule' within the Liberal Party in order to advance the social issues that most concerned Liberal supporters in Wales. His support for Welsh Home Rule within the UK was superficial.

In 1895, just before the fall of the Lord Rosebery's Liberal government, the Cymru Fydd League merged with the North Wales Liberal Federation (41). When a Conservative and Liberal Unionist government was elected shortly afterwards, Lloyd George tried to unite the North and South Wales Liberal Federation (SWLF) on what was effectively the Cymru Fydd League programme.

However, this programme addressed neither the needs of the capitalist coal and steel owners, nor those of the industrial workers of the South Wales valleys, where the majority of the population in Wales now lived. A Newport meeting of the SWLF, held in 1896, completely rejected this merger (42). "The gulf between

---

[11] Beriah Gwynfe Evans had founded the Society for the Utilisation of Welsh. He was a Liberal Imperial Federalist, and later gave his support to the Boer War.

north and mid-Wales on one hand, and mercantile and industrial South Wales on the other seemed alarming and gaping, and the Liberals strove to patch it up by dropping the entire campaign for home rule " (43).

Lloyd George's old flirtation with Liberal Unionism reasserted itself, but now in Liberal Imperialist terms. He "decided that it was as a British Liberal not a future Welsh nationalist that his future was to lie"[12] (44). Some cultural nationalists took solace in the idea that the Irish were not real nationalists since they had given up their own distinctive language. In Wales, the last component of Davitt's 'internationalism-from-below' alliance was derailed.

---

[12] Lloyd George was still to have his anti-imperialist moment, like John Redmond and the Irish Nationalists, during the Boer War (1899-1901). However, like them, he later gave strong support to British Imperialism, particularly during the First World War, when he became Prime Minister leading the War Coalition.

References

(1)   see http://www.liberalhistory.org.uk/item_single.php?item_id=30&item=history

(2)   see Caroline Benn, *Keir Hardie*, p. 89 (Hutchinson, 1992, London)

(3)   see http://www.wakefield.gov.uk/CultureAndLeisure/HistoricWakefield/FeatherstoneMassacre/default.htm

(4)   see Chapter 10, reference 14.

(5)   see Elaine McFarland, *John Ferguson, 1836-1906, Irish Issues in Scottish Politics* p. 237 (Tuckwell Press, 2001, East Linton)

(6)   see http://en.wikipedia.org/wiki/Military_history_of_Uganda

(7)   see *Imposition of taxes* on http://www.sahistory.org.za/pages/hands-on-classroom/classroom/pages/projects/grade8/lesson5/07-gold.htm

(8)   see Chapter 3, reference 21.

(9)   Gordon Lucy, *The Great Convention – The Ulster Unionist Convention of 1892*, pp. 6-8 (Ulster Society Publications, 1995, Lurgan)

(10)   ibid., pp. 9-10.

(11)   ibid., p. 6.

(12)   ibid., pp. 21-3.

(13)   ibid., p. 24.

(14)   ibid., p. 19.

(15)   ibid., p. 32.

(16)   ibid., p. 29.

(17)   ibid., p. 15.

(18)   ibid., p. 64.

(19)   (see http://en.wikipedia.org/wiki/Second_Irish_Home_Rule_Bill# Passed_ by_the_Commons.2C_defeated_in_the_Lords

(20)   see John W. Boyle, *The Irish Labor Movement in the Nineteenth Century,* p. 140 (The Catholic University of America Press, 1988, Washington D.C.)

(21)   ibid., p. 142.

(22)   see David Howell, *British Workers and the Independent Labour Party, 1888-1906* (*BWatILP*) pp. 154-5 (Manchester University Press, 1983, Manchester)

(23)   see Keith Webb, *The Growth of Nationalism in Scotland*, p. 39 (The Molendinar Press, 1977, Glasgow)

(24)   see Allan W. McColl, *Land, Faith and the Crofting Communities: Christianity and Social Criticism in the Highlands of Scotland (1843-93)* (*LFatCC*), p. 198 (Scottish Historical Review Monographs, Edinburgh University Press, 2006, Edinburgh)

(25)   ibid., p. 198.

(26)   see http://en.wikipedia.org/wiki/Free_Presbyterian_Church_of_Scotland

(27)   see Iain Fraser Grigor, *Highland Resistance, The Radical Tradition in the Scottish North,* p. 144 (Mainstream Publishing, 2000, Edinburgh)

(28)   ibid., pp. 147-52.

(29)   ibid., p. 142.

(30)   ibid., p. 148.

(31)   see http://en.wikipedia.org/wiki/Local_Government_(Scotland)_Act_1889

(32)   see http://en.wikipedia.org/wiki/T._E._Ellis

(33)   see Kenneth O. Morgan, *Rebirth of A Nation, Wales, 1880-1980*, p. 33, Oxford University Press, 1981, New York)

(34)   ibid., pp. 113-4.

(35)   ibid., p. 110.

(36)   ibid., p. 83.

(37)   ibid., pp. 41-2.

(38)   ibid., p. 115.

(39)   ibid., p. 116

(40)   ibid., p. 43.

(41)   ibid., p. 115.

(42)   ibid., p. 117.

(43)   ibid., p. 118.

(44)   ibid., p. 118.

20. 1895 - The triumph of 'High Imperialism' and the emergence of James Connolly's Irish Socialist Republican Party

In the 1895 General Election, the Conservatives, under the reactionary leadership of Lord Salisbury, won 341 seats whilst their Liberal Unionist allies won 70 seats, between them a net gain of 98 (1). The Liberal Party lost 95 seats, and although their previous Irish Nationalist allies gained one seat - the City of Londonderry - the issue of Irish Home Rule had already been buried under Lord Rosebery, and the new parliamentary arithmetic ensured that Irish Nationalists had no remaining political purchase upon Westminster.

In Scotland, the Conservatives and Liberal Unionists made considerable gains, nowhere more so than in the Glasgow and the Clyde Valley. To maintain their profits made throughout the British Empire, business leaders depended upon British imperial armed might and a workforce divided on sectarian lines. A Liberal Unionist and Orange Order alliance was cemented[1]. The hostility shown by Conservative landlords, the Orange Order and Liberal Unionist businessmen towards the Irish 'peasant' was extended further, by leading Glasgow Liberal Unionist, Thomas Sinclair. He made a speech against Home Rule in 1895, declaring, "It is just as if it were proposed to transfer the interests of shipbuilders and manufacturers of Glasgow from the Imperial Parliament to the control of a legislature swamped by the crofters of the Highlands" (2).

In Wales, it was the Conservatives who made the biggest gains in the 1895 General Election, winning six new seats, including significantly both Cardiff and Swansea (3). South Wales, like the Clyde Valley in Scotland, and the Lagan Valley in Ireland, had an economy dependent on serving the needs of the British Empire. Liberal Unionism, however, was a redundant notion in Wales, where the Liberal Party itself was strongly pro-British unionist and imperialist. This was soon demonstrated in the debacle involving the Cymru Fydd League's attempted takeover of the Liberal Party in Wales. Furthermore, the

---

[1] One indicator of this alliance was the Chairmanship of Rangers Football Club, by the Liberal Unionist, Lord Provost of Glasgow, John Ure-Primrose.

Conservatives' penetration of the Welsh-speaking Liberal heartlands was limited by their "lobby of marcher squires… {who} made a practice of ridiculing all things Welsh" (4).

The only remaining independent Labour representative in Westminster, ILP member, Hardie, lost his seat in the General Election too. The ILP had fielded 29 candidates, but all were defeated (5). The ILP did make gains at the local government level, but this did not compensate for their disappointed high expectations in the 1895 General Election. The previous two years had seen attempts to promote Socialist unity between the ILP and the SDF (6). These had been unsuccessful, due to opportunist worries of most ILP leaders about the wider electoral appeal of Socialism, and to the sectarian socialist propagandist approach of the SDF leaders.

With the ILP breakthrough thwarted, and with the New Unions in retreat, the old suspicions towards trade unionism reasserted themselves in the SDF. Its members fell back even more on building a separate 'pure' Socialist organisation. Hyndman was fully back in control. Nevertheless, even Eleanor Marx and Aveling, along with other former SL member, William Morris, felt the necessity to rejoin the SDF in 1897, to maintain some contact with other Socialists.

Furthermore, as the influence of 'New Unionism' waned, the supporters of 'Old Unionism' reasserted their influence within the TUC. In 1896, the Parliamentary Committee of the TUC to decided to prevent the participation of trades councils at its conferences (7). Trades councils were seen as one of the main proponents of independent Labour representation. Supporters of the 'Old Unionism' were inveterate Lib-Labers, or even straightforward Liberal Party supporters.

One unforeseen effect of this decision was to confirm the existence of an increasingly autonomous Irish TUC [2] (8), and to spur the formation of a Scottish

---

[2] The Irish TUC had been formed in 1894, not on any nationalist basis, but because of the expense of sending delegates to the UK TUC, and the low priority given to Irish labour issues there. Independent Labour representation was hardly an issue in Ireland where Nat-Labism and Belfast-style 'non-political' trade unionism were prevalent. The loss of effective wider Irish participation in the all-UK TUC was just so much collateral damage as its British leadership resorted to increasingly bureaucratic measures to suppress independent Labour and Socialist challenges. As a result, the Irish TUC became more and more autonomous in practice, up to the point at which it became effectively an independent body.

TUC in 1897 (9). Trades councils were a much more significant part of the trade union movement in both Ireland and Scotland[3]. The STUC recognised some similarities in the ITUC's position. Hardie's ally, Robert Smillie[4], was sent as a fraternal delegate to their conference (10). However, neither the largely accidental formation of the ITUC, nor the more planned setting up of the STUC, were of much political significance at the time. They made little contribution to the renewal of a wider, more working class based 'internationalism from below' alliance.

The politics of the main participants in the ITUC were dominated by the Nat-Labism and the 'non-political' trade unionism found in Ireland. Although the recognition of the need for independent Labour representation continued to be a powerful influence in the STUC, it was Hardie's political thinking over this issue that still prevailed. This view largely accepted the Liberals' and Irish Nationalists' constitutional agenda. In doing so, the STUC became largely sentimental followers of the idea of 'Home Rule-all-round'. Instead it prioritised campaigns on the immediate economic and social interests facing the working class, largely leaving the wider politics to others.

The 1895 General Election signalled the arrival of the period of 'High Imperialism'. The Conservatives and Liberal Unionists were to remain in power until 1906. The retreats of 'New (Trade) Unionism' and the collapse of the Home Rule movement opened the door for further employer attacks on the trade union movement, and for the imperialist triumphalism, highlighted by Queen Victoria's Diamond Jubilee celebrations in 1897. The new Liberal Unionist, Colonial Secretary, Joseph Chamberlain, proposed the Jubilee be made a festival for the entire British Empire (11).

It was only now that Davitt recognised the final defeat of his earlier strategy (12). He was later to recover some of his political judgement and campaign against imperialism (13), racism in the colonies (14) and Tsarist Russian anti-

---

[3] Whilst it was undoubtedly the case that Scottish trades councils were to the forefront in their advocacy of independent Labour representation, this was certainly not the case with the Irish trades councils. Here trades councils were still necessary to coordinate activity, both in industries where trade unions were smaller and more locally based, and in the smaller towns where the overall influence of the working class would have been weaker without them.

[4] Both Hardie and Smillie had earlier shown certain anti-Irish feelings at times when they felt that Irish-born workers, living in Scotland or England, were too much under the influence of Irish Nationalist politicians, who told them to vote Liberal instead of Labour. Smillie's attempt to cultivate fraternal relations with the ITUC, whatever its shortcomings, represented perhaps a more considered attempt to overcome this problem.

Semitism (15). Davitt also went on to challenge the Catholic hierarchy's reactionary stance on education (16). He had not completely abandoned his old anti-imperialism and social republicanism, nor entirely forgotten his Radical past.

However, it was a new figure - the socialist republican, James Connolly - who lifted Davitt's legacy of social republican and Radical politics on to the higher plane needed in a world of 'High Imperialism' (17). Connolly had been a member of the Socialist

James Connolly took up Davitt's 'internationalism from below' legacy

League (SL), the Scottish Socialist Federation (SSF) and the Scottish Labour Party (SLP), and later became a member of the Social Democratic Federation and Independent Labour Party, when the SL disintegrated and the SLP dissolved itself.

Connolly had moved to Edinburgh just at the time when 'New Unionism' was making its impact felt. Davitt's ally, Edward McHugh, addressed the Leith dockers on August 10th, 1889 (18). Attempts were made to organise the Amalgamated Carters' Society in Edinburgh (19).

James Connolly's brother, John, fellow SSP and SLP member, was dismissed from his council carting job for his role in organising an '8 Hour Working Day' demonstration in the city's Queens Park (20).

Support for the 'Plan of Campaign' was also strong amongst Edinburgh's Irish migrant community. One of Connolly's first political interventions in the city was to address both the Edinburgh and Leith (Irish) National League (NL) branches, calling for the reinstatement of prominent local NL member, Michael Flanagan, as Secretary of the Catholic Young Mens Society (21). Flanagan was also a leading light in Hibernian Football Club, which may also have influenced Connolly! He had been victimised by William Smith, the Catholic Archbishop of Edinburgh and St. Andrews, for campaigning very publicly for the 'Plan of Campaign'. Smith was a Scottish Catholic, and as such was far more willing to enforce the Vatican's anti-Campaign anathema, than many of his Irish counterparts.

Connolly, whose own adherence or non-adherence to the Catholic Church, has been the subject of dispute (22), was developing his approach to win over religiously-influenced workers. Here, he was following Davitt's earlier efforts. Connolly also challenged the Catholic hierarchy when necessary.

Connolly wrote for a number of journals. He showed his working class internationalism in Hyndman's and the SDF's *Justice.* He attacked the Master Bottlemakers Association for refusing to meet with striking workers from Portobello in Edinburgh because there were German migrant workers amongst their number (23). In another issue of this journal, he reported that the SSF had agreed to send a delegate to the Zurich Congress of the Second International in 1893 (24).

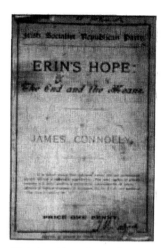

'Erin's Hope' - James Connolly's socialist republican case for Irish independence

Connolly also wrote for the *Edinburgh and Leith Labour Chronicle,* which was effectively the paper of the SSF. On its masthead it carried the words of French Jacobin, Camille Desmoullins, "The great only appear great to us because we are on our knees; let us rise." Translated into Irish, this was to become the masthead of the Irish Socialist Republican Party's better-known journal, *Workers Republic,* published from 1898-1903 (25).

Through Connolly's friendship with SSF Secretary, the Irish-Scot, John Leslie, he became more fully acquainted with the tradition of alliance in Scotland between United Irishmen and Scottish Radicals in the 1798 period, between Young Irelanders and Chartists in the 1840's, and between Fenians, Irish Land Leaguers, Scottish Land Nationalisers and Socialists in the '70's and '80's. This was the time when Leslie gave a series of lectures on Ireland to the SSF (26). The role of Davitt and the Irish Land League figured prominently. This greatly influenced Connolly.

When Connolly stood as an SSF candidate for the Edinburgh St. Giles ward in the City Corporation election in 1894, he wrote a contribution to the *Edinburgh and Leith Labour Chronicle* making the connection between "the landlord who grinds his peasants on a Connemara estate, and the landlord who rackrents them in a Cowgate slum" (27). Connolly had served in the British Army between 1892-9, remembered being on guard duty near Cork the night that Myles Joyce was executed in Galway Jail for his alleged part in the Maamtrasna Murders (28). Like Mayo-born Davitt, he paid keen attention to events in the West of Ireland.

Unable to make a living in Edinburgh, Connolly was invited by Adolphus Shields, a key figure in attempting to bring 'New Unionism' to Ireland, to act as an organiser for the Dublin Socialist Club in 1896 (29). This was probably on the understanding that Connolly would help start a new ILP branch in the city (30).

Connolly had other ideas, and soon set about founding the Irish Socialist Republican Party (ISRP). The new party's programme called for the "Establishment of AN IRISH SOCIALIST REPUBLIC" (31). Edward Aveling formally joined the ISRP, whilst Eleanor Marx expressed her support (32).

Connolly prepared the theoretical grounding, which could shift late nineteenth and early twentieth century working class politics in the UK beyond the almost defunct social republicanism found in Ireland, and the receding but still influential Radicalism found in Britain. Connolly made use of both British Labour and advanced Irish nationalist journals, since the ISRP did not yet have its own press. In publishing articles in Hardie's *Labour Leader* and Alice Milligan's[5] (33) *Shan Van Vocht*, he was following the legacy of Davitt, in his target audiences. However, by 1897, the ISRP was able to combine these articles and produce the pamphlet, *Erin's Hope: The End and the Means* (34).

Connolly made the first bare outlines of an alternative history of Ireland, which he was to develop much further, over a decade later, in his *Labour in Irish History* (35). Influenced by contemporary Irish historians, he outlined the role of primitive communism in Ireland up to the seventeenth century (36), and opened up the prospect of Socialists being able to re-establish a communist society, but based upon a higher level of economic and social cooperation.

Connolly placed anti-imperialism at the centre of his politics. He advocated a 'break-up of the British Union and Empire' strategy. He stated that, "No Irish revolutionist worth his salt would refuse to lend a hand to the Social Democracy of England in the effort to uproot the social system of which the British Empire is the crown and apex, and in like manner, no English Social Democrat fails to recognise clearly that the crash which would betoken the fall of the ruling

---

[5] Alice Milligan was an advanced Irish nationalist and member of the Gaelic League, *Shan Van Vocht* was a literary monthly, published in Belfast.

classes in Ireland would sound the tocsin for the revolt of the disinherited in England" (37). He was over sanguine in his appraisal of English/British Social Democrats.

Connolly, like Davitt, took a keen interest in India, and published an article, *British Rule in India*, which attacked "extravagant ideas about the 'wealth of India'. In reality India was one of the poorest countries in the world, if not the poorest, her population (200 million) in a state of chronic misery. Yet the tribute exacted by the Imperial government amounted to 20 to 27 million pounds sterling" (38).

Furthermore, Connolly was also an organiser and he soon threw himself into the preparations for an outdoor meeting in Dublin to protest against the Diamond Jubilee. The Rank & File 98 Club[6] held a mass meeting, attended by about 6000, under the slogan, "Down with the Monarchy: Long live the Republic!" (39). On Jubilee Day itself, the ISRP organised a demonstration, at the front of which was a black coffin marked 'British Empire'. It challenged all those Conservative, Liberal, Radical and Labour imperialists who believed Victoria's lengthy rule over the British Empire had been marked by continued progress. Banners were flown highlighting the number who had died in the Irish Famine, or who had been forced to emigrate. When Connolly reached the River Liffey, he threw the coffin over the bridge, declaring, "Here goes the coffin of the British Empire. To Hell with the British Empire!" (40).

Connolly very much appreciated the limitations placed upon the self-determination of nations within an imperialist dominated world. The struggle for political liberation had to be linked to social struggle for emancipation. "If you remove the English army tomorrow and hoist the green flag over Dublin Castle, unless you set about the organisation of the Socialist Republic your efforts would be in vain. England would still rule you. She would rule you through her capitalists, through her landlords, through her financiers, through the whole array of commercial and individualist institutions she has planted in this country" (41).

Davitt had run with the 'internationalism from below' baton for the decade from 1879-89, before fumbling with it in 1890, and finally dropping it in 1892. Now, in the darkest days of political and industrial defeats, during the heyday of

---

[6] 1898 was to mark the centenary of the United Irish Rebellion. The Club was a united front between the ISRP and advanced nationalists. It was partly formed to counter the influence of the tame Irish Nationalist Centennial Association, which had the support of William Martin Murphy, later, at the time of the Dublin Lock-Out in 1913 to be a much more significant antagonist for Connolly.

'High Imperialism', Connolly was preparing the grounds for the new 'internationalism from below' alliance in the UK and British Empire, built on the politics of socialist republicanism.

Connolly took up this baton, shortly after Engels' death in 1895. Eleanor Marx was to commit suicide in 1897, whilst her former partner, Aveling died a year later. Whilst personal relationships and medical problems were the immediate causes of death, their demise can be taken as a sign of the times.

Davitt had first pioneered the political strategy in the UK and British Empire – 'internationalism from below' – that would be taken up and further developed by Connolly. It took new struggles before another generation of revolutionary Social Democrats and Communists began to appreciate this 'internationalism from below' approach. In the first two decades of the twentieth century, a truly global opposition arose against capitalist imperialism. The 1904-7 International Revolutionary Wave once more brought 'internationalism from below' into the political arena, announcing the presence of anti-imperialist, revolutionary Social Democracy.

Furthermore, Connolly went on to play a leading role in the 1916 Easter Rising. This heralded the International Revolutionary Wave of 1916-21 and the conscious struggle for genuine communism, based on the principles of, 'From each according to their abilities; to each according to their needs' and, 'Where the free development of each is the condition of the free development of all.' It was Connolly's commitment to **internationalism from below** that enabled him to initiate this International Revolutionary Wave.

Today, the Scottish Socialist Party is trying to re-establish itself as the voice of workers living in Scotland[7], in alliance with socialist republicans living in Ireland, Wales and England[8], and as part of a wider European Anti-Capitalist Alliance[9]. We have the benefit of hindsight, and the knowledge that another world war would be unlikely to open up the prospect of a new society based on human emancipation and liberation. We need to break the power of US and British corporate imperialism before it drags all humanity down into barbarism or annihilation.

---

[7] The SSP gave its support to the 'No One Is Illegal' Campaign at its 2007 Conference, highlighting its commitment to all workers living in Scotland – native-born, newly settled and temporarily domiciled migrant dwellers.

[8] The SSP International Committee organised the Republican Socialist Convention, in Edinburgh, on November 29th, 2008, with participants from England, Ireland, Scotland and Wales.

[9] The SSP agreed, at its 2009 Conference to stand in the June Euro-elections as part of the European Anti-Capitalist Alliance.

References

(1)   **see** http://en.wikipedia.org/wiki/United_Kingdom_general_election,_1895

(2)   **see** Graham Walker and David Officer, *Scottish Unionism and the Ulster Question* **in** Catriona M, Macdonald, edit., *Unionist Scotland, 1800-1997*, p. 18 (John Donald, 1998, Edinburgh)

(3)   **see** Kenneth O. Morgan, *Rebirth of A Nation, Wales, 1880-1980*, p. 30 (Oxford University Press, 1981, New York)

(4)   ibid., p. 57.

(5)   **see** Martin Crick, *The History of the Social Democratic Federation,* p. 87 (Ryburn Publishing, 1994, Keele University)

(6)   ibid., pp. 86-7.

(7)   **see** John W. Boyle, *The Irish Labor Movement in the Nineteenth Century (TILM)* p. 151 (The Catholic University of America Press, 1988, Washington D.C.)

(8)   ibid., p. 153.

(9)   **see** Michael Keating & David Bleiman, *Labour and Scottish Nationalism (LaSN)* pp. 39-40 (The Macmillan Press Ltd, 1979, London)

(10)   **see** John W. Boyle, *TILM,* op. cit., pp. 152-3.

(11)   **see** http://en.wikipedia.org/wiki/Queen_Victoria#Diamond_Jubilee

(12)   **see** David Howell, *British Workers and the Independent Labour Party, 1888-1906 (BWatILP)* p. 142 (Manchester University Press, 1983, Manchester)

(13)   **see** F. Sheehy-Skeffington, *The Counter-Revolution* **in** *Michael Davitt, Revolutionary Agitator and Labour Leader* pp. 165-70 (MacGibbon & Kee, 1967, London)

(14)   ibid., p. 160.

(15)   ibid., p. 185.

(16)   ibid., pp. 199-209.

(17)   **see** http://en.wikipedia.org/wiki/James_Connolly

(18)   **see** Ian MacDougall, *Voices of the Leith Dockers – Personal Recollections of Working Lives,* p. 211 (Scottish Working People's History, Mercat Press, 2001, Edinburgh)

(19)   **see** Angela Tuckett, *The Scottish Carter,* p. 37 (George Allen and Unwin Ltd., 1967, London)

(20)   **see** Donal Nevin, *James Connolly, 'A Full Life', (JC-AFL)* p. 34 (Gill & Macmillan Ltd, 2005, Dublin)

(21)   **see** Alan Lugton, *The Making of Hibernian I*, p. 169 (John Donald Publishing Ltd, 1999, Edinburgh)

(22)   **see** Donal Nevin, *JC-AFL,* op. cit., p. 35.

(23)   ibid., p. 34.

(24)   **see** Manus O'Riordan, *James Connolly Re-assessed: The Irish and European Context*, p. 24 (Aubane Historical Society, 2006, Aubane, Millstreet, County Cork)

(25)   **see** Donal Nevin, *JC-AFL*, op. cit., p.35.

(26)   ibid., p. 42-6.

(27)   ibid., p. 39.

(28)   ibid., p. 16 and Chapter 8, reference 1.

(29)   **see** Fintan Lane, *The Origins of Modern Irish Socialism, 1881-1896*, (*TOoMIS*) p. 215 (Cork University Press, 1997, Cork)

(30)   ibid., p. 215

(31)   *IRSP Programme, 1896*, **in** David Lynch, *Radical Politics in Modern Ireland: The Irish Socialist Republican Party, 1896-1904*, p. 166 (Irish Academic Press, 2005, Dublin)

(32)   **see** Fintan Lane, *TOoMIS*, op. cit., p. 219.

(33)   **see** http://en.wikipedia.org/wiki/Alice_Milligan

(34)   **see** Donal Nevin, *JC-AFL*, op. cit., pp. 75 and 85 .

(35)   **see** http://www.marxists.org/archive/connolly/1910/lih/index.htm

(36)   **see** Donal Nevin, *JC-AFl,* op, cit., pp. 76-7.

(37)   **see** Fintan Lane, *TOoMIS*, op. cit., p. 220.

(38)   **see** Donal Nevin, *JC-AFl,* op, cit., p. 92.

(39)   Fintan Lane, *TOoMIS*, op. cit., p. 221.

(40)   ibid., p. 221.

(41)   James Connolly, *Shan Van Vocht*, 1/1897, quoted **in** P. Berresford Ellis, *James Connolly, Selected Writings*, p. 124 (Penguin Books Ltd, 1973, Harmondsworth)

Bibliography

Since many of the books referred to are long out-of-print and difficult to get, I have also provided website references, after each chapter, particularly from the easily accessible Wikipedia. The advent of so much material on the website is a real gain for Socialists, particularly given the rising costs of books. There can be a problem due to particular website references being removed or altered. Therefore, website references are only accurate up to October 1st 2010. Many academics take quite a sniffy approach to the use of website references, claiming they are often unreliable and extremely biased. In my experience these problems apply just as much to books. As far as possible, website references have been used which seem to provide accurate information.

Baylen J. O. and Gossman, N. J., *Biographical Dictionary of Modern British Radicals*, Vol. 3. 1830-1914 (Harvester Wheatsheaf, 1988, Hemel Hempstead)

Bellamy, J.M, and Saville, J., *Dictionary of Labour Biography*, Vol. VII (Macmillan Press, 1982, London)

Bell. G., *Troublesome Business - The Labour Party and the Irish Question* (Pluto Press, 1982, London)

Benn, C., *Keir Hardie* (Hutchison, 1992, London)

Bew, P., *C. S. Parnell* (Gill and Macmillan, 1980, Dublin)

Biggs-Davidson J. and Chowdharay-Best, G., *The Cross of St. Patrick - the Catholic Unionist Tradition in Ireland* (The Kensal Press, 1984, Bourne End)

Bowman, T., *People's Champion, The Life of Alexander Bowman, Pioneer of Labour Politics in Ireland* (Ulster Historical Foundation, 1997, Belfast)

Boyd, A., *Jim Connell - Author of the Red Flag* (Donaldson Archives/Socialist History Society, 2001, Oxford)

Boyle, J. W, *The Irish Labor Movement in the Nineteenth Century* (The Catholic University of America Press, 1988, Washington D.C.)

Cameron, E. A., *Land for the People, The British Government and the Scottish Highlands, 1880-1925* (Tuckwell Press, 2000, East Linton)

Campbell, C., *Fenian Fire - The British Government Plot to Assassinate Queen Victoria* (Harper Collins, 2002, London)

Collins, H and Abramsky, C, *Karl Marx and the British Labour Movement* (Macmillan, 1965, London)

Connolly, J., *Labour in Irish History* (Bookmarks, 1987, London)

Crick, M., *The History of the Social Democratic Federation* (Ryburn Publishing, 1994, Keele University)

Crouch, D. and Ward, C., *The Allotment, Its Landscape and Culture* (Faber and Faber, 1988, London)

Crowley, D. W., *The Crofters Party* in *The Scottish Historical Review*, Volume 35 (Edinburgh University Press, 1956, Edinburgh)

Curtis, L., *The Cause of Ireland, From the United Irishmen to Partition* (beyond the Pales Publications, 1994, Belfast)

Davidson, J. M., *Grand Old Man of Fleet Street* in *Politics for the People* (William Reeves, 1892, London)

Davidson, J. M., *Scotia Rediviva - Home Rule for Scotland* (William Reeves, 1890, Scotland)

Davitt, M., *The Fall of Feudalism - or the Story of the Land League Revolution* (Harpers & Brothers Publishers, 1904, London)

Douglas, R., Land, *People and Politics, A History of the Land Question in the United Kingdom, 1878-1952* (Allison & Busby, 1976, London)

Duncan, R*., James Leatham, 1865-1945 - Portrait of a Socialist Pioneer* (Aberdeen Peoples Press, 1978, Aberdeen)

Ellis, P. B, *James Connolly, Selected Writings* (Penguin Book s Ltd, 1973, Harmondsworth)

Ellis, P. B., *The History of the Irish Working Class* (Pluto Press, 1985, London)

Engels, F., *Selected Works*, Vol. 3 (Lawrence & Wishart, 1985, London)

Evans, P. J., *Euan Pan Jones - Land Reformer* in *Welsh History Review*, Vol, 4, no. 2 (University of Wales, June 1968, Cardiff)

Fraser, W. H., *Conflict and Class, Scottish Workers, 1700-1830* (John Donald, 1988, Edinburgh)

Geary, L., *The Plan of Campaign, 1886-1892* (Cork University Press, 1986, Cork)

George, H, jr., *The Life of Henry George* (Double Day, Doran & Company Inc, 1930, Garden City)

Greaves, C. D., *The Life and Times of James Connolly* (Lawrence & Wishart, 1986, London)

Grigor, I. F., *Highland Resistance, The Radical Tradition in the Scottish North* (Mainstream Publishing, 2000, Edinburgh)

Hobsbawm, E., *The 'New Unionism' in Perspective* in *Worlds of Labour - Further studies in the history of labour* (Weidenfield & Nicholson, 1984, London)

Howell, D., *British Workers and the Independent Labour Party, 1888 - 1906* (Manchester University Press, 1984, Manchester)

Hunter, J., *For the People's Cause - From the Writings of John Murdoch* (HMSO Books, 1986, Edinburgh)

Hyslop, J., *The Notorious Syndicalist, J. T. Bain: A Scottish Rebel on Colonial South Africa* (Jacana Media (Pty) ltd, 2004, Johannesburg)

Jenkins, R., *Dilke - A Victorian Tragedy* (Papermac, 1996, London)

Jones, G. J. Michael Davit,t David Llloyd George and T. E. Ellis - The Welsh Experience, 1886 in Welsh Historical Review, Vol, 18, no. 3 (University of Wales, 1997, Cardiff)

Kapp, Y, *Eleanor Marx. Volume II - the Crowded Years, 1886-1898* (Virago press, 1979, London)

Kapp, Y., *The Air of Freedom: The Birth of New Unionism* (Lawrence & Wishart, 1989, London)

Keating. M., and Bleiman, D., *Labour and Scottish Nationalism* (Macmillan Press Ltd, 1979, London)

Kelly, J. S., *The Bodyke Evictions* (Fossbeg Press, 1987, Scariff, County Clare)

Kenefick, W, *Red Scotland! The Rise and Fall of the Radical Left, c. 1872 to 1932* (Edinburgh University Press, 2007, Edinburgh)

King, C., *Michael Davitt*, Life and Times, no. 15 (Historical Association of Ireland, Dundalgan Press, 1999, Dundalk)

Lane, F., *The Origins of Modern Irish Socialism, 1881-1896* (Cork University Press, 1997, Cork)

Lawrence, E. P., *Henry George in the British Isles* (Michigan State University Press, 1953, East Lansing)

Leslie, J., *The Irish Question* (The Cork Workers Club Historical Reprints, no, 7, 1974, Cork)

Lowe, D., *Souvenirs of Scottish Labour* (W. & R. Holmes, 1919, Glasgow)

Lucy, G., *The Great Convention - The Ulster Unionist Convention of 1892* (Ulster Society Publications, 1995, Lurgan)

Lugton. A., *The Making of Hibernian I*, (John Donald Publishing Ltd, 1999, Edinburgh)

Lynch, D., *Radical Politics in Modern Ireland: The Irish Socialist Republican Party, 1896-1904* (Irish Academic Press, 2005, Dublin)

MacColl, A. *Land, Faith and the Crofting Communities: Christianity and Social Criticism in the Highlands of Scotland (1843-93)* (Scottish Historical Monographs, Edinburgh University Press, 2006, Edinburgh)

MacDougall, I., *Voices of the Leith Dockers - Personal Reflections of Working Lives* (Scottish Working People's History, Mercat Press, 2001, Edinburgh)

Maclean, R., *Labour and Scottish Home Rule, part 1, Mid-Lanark to Majority Government* (Scottish Labour Action, undated, Broxburn)

Maclean, S., *Mhairi Mhor nan Oran* in *Calgacus* (West Highland Publishing Co. Ltd., 1975, Breakish, Isle of Skye)

Marley, L., *Michael Davitt - Freelance Radical and Frondeur* (Four Courts Press, 2007, London)

Marx. K. and Engels, F., *Articles on Britain* (Progress Publishers, 1975, Moscow)

Marx, K. and Engels, F., *Ireland and the Irish Question* (Lawrence & Wishart, 1978, London)

McCartney, T., *The Great Dock Strike, 1889 - The Story of the Labour Movement's First Great Victory* (Weidenfield & Nicholson, 1988, London)

McFarland, E., *John Ferguson, 1836-1906, Irish Issues in Scottish Politics* (Tuckwell Press, 2001, East Linton)

Miller, J, *The Lithuanians in Scotland* (House of Lochar, 1998, Isle of Colonsay)

Moody, T.W., *Davitt and Irish Revolution*, 1846-82 (Oxford University Press, 1990, Oxford)

Morgan, K., *The Rebirth of a Nation - Wales, 1880 -1980* (University of Wales Press, 1981, Oxford)

Nevin, D., *James Connolly - A Fine Life* (Gill & Macmillan, 2005, Dublin),

Newby, A., *Landlordism is Going Skye-High - Michael Davitt and Scotland, 1882-1887* in *History Scotland*, Vol 3. no. 4 (History Scotland, 2003, Edinburgh)

Newby, A., *The Life and Times of Edward McHugh (1853-1913)* (Edward Mellen Press, 2004, Ceredigion)

O'Brien, R. B., *The Life of Charles Stewart Parnell* (Thomas Nelson & Sons, 1910, London)

O'Neill, B., *The War for Land in Ireland* (Martin Lawrence, 1933, London)

O'Riordan, M., *James Connolly Re-assessed: The Irish and European Context* (Aubane Historical Society, 2006, Aubane, County Cork)

Oxford Dictionary of National Biography, Volume 53 (Oxford University Press, 2004, Oxford)

Parry, C, *The Radical Tradition in Welsh Politics - a study of Liberal and Labour politics in Gwynnedd, 1900-1920* (University of Hull Publications, 1970, Hull)

Parnell, A., *The Tale of the Great Sham* (edited by Hearn, D (Arleen House, 1986, Dublin)

Reid, A, *United We Stand - A History of Britain's Trade Unions* (Penguin Books, 2004, London)

Republican Socialist Convention Report (International Committee, Scottish Socialist Party, 2009, Dundee)

Ryan, W.P., *The Irish Labour Movement, From the Twenties to Our Own Day* (The Talbot Press, 1919, Dublin)

Semmel, B., *The Rise of Free Trade Imperialism - Classical Political Economy and the Empire of Free Trade and Imperialism, 1750-1850* (Cambridge University Press, 1970, London)

Sheehy-Skeffington, F., *Michael Davitt, Revolutionary Agitator and Labour Leader* (MacGibbon & Kee, 1967, London)

Smith, D., editor, *A People and a Proletariat - Essays in the History of Wales, 1780-1980* (Pluto Press, 1980, London)

Talpin, E., *Liverpool Dockers and Seamen, 1870 - 1890* (Univserity of Hull, 1970, Hull)

Tuckett, A., *The Scottish Carter* (George Allen and Unwin Ltd., 1967, London)

Waldron, J., *Maamtrasna, the Murders and the Mystery* (Edmund Burke Publisher, 1992, Blackrock)

Walker, G, and Officer, D., *Scottish Unionism and the Ulster Question* in Macdonald, C, edit, *Unionist Scotland, 1800-1997* (John Donald, 1998, Edinburgh)

Walsh, P, *The Rise and Fall of Imperial Ireland* (Athol Books, 2003, Belfast)

Williams, G. A., *When Was Wales?* (Penguin Books, 1985, London)

Wood, J. D., *Henry George's Influence on Scottish Land Reform* in *The Scottish Historical Review*, (Edinburgh University Press, April 1984, Edinburgh)

Index

Aberdeen, 137n
Aberdeen Socialist Society, 100
Aberdeen South constituency, 138n
Aberystwyth (Mid-Wales), 153
Abraham, W (Mabon), 82, 82n
Address to the Electors of Tyrone, 48
advanced nationalism/ts, 31n, 161, 161n, 162
advanced Radicals, 27, 40n, 45, 46, 56, 62, 62n, 63, 88, 96, 97, 98, 109
African Americans, 38n, 105n
Africans, 148
agricultural cooperation (also see Irish farmers cooperative movement), 56
Aliens Act (1905), 80n
Allan, F, 122, 130
all-Britain organisation, 23, 25, 26
All for Ireland League, 86n
Alliance for Workers Liberty, 18, 18n
all-UK/English/British-based organisation, 25, 26, 49, 56, 61, 120, 122, 123, 125, 140, 141n, 143, 157n
all-UK Radical and social republican alliance (see Radical and social republican alliance)
all-UK reactionary block, 79
Amalgamated Carters Society, 159
Amalgamated Society of Engineers, 119n, 143n
Amalgamated Society of Railway Servants, 143, 144
American (see USA)
American Civil War (1861-5), 5n
American Federation of Labour, 106, 106n
American Society of United Irishmen, 37
Anarchism/ists, 21, 89n, 91, 94, 98, 104, 105, 105n, 114
Ancient Order of Hibernians, 86n
An Comunn Gaidhealach, 65n
Anglo-Irish/Protestant Ascendancy, 41, 55, 72, 79, 136n, 148n
'Anglo-Saxon'/'Teuton'/'English' race, 9, 61n, 75, 107, 107n, 111
anti-Catholicism (see sectarianism)
anti-coercion, 48, 111, 125
Anti-Coercion League, 45

Bechuanaland, 91

Belfast (also see North Belfast/South Belfast/West Belfast constituency), 63, 64, 64n, 73, 75, 118n, 123n, 124, 130, 131, 139n, 140, 143n, 144, 145, 149n, 150, 150n, 157n, 161n

Belfast Anti-Home Rule Riots (1886) 75, 149

Belfast-Glasgow-Liverpool triangle, 118n

Belfast North constituency, 70n

Belfast pogroms (1920-2), 12

Belfast Riots (1857), 64n

Belfast South constituency, 74

Belfast Trades Council, 64n, 123

Belfast Weekly Star, 64

Belfast West constituency, 137

Berlusconi, S, 16

Besant, A, 116, 116n

Biggar, J, 31

binworkers - strike of Glasgow (1977), 13

Birmingham, 46n

birth control, 116

Black Americans (see African Americans)

blacklegs/strikebreakers (also see scab unions), 99, 143

blanket protests, 80n, 88n

Blaenau Ffestiniog (North Wales), 81, 120

'Bloody Sunday' (London) (1887), 91, 95n, 116n, 119n

'Blue Books' controversy, 112

Blunt, W. S, 80, 80n, 88n

Bodyke Evictions (1887), 87

Bodyke Eviction Fund, 87

Boers, 41, 43, 46n, 48, 54n, 107n

Boer War - First (1880-81), 42, 43

Boer War - Second (1899-1902), 153n, 154n

Bonar Bridge (Sutherland), 81, 84

Bootle (Merseyside), 117n

Bowman, A, 64, 64n, 70n, 75, 113n, 140

Boycott, Captain, 34n, 35

boycott action, 34, 41, 87, 117

Bradford (Yorkshire), 138, 139, 144

Bradford West constituency, 138

Bradlaugh, C, 62, 62n, 75n, 116n

Braes (Battle of) (Skye) (1882), 56, 57

Bray, J. F, 39n

break-up of the UK and British Empire, 27, 110

'break-up of the UK and British Empire road to socialism', 21, 110n, 161

Brennan, T, 33, 42, 49

brickworkers, 120

Bright, J, 46, 46n, 62, 107

Britain/Great Britain/British (also see United Kingdom), 6, 8, 9, 10, 11, 12, 13, 15, 16n, 19, 23, 26n, 39n, 41, 42, 45, 46, 47, 48, 54, 54n, 55, 56, 58n, 61, 62, 62n, 70, 71, 72, 86, 91n, 99n, 108, 109, 112, 113, 114, 117n, 122n, 124, 125, 126, 128, 129, 132n, 145, 148, 149, 150, 154, 157n, 161, 162

British Army/military/officers, 12, 20, 46n, 91, 99n, 114, 151, 156, 162

British East Africa Company, 148

British Empire/imperialism/ists, 6, 8, 10, 15, 22, 24, 25, 26, 26n, 27, 28, 29, 31n, 39, 39n, 46n, 61n, 62, 62n, 73, 79, 80n, 88, 82, 94, 97, 98, 107, 107n, 108, 110, 110n, 114, 116, 117n, 122n, 137n, 139, 148, 148n, 149, 150, 154n, 156, 158, 161, 162, 163,

British Imperial Parliament (also see Imperial Federation/Westminster), 97, 107, 108, 109, 110, 156

'British Federal Republic' (see federation of England Scotland and Wales'

'British Free Trade Empire', 6n, 6, 10

British Labourist Socialism, 139

British National Party (BNP), 16

British Radical/s, 17, 31, 145

'British road to progress', 17, 18

'British road to socialism' 17, 18, 21, 141

British Rule in India (James Connolly), 162

British ruling class, 5, 6, 7, 11, 12, 13, 15, 17, 21, 24, 27n, 114

British security services, 54, 54n

British Socialism/ists (also see Left unionism, 'Marxist Radicals'), 64, 91, 114

British Union (see United Kingdom)

British Unionism/t (also see Conservative & Unionist Party, Democratic Unionist Party, Irish Liberal Unionists, Irish Unionist Party, Liberal Unionists, Progressive Unionist Party, True Unionist Voice, Ulster Unionist Party), 8, 14, 24, 80n, 123, 132n, 136n, 144, 150, 156

'British Welfare State Empire', 10

Broad Left (strategy), 11, 16

Brodie, R, 137n

Brotherhood, 64, 64n

Brown, G. 21

Broxburn, 137n

Broxburn Shaleminers' Strike (1887), 98, 116, 137n

Buganda, 148

building workers (also see Dublin United Building Labourers' Strike), 123

Bullock Report (1975), 13

Burke, T, 54, 86

Burleigh, B, 137n

Burma, 73

Burns, J, 100n, 119, 119n, 138, 147

Butt, I, 30n, 31, 34n, 39

'ca' canny' methods, 117, 117n

Caithness (Highlands), 63

Caithness constituency, 67, 81

Calvinist Methodist/s, 7, 82

Camberwell Radicals, 67

Camborne constituency, 88n

Cambrian Miners Association, 82n

Cameron, D, 15

Canada, 26n, 30n, 37, 41, 108, 110

Canadian Confederation, 73, 73n

Cape Colony, 148, 148n

Capital (Karl Marx), 88

'Captain Moonlight', 35, 50

Canty, M, 122, 124, 125, 130, 131, 133, 145

Cardiff (South Wales), 153, 156

Cardiff Bay (see Welsh Assembly)

Cardiff docks, 120

Carnarvon, Lord, 69

Carroll W, 30, 41, 57, 57n

Carson, Sir E, 86n

carters, 20, 117, 123, 159

'Castle Catholic', 136n

Catalans, 27n

Catholic Church, 12, 152, 160

Catholics/Catholicism, 7, 12n, 32, 34, 55n, 56n, 67, 71, 73, 80n, 84, 86n, 91, 117, 118, 126n, 130, 131, 133n, 136n, 139n, 150n

Catholic hierarchy, 7, 49, 53, 55, 56n, 57, 59n, 89, 129, 130, 133, 133n, 159, 160

Catholic Young Mens Society (Edinburgh), 159

Cavendish, Lord, 54

'Celtic Fringe', 112n

Celtic Studies, Chair of (Edinburgh University), 65n

Celtic Literature (Matthew Arnold), 112n
Celtic Scotland (William Skene), 109n
Celts/clans, 84, 109n, 112n
Centennial Association, 162n
Central Belt (Scotland) (also see Clydeside), 70, 94, 94-5, 98
Chamberlain, J, 46, 46n, 62, 73n, 74, 75, 76, 76n, 114n, 137, 149n, 158
Champion, H, 9, 46, 62, 63, 89, 96, 96n, 97n, 119n, 137, 137n, 139, 141, 141n
Chartism (also see Scottish Chartists, Chartist Left), 11n, 24n, 39n, 81n, 90n, 103, 160
Chartist Left and Irish Confederate alliance, 37
chauvinism (also see anti-Irish/anti-Welsh/racism/supremacism), 61
Chester (Cheshire), 81
Chicago USA), 105, 120
child labour, 6, 20
Chinese labour immigration, 38 88, 104
Christian Socialist/Societies, 46n, 97, 139
Chubut Valley (Patagonia), 81
Churchill, R (Lord), 8, 69, 72, 73, 74, 76, 76n
Church of Ireland, 35n, 72n
Church of Scotland, 65, 98, 149n
Church of Wales, 82n, 112, 149n, 153
Cincinnati (USA), 105
Civil Rights Movement, 14
Clan-na-Gael (see Fenians)
Clark, Dr. G.B, 40, 40n, 47, 67, 81, 97, 109, 152
Clearances (Highland), 41, 65
Clydach (South Wales) 83
Clydeside/Clyde Valley, 24n, 27, 94, 117, 143n, 156
coachmakers, 122
Cobden, R, 46n, 107
coercion (see state coercion)
Coercion Act, 54
Collins, J, 73n, 103
Committee for a Workers International (CWI), 18, 18n
Commonweal, 90, 141n
communal and republican club tradition, 90n, 110, 114
Communist Party (of Great Britain), 18
Communist Party of Great Britain (*Weekly Worker*), 18
communist society (also see genuine communism), 109n, 161
community control of land, 56

Congested Districts Board, 130

Congregationalist (Church), 112n

Connacht (Ireland - West) 42n

Connell, J, 37, 37n, 47, 120

Connemara (Ireland - West), 162

Connolly, James, 20, 21, 22, 33n, 70n, 90n, 91n, 99, 100n, 125n, 137n, 159, 160, 161, 162, 162n, 163

Connolly, John, 99, 100n, 159

Conservative and Liberal Unionist alliance, 12, 26, 64n, 79, 82, 107, 108, 114, 139

Conservative (and Liberal Unionist/Unionist) government, 5, 7, 13n, 14, 15, 72, 76, 79, 80n, 86n, 87, 91, 130, 147, 149n, 152n, 153, 158

Conservative Labour (Con-Lab) (see Labour Unionist)

Conservative (and Unionist) Party/Tories 8, 9, 10, 12, 12n, 15, 16, 21, 22, 23, 26, 26n, 27, 45, 46, 46n, 49, 64n, 69, 70, 70n, 71, 71n, 72, 72n, 73, 74, 74n, 75, 75n, 76, 79, 82, 86, 88, 89, 107, 108, 114, 118n, 123, 128, 136, 139, 141, 150, 152, 156, 157, 158, 159, 162

conservative (direct rule) unionist (approach), 8n, 11, 13, 15, 25, 26n, 27, 79, 108, 149, 150

constitutional nationalism/ists (also see Irish Nationalists, Scottish National Party, Plaid Cymru), 12, 13n, 21, 57, 58, 80, 108, 110, 113

Continuity IRA, 19

Conybeare, C, 88n, 99n

Cork City, 125, 162

Cork Trades Council, 133

Cornwall, 88n

cottars, 7, 9, 65, 79, 84, 104, 152

Councils of Action, 90n

'counter-revolution within the revolution', 7, 42, 49, 71

County Antrim, 149n

County Carlow,

County Clare, 48

County Cork, 39, 41, 88

County Down, 74n, 149n

County Mayo, 32, 69, 148, 161

County Mayo/constituency, 34, 88

County Meath by-election (1882), 53n

County Meath constituency (also see Meath North constituency and Meath South constituency), 31n

County Tipperary, 91n

County Tyrone constituency by-election (1881) 48

County Wexford constituency, 34

Dundee Radical Association, 100n
Durham Miners Association, 40
Dynamiters/'Dynamite Campaign', 19, 49, 57n

Easter Rising (1916), 86n, 163
East Midlands, 139n
economic protectionism/tariffs, 73, 120
Edinburgh, 20, 21, 22, 64, 66, 82, 84, 87, 90n, 97, 99n, 133, 134, 160, 162n
Edinburgh and Leith Labour Chronicle, 160
Edinburgh Central constituency, 137n, 143
Edinburgh City Corporation, 20
Edinburgh Cowgate/'Little Ireland', 20, 87, 161
Edinburgh Evening News, 20
Edinburgh Hibernian F.C., 91n, 159
Edinburgh (Irish) National League, 87, 159
Edinburgh, Portobello, 161
Edinburgh Queens Park, 87, 89
Edinburgh St. Giles ward, 160
Edinburgh Trades Council, 99
Edinburgh University, 65n
Educational Institute of Scotland, 11
Egan, P, 33, 42, 50
Egypt, 46n, 62, 70, 79, 80n
eight hour day/campaign, 95n, 96, 97, 100, 103, 104, 105, 106, 114, 118, 120, 130, 147, 159
electoral gerrymandering, 12
Ellis, T, 111. 153
Engels, F, 31, 40n, 41, 47n, 56, 70, 80n, 88, 95, 109, 125, 126n, , 132, 132n, 163
engineers, 122
Engineering Employers Federation, 143
England/English, 6, 18,19n, 22, 24, 25, 26, 29, 31, 40, 42, 46, 56, 62n, 63, 80, 88, 88n, 91, 98, 100, 109, 110, 111n, 112n, 113, 114, 116, 117, 120, 124, 128, 132, 136, 138, 139, 140, 141, 143, 151, 158n, 163, 163n
England for All and the Historical Basis of Socialism in England (Henry Hyndman), 88n
English Civil War (1642-51), 88n
English Land Restoration League, 62, 66
English republic, 62n
Erin's Hope: The End and the Means (James Connolly), 161
'ethical imperialism'(also see social imperialism), 25

Glasgow police, 56, 63
Glasgow (port of), 94
Glasgow Rangers F.C., 156n
Glasgow Trades Council, 97, 117, 137n
Glasgow Tradeston constituency, 137n
Glasier, B, 66, 66n, 90, 97, 98, 139, 140
Glendale (Skye), 56, 63
'Glendale Martyr' (John Macpherson), 63
Glen Grey Act (1894), 148
Glyncorrwg (South Wales) 83
'gombeen men', 56n
Good Friday Agreement (1998), 15, 19
Grawhill killings (1881) (County Mayo), 50, 88
Great Famine ('Gorta Mor'), 29, 32n, 45, 55n, 162
Great Plains (USA), 105n
Greaves, D, 100n
Greenock constituency, 109
Griffiths, A, 86n, 145
gung ho/jingoism, 23, 24, 25, 27, 73, 79, 80n, 89

Haldane, R. B, 99, 99n
Hamilton (Lanarkshire) 84
Hamilton, F, 99
Hammersmith Socialist Society, 89n
Hanna, Rev. H ('Roaring'), 64, 64n, 73, 74n
Harcourt, Lord, 43
Hardie, K, 8, 29, 29n, 62n, 66n, 95, 95n, 96, 97, 100, 109, 110, 111, 113, 132n, 137, 139, 140, 147, 151n, 157, 158, 158n, 161
Harris, M, 42, 42n
Hartington, Lord, 75, 75n, 76
Haslingsen (Lancashire) 29
'Hawardan Kite', 72
Haymarket Square (Chicago), 106
Haymarket Martyrs, 105, 106, 120
Healey, T, 86, 86n
hereditary system, abolition of, 97
'High Imperialism', 21, 158, 159, 163
Highlands/and Islands, 6, 79, 94, 117, 156
Highland Land Law Reform Association (HLLRA)/Highland Land League, 6, 7, 64, 65, 66, 70, 76, 81, 82, 96, 99, 152

Highland Land Reform Association, 152

Hillsborough Agreement (2010), 15, 19

Holyrood Parliament, 22

Home Rule (also see Devolution, Irish Home Rule, Scottish Home Rule and Welsh Home Rule), 8, 26, 27, 41, 91, 97, 108, 109, 110, 110n, 111, 126, 139, 140, 147, 148n, 151

'Home-rule-all-round', (also see Devolution-all-round') 15, 26, 81, 108, 108n, 109, 113, 114, 151, 158

Home Rule Confederation of Great Britain (HRCGB), 31, 31n

Home Rule League (HRL) (also see Independent Irish Party), 30, 30n, 31, 31n, 47

'home rule' (national autonomy) within trade unions, 11, 124, 125,126, 126n, 141n, 143, 144, 144-5, 145n, 157, 157n

'home rule' within political parties, 141, 141n, 153

'Hottentots' (Khoikhoi) - 75

House of Commons (also see Westminster), 72n, 75, 114, 150

House of Lords (also see Westminster), 72, 72n, 76, 150

House of Lords, abolition of, 95, 97

'house of lords' - Irish, 74

House of Lords, reform of, 61, 76

Hunger Strikes (1980/1981), 13n

Hyndman, H, 9, 40n, 46, 47, 63, 88, 88n, 89, 89n, 90, 94, 132n, 139, 160

Imperial Federation/League (also see British Imperial Parliament), 107, 108, 109, 110, 139, 151, 153n

imprisonment, 6, 29, 43, 48, 50, 53, 80, 88

Independence First, 18n

Independent Irish Party (IIP) (also see Home Rule League), 30, 31, 31n, 42n, 47

independent Labour organisation (also see Independent Labour Party and Movement, Irish Land and Labour Association, Scottish Labour Party), 25, 46n, 47, 47n, 66, 72, 80n, 95, 95n, 96, 113, 116n, 118n, 120n, 123, 125n, 131, 137, 138, 138n, 140, 140n, 147, 151, 151n, 152, 157n, 158, 158n

Independent Labour Party, 10n, 18, 20, 23, 25, 35n, 37n, 66n, 95n, 117n, 118n, 132n, 139, 139n, 140, 141, 141n, 151, 157, 161, 162

independent women's labour organisations (also see Womens Protective and Provident League, Womens Trade Union League), 125n

India/n, 61, 62, 89, 110, 111n, 116n, 162

Indian Rebellion (1857), 111

industrial accident, 6

Industrial Workers of the World, 105n

'internationalism from above', 7, 113, 151

Irish Land Purchase Act (1903), 86n
Irish language (see Gaelic language)
Irish Land Restoration Society, 63-4, 64n, 70n
Irish Land War, 5n, 9, 29n, 31, 87
Irish Liberal Party (see also Ulster Liberal Party), 32n, 48, 64
Irish Liberal Unionists (see also Ulster Liberal Unionists), 74, 76n, 79n, 113n
Irish Loyal and Patriotic Union, 72n
'Irish methods', 65, 83
Irish migrants(also see Irish Americans/Irish-Scottish), 7, 29, 159
Irish National Federation (INF), 122n, 129, 130, 131, 133, 134, 134, 136, 149
INF/Liberal Imperialist alliance, 151
Irish N/nationalists/Green (see also All-for Ireland League, National League, Irish National Federation, United Irish League) 12, 12n, 19, 20, 26, 31, 50, 53, 55n, 71, 72, 76n, 79, 91n, 122n, 128, 132, 136, 136n, 150, 150n, 151, 152n, 154n, 156, 158, 158n, 161, 161n, 162
Irish National Land League (INLL) (Irish Land League/rs) (also see National Land League of Great Britain, Ladies Land League), 5n, 6, 9, 10, 19, 20, 32, 32n, 33, 34, 34n, 35n, 37, 39, 40, 40n, 41, 42, 45, 45n, 47, 48, 49, 50, 53, 54, 55, 56, 57, 58, 58n, 59n, 63, 66, 71, 80n, 82, 86n, 87, 89, 90, 94, 99, 103, 109, 117n, 118, 129, 133, 149, 150n, 151, 160
Irish National League (see National League)
'Irish only' exclusivism/organisation, 71, 89, 91n
Irish parliament, 12n, 26n, 41, 73, 74, 108, 148n
Irish Parliamentary Party (IPP) (also see National League), 44n, 57n, 58n, 59, 69, 73, 76n, 86n, 111, 124, 140n, 148
Irish Presbyterians, 35n, 54n, 70n, 73, 79 (also see Presbyterian Unitarians)
Irish Protestant Home Rule Association (IPHRA), 64n, 75, 76, 76n, 113n
Irish Purchase of Land Act (1885), 69, 87
'Irish Question', 91
Irish Republic, 24n, 30, 31, 32, 33n, 42, 57n, 132, 133, 151
Irish Republican Brotherhood (IRB) (see Fenians)
Irish Republicans (Movement) (also see Sinn Fein), 12, 13, 14, 15, 19, 24n, 132, 132n
Irish Revolution, 5, 5n, 23, 24, 28, 32, 55, 110n, 132
Irish Rising (1867), 30n
Irish ruling class, 12
Irish-Scottish/mixed background, 21, 99, 160
Irish Socialist Republican Party, 21, 161, 162
Irish Socialists, 23, 146
Irish Socialist Union, 123
Irish sports, 91n

Irish Tenants Defence Association, 130
Irishtown (County Mayo) 32
Irish Trade Union Congress, 64n, 144, 157, 157n, 158, 158n, 159n
Irish Transport and General Workers Union, 70n
Irish Unionism/ts (Party), 74, 79, 79n, 113, 113n, 124, 130, 136, 149, 151
Irish War of Independence (1919-23), 12
Irish World, 30, 38
Italy, 16

Jackson, President, 38n
Jacobin, 160
Jamaica, 82n
Japan, 5n
Jefferson, President, 38n
Jewish migrants, 97, 111
Jewish Tailors Union, 97
jingoism (see gung ho/jingoism)
Johnson, P, 32
Johnston, H, 117
Johnston, W, 74, 74n
Jones, Dr. E. P, 81
Jones, M, 81
Joyce, M, 69, 162
Justice, 89, 160

'Kaffirland' (Cape Province, South Africa), 32, 148
Kanturk (County Cork), 32,
Kanturk Democratic Labour Federation, 131
Kautsky, K, 89n
Kennedy, C, 117
Kenny, W, 136n
Kettle, A, 32, 42
Kilbrandon Commission (1973), 13n
Kilkenny by-election (1891), 133
Kilmainham Jail, 50
Kilmainham Treaty, 53, 54
Kinsale (County Cork), 41
Kirkintilloch (Dunbartonshire), 84
Knights of Labour, 104, 105, 117n, 122
Knock (County Mayo) 32n

Kropotkin, P, 40n

Labour government, 13, 99n
Labour in Irish History (James Connolly), 161
Labour Leader, 95n, 139, 161
Labour League (Ireland), 130, 131, 132, 133
Labour (New Labour) Party and Movement (British) (also see Independent Labour Party and New Labour Party) 13, 13n, 14, 15, 16, 17, 18, 22, 24, 25, 26, 80n, 95n, 152n, 161
Labour Party and Movement (Ireland), 23, 125
Labour Representation Committee, 25
Labour Standard, 47
Labour Theory of Value, 39n
'Labour Unionism' (Northern Ireland), 141, 145, 151n
Labour World, 124
Ladies Land League, 33, 38, 48, 49, 53, 54, 58, 67
Lagan valley (north east Ulster), 123, 144, 156
Lalor, J. F, 30
Lanarkshire (Central Belt), 99, 111
Lanarkshire, Mid by-election (1894), 151
Lanarkshire, Mid constituency, 29n, 96
Lanarkshire miners, 95, 117n, 139
Lanarkshire Miners' Strike (1888), 99
Lanarkshire North West constituency, 95, 138n
Lancashire (also see Haslingden), 34, 117n
Land Act (1881), 49, 50, 87
land and labour alliance (also see mining royalties), 6, 37, 71
Land and Labour League, 39
'Land for the People', 32, 84
land grabbers, 34
Land Law Reform Association, 40
Land Leagues (also see Irish National Land League, Highland Land Law Reform Association, Welsh Land League), 6, 10, 56, 143
(the) landless (also see cottars), 7, 24, 32, 39, 55, 57, 73n, 84, 86n, 129, 152
landlords/landlordism, 7, 38, 41, 42, 42n, 45, 45n, 49, 58, 63, 65, 72, 73n, 79, 82, 83, 84, 99, 162
land nationalisation (also see nationalisation of land and minerals), 39, 40, 47, 55, 56n, 57, 58, 64, 66, 76, 81, 97, 103, 104, 120, 130
Land Nationalisation League, 66, 67
Land Nationalisation Society (also see Cymdeithas y Ddaear i'r Bobl), 40, 56

Macfarlane, D, 56-7, 76n
Maclean, J, 110n, 141n
Macpherson, J ('Glendale Martyr'), 63
Macpherson, M (Mairi Mhor nan Oran), 65
MacRae, D, 84
Mahon, J, 90, 90n, 94, 97, 98, 100, 137n, 141, 141n
Major, J, 15
Majuba Hill (Battle of) (1881), 42, 43, 48
Maloney, H, 58n
Manchester, 46n
Manchester School of political economy, 39, 104, 112, 113
Mann, T, 119, 119n, 138n, 139, 143
Manningham Mills Strike (1890-1), 138, 143
Master Bottlemakers Association (Edinburgh), 161
Marx, K, 30, 39, 40n, 47n, 80n, 88, 132
Marx/Aveling, E, 21, 28, 80, 80n, 90, 90n, 100, 116, 125, 125n, 131, 138n, 139, 157, 161, 163
Marxist, 46n, 88, 88n, 99n
'Marx Party', 28, 80n
'Marxist Radicals', 16, 17, 18
Mason, R, 14
May Day/demonstrations, 100, 106, 114, 123, 130, 144
Maxwell, J. S, 66, 71, 97
Mazzinian, 111
McCarthy, J, 47
McCormick plant (Chicago), 105, 105n
McGee, T D'A, 73n
McGhee, R, 37, 97, 105, 117, 125
McHugh, E, 37, 57, 63, 66, 96, 117, 117n, 118, 125, 145, 159
McKeown, M, 123
McKinley Tariffs, 120
Meath North constituency, 133
Meath South constituency, 133
Meillet, L, 100n
Merionydd/Merioneth (North Wales), 111
Mersey/side, 24n, 27, 117, 117n, 118
Merthyr Tydfil (South Wales), 80
Merthyr Tydfil constituency, 29n, 112
metalworkers, 120
Mexican, 105n

middle class and better-off peasant alliance, 70

Middlesborough constituency, 138, 145

Midlothian campaign, 45

Mid Wales (also see Aberystwyth), 80, 81, 112

migrant labour/workers (also see German migrant workers/Irish migrants/Jewish migrants/Lithuanian labourers/Chinese migrant labour), 11, 15, 24, 94, 97, 105, 106, 106n, 111, 160, 163n

Militant (see Socialist Party)

Milligan, A, 161n, 161

Mill, J, 111

Mill, J. S, 40n, 111

millworkers, 143

Miners Association (also see Durham Miners Association), 40

'Miners National Labour League', 84

minimum wage, 97

Mining Federation of Great Britain (also see Scottish Miners National Federation and South Wales Miners Federation), 82n, 95n

mining royalties (also see nationalisation of), 38, 40, 66, 83, 84

'Mitchelstown Massacre' (1887), 88, 100, 130

Mochdre (Flintshire), 83

monarchy - abolition of (also see republicanism), 47

Monyrea (County Down), 35n

Moody, T, 5n

Morris, J, 80n

Morris, W, 40n, 80n, 89, 89n, 90, 90n, 100n, 137n, 157

Moscow (Russia), 50

Motherwell (Central Belt), 143, 144

Munster, 140

Murdoch, J, 41, 57, 65, 65n, 66, 70, 84, 96, 109

Murphy, W. M, 70n, 86n, 133n, 144, 144n, 162n

Mutiny, Prison and Army Reform Bill, 31n

Naoroji, D, 61, 61n, 62

Napier Commission (1883), 65

National Agricultural Labourers Union, 35n

National Amalgamated Sailors and Firemens Union (NAS&FU), 116, 116n

National Amalgamated Union of Labour (NAUL), 123n, 144

national democratic movements, 13, 17, 92, 139

nationalisation of capital, 62

nationalisation of land and minerals, 97, 98

nationalisation of railways, waterways and tramways (docks, harbours and other transport facilities), 97, 98, 130

N/nationalists (see also Irish Nationalists, Plaid Cymru, SNP, Sinn Fein), 17, 21, 22, 58n

(Irish) National Land League of Great Britain (NLLGB), 37, 41, 47, 89

National Land League of Great Britain, Poplar branch, 37

(Irish) National League (NL), 58, 59, 61, 69, 70, 70n, 72, 76, 86, 82, 92, 113, 122n, 124, 128, 129, 130, 131, 133, 133n, 136, 148, 151n

National League/NL/Home Rule Liberal (Parnell-Gladstone) alliance, 71, 76, 82, 86, 107, 129, 140

National League of Great Britain (also see Edinburgh NL and Leith NL), 66, 71, 96, 97

'National Question', 15, 17, 17n, 18, 90, 91, 92

National Radical Union, 76n

national self-determination (also see Irish self-determination/right of national self-determination/Scottish self-determination), 5, 15, 19n, 27, 108, 110n, 140,167

National Union of Dock Labourers (NUDL), 117, 117n, 119, 125n, 145, 145n

National Union of Gasworkers and General Labourers (NUG&GL), 118n, 119, 123, 124, 130, 144, 145

National Union of General and Municipal Workers, 123n

National Union of Miners, 14

Native Americans, 32, 38n, 103, 105n

Nat-Lab/ism, 86, 113, 122, 122n, 123, 125, 128, 130, 131, 133, 136, 144, 147, 157n

Neilan, Dr, P. J, 131

neo-colonial, 12

neo-conservatives (USA), 27

neo-liberalism, 22

Newcastle-upon-Tyne, 31, 117, 148

Newcastle-upon-Tyne constituency, 46n

Newcastle Chronicle, 50

'New Departure' (1878), 6, 30, 31, 32, 37, 42, 55, 57n, 132

'New Imperialism', 5, 5n, 8, 19, 23, 25, 27, 72, 79, 89, 92, 107, 113, 120, 132n, 139, 149, 152n

'New Ireland Forum', 14n

New Labour (Party), 8, 11, 14, 15, 16, 21

New Model Unions, 11, 11n, 24n, 118n, 120, 120n

Newport (South Wales), 153

'New Realism', 14

New Unions, 20, 95n, 100n, 105, 123n, 126, 126n, 133, 144, 145, 157

New Unionism, (Tom Mann and Ben Tillet), 138

Plunkett, Sir H, 136n

poaching, 63n, 104n

political bans/proscriptions, 49, 50

poll tax (see Anti-Poll Tax struggle)

Polynesia, 32

Pontycymmer (South Wales) 83

'Popes Brass Band', 86n

populism/t, 8, 18, 31, 59

Port, Wharf, Riverside and General Workers Union (PWR&GWU), 117n, 119, 119n, 120

Possibilists, 100

Portland Prison, 29, 43

Portobello (see Edinburgh, Portobello)

Portree (Skye), 64, 84

Powderley, T, 104

Presbyterian (see Calvinistic Methodists, Church of Scotland, Free Church of Scotland, Free Presbyterian Church of Scotland, Irish Presbyterians)

Presbyterian Unitarian, 35n

prison censorship, 43

privatisation, 12

Progress and Poverty (Henry George) 37, 38, 40-1

Progressive Unionist Party, 16n

prohibition of liquor traffic, 97, 98

pro-monarchist nationalists, 144, 144n, 145

Property Defence Leagues (also see Liberty and Property Defence League, Orange Emergency Committee, North Wales Property Defence League) 143

Protection of Persons and Property Act (1881), 45

Protestants (also see Calvinists Methodists, Church of England, Church of Ireland, Church of Scotland, Church of Wales, Free Church of Scotland, Free Presbyterian Church, Irish Presbyterians, Nonconformists), 7, 12, 131, 32, 45n, 64, 67, 70n, 73n, 74, 75, 79, 84, 100, 108, 117, 123, 129, 150, 150n

Protestant Working Men's Association of Ulster, 74n

public sector cuts, 21

racism/supremacism (also see anti-Semitism, chauvinism), 8, 9, 15, 16, 24n, 46n, 89, 108, 111, 137n

rack-renting, 55n

Radical, 45

Radical/s/Radicalism, 6, 8, 16, 18, 24, 24n, 25, 26, 29, 30n, 31, 34, 40n, 46, 46n, 47, 47n, 61, 62, 62n, 65, 65n, 70, 72, 74, 75, 75n, 79, 80, 86, 88, 89, 91, 92, 97, 99, 99n, 103, 109, 110, 111n, 113, 116n, 118n, 125n, 128, 139, 139n, 159, 162

Radical and social republican alliance, 49, 151

Radical Liberals/ism, 9, 10, 46, 46n, 50, 61, 62, 62n, 64, 64n, 74, 76, 99n, 107, 110, 112, 112n, 113n, 114, 137, 140, 141, 149n, 152

Radical Liberal-Tory Democrat imperial alliance, 76

Radical Programme (1885), 46n

Radical Reconstruction in USA (1865-77), 5n

Radical Secularist, 116n

Radical Unionism, 149n

railway workers (also see Scottish Railworkers' Strike), 128, 143, 144

Rank and File '98 Club, 162, 162n

rank and file trade union (strategy), 11

rates, 104

Real IRA, 19, 54n

'real Labour', 16

'real Radicals/ism' (also see 'sham Radicals'), 16, 45, 48, 56, 71

Redmond, J, 131, 133, 154n

Reform Act (1867) 40n, 112n

Reform Act (1884), 61

reform of House of Lords (see House of Lords, reform of)

republic/an (also see Irish Republic, Irish Republican Movement, social republicanism, socialist republicanism), 19, 40n, 97, 109, 114, 141, 141n

rent strike (also see *No Rents Manifesto*), 49, 50, 87

Republican Club, 90n

Republican Communist Network (RCN), 18

Republican Socialist Convention, 22, 163n

revolutionary Social Democracy, 163

Rhodes, C, 107, 108, 149, 154

Rhondda (South Wales), 82

Rhondda constituency, 81n

Rhyl (North Wales) 82n

Ribbonmen, 34

Ricardo, D, 39n

Richard, H, 112, 112n

right of self-determination , 17, 91

River Liffey (Dublin) 162

Robertson, C, 137, 137n

'Rome Rule', 73

Rosebery, Earl of, 107, 107n, 151, 153, 156

Ross-shire constituency, 67

Royal Commission on Labour, 147

Royal Commission on Land, 157
Royal Irish Constabulary, 33, 88
Royal Irish Fusiliers, 74n
Royal Naval Marines, 63
Russell, G, 136n
Russia/Russian, 99n, 111, 139, 158
Rylett, Rev. H, 35, 35n, 47, 48

St. Andrews Agreement (2006), 15, 19
St. Louis (USA), 106
Salisbury, Lord, 7, 69, 72, 75, 76, 149, 149n, 156
San Francisco (USA), 38
Saunderson, Colonel, 74, 74n, 130
scab unions, 144, 145
Scheu, A, , 90, 90n, 94, 100n
Schnadhorst, J, 96
'scientific socialism', 88
Scotland/Scottish (also see Highlands and Islands) , 5, 6, 10, 11, 13, 13n, 15, 17, 18, 18n, 19n, 20, 22, 23, 24, 25, 26, 27, 27n, 29, 29n, 31, 40, 46n, 56, 62, 63, 64, 67, 71, 83, 84, 91n, 94, 95, 99, 100, 108, 109, 109n, 110, 110n, 113, 114, 116, 117, 120, 120n, 122, 123, 124, 125n, 132, 136, 137, 137n, 139, 139n, 140, 143, 144, 145, 145n, 146, 148, 151n, 152n, 156, 157, 158, 158n, 159, 160, 163, 163n
Scotland & Wales Act (1976), 13n
Scottish Chartists, 20
'Scottish Council' (of the ILP), 141
Scottish Football League, 91n
Scottish Home Rule, 25, 76, 95-6, 110, 114n, 151
Scottish Home Rule Association, 96, 109, 110, 151
Scottish Labour Party (SLP), 10, 18, 20, 96, 97, 98, 99, 99n, 100, 110, 116, 117, 122, 132n, 137, 137n, 139, 140, 141, 144, 149, 159
Scottish Land and Labour League (SLLL), 9, 17, 20, 21, 90n, 94, 95, 97, 98, 99, 110, 118, 137n, 141, 141n
Scottish Land League of America, 66
Scottish Land Nationalisers, 20, 160
Scottish Land Restoration League, 63, 66, 71, 76, 90, 94, 96, 97, 109
Scottish Miners Anti-Royalty and Labour League, 84
Scottish Miners National Federation, 95, 96, 98, 99, 116
Scottish National Council (of the SDP), 141n
Scottish Nationalists (also see Left nationalists, SNP), 21
Scottish National Party (SNP), 18n, 21, 22, 144n
Scottish Parliament (Holyrood) (also see devolution, Scottish Home Rule), 21

South Wales (also see Bargoed, Cardiff, Clydach, Glyncorrwg, Llandysul, Merthyr Tydfil, Newport, Pontycymmer, Seven Sisters, Swansea, 80, 83, 112, 153, 156
South Wales Liberal Federation, 153
South Wales Miners Federation, 82n
South Yorkshire, 147
Spain, 27n
Spies, A, 105, 105n
state coercion (also see Coercion Act/Criminal Law and Procedure Act), 9, 42, 45, 58, 62, 69, 70
state insurance, 97
state socialism/Socialists, 87, 90
Stirlingshire constituency, 137n
Stirlingshire miners, 137n
Stormont, 12, 12n, 19, 22
Straide (County Mayo), 29
Strange, L, 133
strike action, 13, 39, 42, 98, 99, 105, 106, 116, 117, 118, 118n, 129, 138, 160
Sudan, 91
Sunderland, 116
Sunningdale Agreement (1973), 13n
Sutherland, 81
Sutherland, A, 67, 76, 83
Sutherland constituency, 76
Swansea, 156

tariffs (see economic protectionism)
Taylor, H, 40, 40n, 46, 48, 63, 66, 67, 81, 120
Temperance Movement, 98
tenant farmers, 7, 24, 34, 39, 49, 80, 84, 88, 112, 113, 149, 152
- better off/larger, 32, 42, 49, 55, 70, 129, 130
- poorer/smaller, 32, 39, 49, 55, 57, 59, 70n, 86n, 103, 129, 140, 152
Tenants Defence Association (also see Irish Tenants Defence Association), 32
Tenants Relief Bill (1886), 87
tenants rights struggles (also see Irish National Land League), 42n
Thatcher, M, 13n, 14
Thiers, A, 62n
The Highlander, 41
The Highland Jubilee - The Land Question answered from the Bibble (Iubile nan Gaidheal, Fuasgladh an-Fhearainn a-rair a' Bhuibuil) (John Murdoch), 65n
The Irish land question: what it involves and how it can be settled (H. George), 38

In early 2011 Intfrobel Publications will be making the following available online at *www.internationalismfrombelow.com*:

Internationalism From Below
Reclaiming a hidden communist tradition
to challenge the nation-state and capitalist empire

Ready for publication

Volume 1
The Historical Development of Nation-States and Nationalism up to 1848

Volume 2
The World of Nation-States and Nationalism between the Communist League and the early Second International (1845-1895)

In preparation

Volume 3
Revolutionary Social Democracy, Nation-States and Nationalism in the age of the Second International (1889-1916)

Volume 4
Communists, Nation-States and Nationalism during the International Revolutionary Wave of 1916-21